중세영어

중세 영어

전 상 범

2007년	5월	25일	초판 1쇄 인쇄
2007년	6월	4일	초판 1쇄 발행
2008년	10월	10일	초판 2쇄 발행

펴낸이 김 진 수
편 집 진 정 미
펴낸곳 한국문화사

133-823 서울시 성동구 성수1가 2동 656-1683 두앤캔B/D 502호
전화 • 02)464-7708(대표) 3409-4488(편집부) 468-4592~4(영업부)
팩스 • 02)499-0846
등록번호 • 제2-1276호(1991.11.9 등록)
e-mail • hkm77@korea.com
homepage • www.hankookmunhwasa.co.kr

가 격 15,000원

ISBN 978-89-5726-461-4 93740

잘못된 책은 바꾸어 드립니다.

이 책의 내용은 저작권법에 따라 보호받고 있습니다.

이 도서의 국립중앙도서관 출판시도서목록(CIP)은 e-CIP 홈페이지
(http://www.nl.go.kr/cip.php)에서 이용하실 수 있습니다.
(CIP제어번호: CIP2007001611)

MIDDLE ENGLISH
책머리에

 흔히 영어의 역사를 고대(450~1100), 중세(1100~1500), 현대(1500~)의 세 단계로 나눈다. 중세영어는 고대영어에서 현대영어로 넘어오는 과도기적인 중간 단계의 언어이다.
 고대영어에는 대표적인 세 방언이 있었으나 바이킹족들의 침략으로 색슨(Saxon) 방언의 문헌을 제외하고는 거의 모두 소실되었다. 그 결과 우리에게 전해진 고대영어는 매우 동질적이다. 따라서 고대영어를 앵글로-색슨어(Anglo-Saxon)라고 부르는 것은 정확하지 않다.
 거기에 비해 중세영어는 거의 모든 방언의 문헌이 상존하여 매우 이질적이다. 비록 그 기간은 400년 밖에 되지 않으나 초기와 후기의 모양은 판이하다. 초기의 중세영어는 아직도 고대영어의 모습을 간직하고 있는데 비해 후기 중세영어는 거의 현대영어에 가깝다.
 중세영어는 고대영어 시대의 풍부하던 굴절형이 거의 사라지고 모든 품사의 굴절형이 한두 개의 어미로 평준화된 시기이기도 하다.
 중세영어에서 쵸서(Chaucer)가 차지하는 비중이 하도 막중하여 중세영어와 쵸서는 거의 동의어에 가깝다. 쵸서의 작품 가운데서도 *Canterbury Tales*는 영문학의 백미라고 할 수 있다. 쵸서를 영시의 아버지라고 부르는 까닭이다. 교양으로 중세영어를 읽거나 영문학적 관심으로 쵸서를 읽으려는 사람들은 우선 *Canterbury Tales*의 Prologue를 읽어야 한다. 본서의 절반을 Prologue로 채운 것은 그 까닭이다.

그러나 중세영어를 어학적 관심에서 읽으려는 사람들은 보다 초기의 중세영어와 쵸서가 글을 쓴 런던 이외의 방언에 대한 지식도 필요해진다. II부는 그와 같은 목적으로 중세영어를 공부하려는 독자들을 위한 것이다.

어학적으로 볼 때 본서는 필자의 『고대영어』의 후속편이다. 고대영어의 지식이 있으면 II부를 읽기가 수월하겠지만 고대영어의 지식이 없는 경우에는 시대적으로는 거꾸로가 되겠지만 I부의 쵸서부터 읽는 것이 좋다.

『고대영어』때와 마찬가지로 본서를 집필할 때의 필자가 마음속에 새겨둔 구호는 세상에서 가장 쉽게 중세영어를 배울 수 있는 책을 쓰자는 것이었다. 궁극적인 평가는 독자들의 몫이지만 필자의 경험으로 미루어 이 책 하나면 중세영어를 혼자 공부하기에 거의 미흡함이 없을 것이다.

이런 학술서적의 집필이 늘 그렇듯이 선행연구서들에게 빚진 바가 적지 않다. 무엇보다도 Sanki Ichikawa & Tamotsu Matsunami, 2005, *Chaucer's Canterbury Tales: General Prologue*, Tokyo : Kenkyusha에서 발음기호의 전재를 허가해준 겐큐샤(硏究社)와 그 필자들에게 감사의 뜻을 전하는 바이다. (An acknowledgement is due to Kenkyusha (Japan) and the writers of *Chaucer's Canterbury Tales: General Prologue* (2005) for the generous permission to reproduce the phonetic transcription of *Prologue*.)

『고대영어』와 본서의 집필로 필자는 학계에 대한 작은 책임과 숙제를 다한 셈이다. 작으나마 필자의 노력이 우리나라의 영어학 발전을 위한 하나의 초석이 될 수 있다면 더 없는 기쁨으로 여길 것이다.

2007년 초 여름에
田 相 範 적음

MIDDLE ENGLISH CONTENTS

책머리에 / v

I. Chaucer / 1
- Chaucer의 생애 _ 3
- *Canterbury Tales*의 문법 _ 5
  - 철자와 발음 ··5
  - 굴절 ···7
  - 작시법 ··10
- *General Prologue* _ 12
  - 본문 ··12
  - 음성기호 ··13
  - 주석 ··74
  - 번역 ··140

II. Minor Works / 159

- 12th Century _ 161
  1. *Peterborough Chronicle* ···161
  2. *Ancrene Wisse* ··174
- 13th Century _ 187
  1. *The Owl and the Nightingale* ···187
  2. *Havelock the Dane* ··200
- 14th Century _ 211
  1. *The Bruce* ···211
  2. *John of Trevisa's Translation of Ranulf Hidgen's Polychronicon* ··222
  3. The Wicliffite Bible ···232
     - The Lord's Prayer ···232
     - The Ten Women ··232
     - The Prodigal Son ···233
- 15th Century _ 241
  - Caxton's Prologue to *Eneydos* ··241

참고문헌 / 245
어휘사전 / 247

I MIDDLE ENGLISH CHAUCER

- Chaucer의 생애
- Canterbury Tales의 문법
  1. 철자와 발음
  2. 굴절
  3. 작시법
- General Prologue

Chaucer의 생애

　유명한 사람들이 대개 그렇듯 Chaucer도 사망한 때는 분명한데 비해 태어난 해는 정확히 알지 못한다. 여러 증거로 미루어 1343년 아니면 그 이듬해에 태어났을 것으로 짐작된다.
　조부와 부친은 양조업에 종사했으며, 부친은 궁정에 출입한 것으로 알려져 있다. 그런 인연으로 Chaucer는 Edward III세의 셋째 며느리(Prince Lionel의 아내)의 시동(page)이 되는데, 이것은 출세를 추구하는 젊은이들이 부러워하는 자리였다.
　Chaucer는 1359년에 10대의 어린 나이로 프랑스와의 싸움에 참전했다가 포로가 되어 왕이 치러준 몸값(ransom)으로 풀려나는 일이 있었다. 귀국하고 나서는 왕을 직접 모시게 되며, 얼마 뒤 1366년에 Philippa와 결혼하게 되는데, Philippa는 좋은 집안 출신으로 스스로는 여왕의 시녀였다. 한편 Philippa의 동생은 왕의 넷째 아들인 John of Gaunt의 아내로서, 세력가였던 그는 평생 Chaucer의 후견인 노릇을 한다.
　Chaucer는 1372년과 1378년에 두 번 외교적 임무를 띠고 이태리로 출장을 가는데, 첫 번째는 Genoa와 Florence로, 그리고 두 번째는 Milano에 갔다. 문예부흥의 발상지였던 당시 이태리는 구라파에서 가장 앞선 나라였다. 그가 이태리에서 누구를 만나고 무엇을 했는지는 정확히 알려져 있지 않으나 Petrarch를 만났을 가능성이 있으며, 더욱이 Dante의 *Divina Commedia*(신곡)나 Boccaccio의 *Decameron*에 대해 알게 되었을 가능성은 높다.
　1374년부터 시작한 세관의 감독관(controller)의 일을 시작으로 중견 공무원으로서의 업적을 쌓아나간다. 뒤에 가서는 Kent의 치안판사(Justice of the Peace) 노릇도 하며, 말년에는 왕의 부동산 관리를 맡는 일(Clerk for the King's Works)이나 명예직(sinecure)인 산림 관리 같은 일도 했다.

그는 Edward III세와 Richard II세는 물론 Henry IV세에 이르기까지 왕들의 총애를 늘 받아 왔다. Henry IV세는 John of Gaunt의 아들로서 아버지를 따르던 Chaucer를 소홀히 하지 않았다.

그러나 Chaucer는 한 때 그의 후견인인 John of Gaunt가 잠시 권력의 자리에서 밀려났을 때 그도 낙향한 적이 있는데, 이 때 그가 불후의 명작인 *Canterbury Tales*를 썼다는 것은 역사의 아이러니이다.

그는 1400년 10월 25일 57세의 나이로 세상을 하직했다. 죽은 뒤 그는 Westminster Abbey에 묻히는데 그가 Poets' Corner에 묻힌 최초의 시인이 되었다.

Chaucer는 대단한 독서가(prodigious, voracious reader)로 알려져 있으며, 많은 것에 한없는 관심을 가졌던 것으로도 유명하다. 그의 작품을 통해 우리는 그가 천문학(astronomy), 점성술(astrology), 의학(medicine), 심리학(psychology), 물리학(physics), 야금술(alchemy), 심지어는 관상학(physiognomy)에 이르기까지 폭넓은 지식의 소유자였던 것을 알게 된다. 그는 *The House of Fame*이라는 시에서 음파에 대해 자세하고 해박한 설명을 하고 있다. 그는 Latin어를 비롯해 프랑스어, 이태리어 등에도 통달했던 것으로 알려져 있다.

그는 평생 관직에 있었고 때로는 겸직도 마다않는 바쁜 생활을 해온 사람으로서 문학은 그에게는 어디까지나 부업이었다. 그런 그가 그처럼 훌륭한 작품을 많이 남겼다는 것은 놀라울 뿐이다.

Canterbury Tales의 문법

1. 철자와 발음

우리가 간단히 중세영어라고 말하는 언어는 1100년에서 1500년까지의 400년에 걸치며, 또 방언도 여럿이 있다. 고대영어의 경우에는 현존하는 문헌의 대부분이 후기 West Saxon 하나의 방언이었으므로 비교적 동질적이라고 할 수 있으나 중세영어의 경우에는 그렇지가 않다. 시대와 장소에 따라 그 모양이 다양하다. 따라서 대개의 경우 표준적인 교과서에서의 중세영어에 대한 설명은 중세영어의 대표적인 시인 Chaucer(1340?-1400)의 영어를 기준으로 설명하는 것이 관례이다. 여기서도 그 관례를 따를 것인데, 설명은 주로 Kökeritz(1954), *A Guide to Chaucer's Pronunciation*을 근거로 했다. Kökeritz(1954)는 그 얄팍한 부피(32쪽)에도 불구하고 Chaucer의 발음에 대한 가장 권위 있는 참고서 가운데 하나이다.

1) 모음
  (1) 단모음
      a [a] : fast [fast], harm [harm], walk [walk]
      e [e] : bed [bed], brest [brest], herte [hertə]
      i, y [i] : sittten [sitən], kyng [kiŋ], byrth [birθ]
      o [ɔ] : God [gɔd], ofte [ɔftə], port [pɔrt]
         [u] : love [luvə], monk [muŋk], yong [yuŋg]
      u [u] : hungere [huŋgər], but [but], just [dʒust]
  (2) 장모음
      a, aa [aː] : maken [maːkən], smale [smaːlə], caas [kaːs]
      e, ee, ie [eː] : seke [seːkə], deeme [deːmə], grief [greːf]

e, ee [ɛː] : deel [dɛːl], eten [ɛːtən], deed [dɛːd]
i, y [iː] : lik [liːk], wild [wiːld], bynden [biːndən]
o, oo [oː] : doo [doː], good [goːd], blood [bloːd]
o, oo [ɔː] : stoon [stɔːn], smoke [smɔːkə], noon [nɔːn]
u [ü] : duc [düːk], fur [füːr], vertu [vertüː]
ai, ay, ei, ey [æi] : plain [pæin], mayden [mæidən], wey [wæi]
au, aw [ɑu] : chaumbre [tʃɑumbrə], saugh [sɑuf], lawe [lɑuə]
eu, ew [iu] : newe [niuə], trewe [triuə], blew [bliu]
　　　[ɛu] : fewe [fɛuə], lewed [lɛuəd], shewen [ʃɛuən]
ou, ow, ough [uː] : house [huːs], how [huː], proud [pruːd]
　　　[ɔu] : knowen [knɔuən], soule [sɔulə], thought [θɔuxt]

2) 자음
c [k] : cost [kɔst]
　[s] : certain [sertæin]
g [g] : goos [goːs], frogge [frɔgə]
　[ʤ] : gentil [ʤentil], jugge [ʤuʤə]
gh [x] : thought [θɔuxt]
　[ç] : night [ni·çt]
gn [gn] : gnawen [gnɑuən]
kn [kn] : knowen [knɔuən]
j [ʤ] : just [ʤust]
lf [lf] : half [half]
lk [lk] : folk [folk]
lm [lm] : palmer [palmər]
ng [ŋg] : singen [siŋgən]
r [ř] : 약한 연탄음 (trill)
s [s] : hous [huːs]
　[z] : rise [riːsə]
th [θ] : bath [baθ]
　[ð] : bathen [baːðən]
wr [wr] : writen [wriːtən]

ㄹ. 굴절

1) 대명사 : 중세영어의 대명사는 대부분 고대영어의 모습을 그대로 간직하고 있다. 비교의 편의를 위해 고대영어를 괄호 안에 제시해 놓았다.

(a) 1인칭

	단수		복수	
주격	I, ich, ik	(iċ)	wē	(wē)
속격	my, myn	(mīn)	oure	(ūre)
여격	me	(mē)	us	(ūs)
대격	me	(mē)	us	(ūs)

(b) 2인칭

	단수		복수	
주격	thou	(aū)	ye	(ġe)
속격	thy, thyn	(aīn)	youre	(ēower)
여격	thee	(aē)	yow, you	(ēow)
대격	thee	(aē)	yow, you	(ēow)

(c) 3인칭

	단수					복수	
	남성		여성		중성		
주격	he(e)(hē)		she	(heo)	hit (hit)	they	(hīe)
속격	his (his)		hir(e), her(e)	(hiere)	his (his)	hir(e), her(e)	(hiera)
여격	him (him)		hir(e), her(e)	(hiere)	him (him)	hem	(him)
대격	him (him)		hir(e), her(e)	(hīe)	hit, hyt(hit)	hem	(hīe)

2) 형용사 : 고대영어의 복잡했던 굴절형은 다음과 같은 5개의 어미로 줄어들었다.

-a, -e, -an, -ena, -um

이들 어미의 모음은 모두 무강세 단모음이므로 이들은 다음과 같은 약화 과정을 거쳐 모두 -e로 평준화되었다.

-a >   -e
-an > -en > -e
-um > -en > -e
-ena > -ene > -e

3) 명사 : 어미의 평준화는 궁극적으로 명사 굴절 체계의 간소화를 가져왔다. 명사에서 흔히 볼 수 있던 -an, -on, -en 등은 우선 -en으로 평준화 되었던 것이, 어말의 n 탈락에 의해 -e([ə])가 되었다가, 그나마도 탈락하여 현재와 같은 모습을 갖게 되었다. 강변화 명사의 고대, 중세영어의 굴절형을 비교해보기 바란다.

	단수		복수	
	OE	ME	OE	ME
주격/대격	stān	stōn	stān-as	stōn(e)
속격	stān-es	stōnes	stān-a	stōnes
여격	stān-e	stōn	stān-um	stōnes

4) 동사 : 강변화 동사 bindan(=to bind)의 굴절
　[직설법 현재]
　　단수　1. bind-e
　　　　　2. bind-est
　　　　　3. bind-eþ
　　복수　　bind-eþ, bind-en
　[직설법 과거]
　　단수　1. band
　　　　　2. bund-e
　　　　　3. band
　　복수　　bund-en

약변화동사 dēman(=to deem)의 굴절
　[직설법 현재]
　　단수　1. dēm-e
　　　　　2. dēm-est
　　　　　3. dēm-eþ, dēm-es
　　복수　　dēm-eþ, dēm-es
　[직설법 과거]
　　단수　1. dēm-de
　　　　　2. dēm-dest
　　　　　3. dēm-de
　　복수　　dēm-den

3. 작시법

압운(rhyme)을 맞추는 Chaucer의 작시법은 두운(alliteration)을 맞추던 고대영어 이래 지금까지의 작시법에 비해 대단히 신선하게 보였을 것이다. 압운은 지중해의 작시법이다.

두운이란 하나의 시행을 전후반으로 나누고 전반부에 후반부의 첫 자음과 동일한 자음으로 시작하는 단어를 사용하는 시작법이다. 아래에 인용한 Beowulf의 처음 시행들을 보자.

1 Hwæt wē Gār-Dena   in ġeār-dagum
2 bēod-cyninga   brym gefrunon,
3 hū ða æbelingas   ellen fremedon.
4 Oft Scyld Scēfing   sceabena brēatum,
5 monegum mægbum   meodo-setla oftēah;

밑줄 쳐놓은 음들의 두운이 맞는 것을 확인하기 바란다(자세한 설명을 위해서는 전상범 2006『고대영어』, 81-2쪽을 참조하기 바란다.)
여기에 비해 다음 예에서 볼 수 있듯이 Chaucer의 경우에는 시행의 끝들이 동일한 운모로 끝나고 있다.

    Whan that Aprill with his shoures soote
    The droghte of March hath perced to the roote,
    And bathed every veyne in swich licour
    Of which vertu engendred is the flour;

1,2행은 모두 -oote로, 3,4행은 모두 -our로라는 동일한 운모로 끝나고 있다. 이처럼 두 행씩 운을 맞춘 것을 2행연구(couplet)라고 부

르며, 이른바 heroic couplet라고 불리는 것이다. 이와 같은 형식으로 영웅들의 행적을 노래한 경우가 많아 이런 이름이 붙었을 것이다. 이 밖에도 위의 aabb 이외에도 abab, abba등 다양한 모양들이 있다.

한편 하나의 시행에는 약강(˘ ´)의 두 음절로 이루어진 운각(foot)이 다섯 개 씩 들어있다. 약강5음보(iambic pentameter)라고 불리는 이와 같은 시작법은 이후 영시의 대표적인 시형이 된다. Chaucer가 영시의 아버지라고 불리는 연유가 여기에 있다.

약강(iambic)음보가 가장 흔한 형태이지만 경우에 따라서는 강약(trochaic)의 음보도 사용된다. 위의 예에서 첫 행은 강약5음보, 둘째 행 이하는 약강5음보이다. 다음을 참조하기 바란다.

> Whán thăat Áprĭll wíth hĭs shóurĕs sóotĕ
> Thĕ dróghte ŏf Márch hăth pércĕd tó thĕ róotĕ,
> Ănd báthĕd évĕrў véyne ĭn swích lĭcóur
> Ŏf whích vĕrtú ĕngéndrĕd ís thĕ flóur;

위의 예에서 2행은 10음절이 아니라 11음절로 이루어졌는데, 이처럼 시행 끝에 가외의 음절이 하나 첨가된 시행을 feminine ending 이라고 부른다. Chaucer는 기본적으로는 약강5음보를 지키면서도 여기에 억매이지 않고 비교적 자유롭게 시를 쓰고 있다.

General Prologue

Here bygynneth the Book of the Tales of Caunterbury.

1   Whan that Aprill with his shoures soote
       The droghte of March hath perced to the roote,
       And bathed every veyne in swich licour
       Of which vertu engendred is the flour;
5   Whan Zephirus eek with his sweete breeth
       Inspired hath in every holt and heeth
       The tendre croppes, and the yonge sonne
       Hath in the Ram his halve cours yronne,
       And smale foweles maken melodye,
10   That slepen al the nyght with open yë
       (So priketh hem nature in hir corages),—
       Thanne longen folk to goon on pilgrimages,
       And palmeres for to seken straunge strondes,
       To ferne halwes, kowthe in sondry londes;
15   And specially from every shires ende
       Of Engelond to Caunterbury they wende,
       The hooly blisful martir for to seke,
       That hem hath holpen whan that they were seeke.
       Bifil that in that seson on a day,
20   In Southwerk at the Tabard as I lay
       Redy to wenden on my pilgrymage
       To Caunterbury with ful devout corage,
       At nyght was come into that hostelrye

Here bygynneth the Book of the Tales of Caunterbury

(The stress is marked only when it is not on the first syllable.)

1   hwɑn ðat ɑːpril wiθ (h)is ʃuːrəs soːtə
       ðə druxt ɔf martʃ haθ peːrsəd toː ðə roːtə
       and bɑːðəd ɛvriː væin in switʃ likúːr
       ɔf hwitʃ vərtíu ɛnʤéndrəd is ðə fluːr
5   hwɑn zɛfirus ɛːk wiθ (h)is sweːtə brɛːθ
       inspíːrəd haθ in ɛvriː hɔlt and hɛːθ
       ðə tɛndrə krɔppəs and ðə juŋgə sunnə
       haθ in ðə ram (h)is halvə kuːrs irúnnə
       and smɑːlə fuːləs mɑːkən mɛlɔdíːə
10   ðat sleːpən al ðə niçt wiθ ɔːpən iːə
       sɔː prikəθ hɛm nɑːtíur in hir kurɑ́ːʤəs
       ðan lɔːŋgən fɔlk toː goːn ɔn pilgrimɑ́ːʤəs
       and palmɛrs fɔr toː seːkən straunʤə strɔːndəs
       toː fɛrnə halwəs kuːð in sundriː lɔːndəs
15   and spɛsyəliː frɔm ɛvriː ʃiːrəs ɛndə
       əf ɛŋgəlɔːnd toː kauntərbriː ðæi wɛndə
       ðə hɔːliː blisful martir fɔr toː seːkə
       ðat hɛm haθ hɔlpən hwan ðat ðæi wɜːr seːkə
       bifíl ðat in ðat sɛːzuːn ɔn a dæi
20   in suːðwɛrk at ðə tɑːbard as iː læi
       rɛdiː toː wɛndən ɔn miː pilgrimɑ́ːʤə
       toː kauntərbriː wiθ ful deːvúːt kurɑ́ːʤə
       at niçt was kum intoː ðat ɔstəlríːə

Wel nyne and twenty in a compaignye,
25 Of sondry folk, by aventure yfalle
In felaweshipe, and pilgrimes were they alle,
That toward Caunterbury wolden ryde.
The chambres and the stables weren wyde,
And wel we weren esed atte beste.
30 And shortly, whan the sonne was to reste,
So hadde I spoken with hem everichon
That I was of hir felaweshipe anon,
And made forward erly for to ryse,
To take oure wey ther as I yow devyse.
35 But nathelees, whil I have tyme and space,
Er that I ferther in this tale pace,
Me thynketh it acordaunt to resoun
To telle yow al the condicioun
Of ech of hem, so as it semed me,
40 And whiche they weren, and of what degree,
And eek in what array that they were inne;
And at a knyght than wol I first bigynne.

A KNYGHT ther was, and that a worthy man,
That fro the tyme that he first bigan
45 To riden out, he loved chivalrie,
Troughte and honour, fredom and curteisie.
Ful worthy was he in his lordes werre,
And therto hadde he riden, no man ferre,
As wel in cristendom as in hethenesse,
50 And evere honoured for his worthynesse.
At Alisaundre he was whan it was wonne.

weːl niːn and twɛntiː in a kumpæiníːə
of sundriː fɔlk biː aːvəntíur ifallə
in fɛlauʃip and pilgrims wɛːr ðæi allə
ðat toːward kauntərbiuriː wɔldən riːdə
ðə tʃaːmbrəs and ðə staːbləs wɛːrən wiːdə
and weːl weː wɛːrən ɛːzəd attə bɛstə
and ʃɔrtliː hwan ðə sunnə was toː rɛstə
sɔː hadd iː spɔːkən wiθ (h)ɛm ɛvritʃɔ́ːn
θat iː was of (h)ir fɛlauʃip anɔ́ːn
and maːdə fɔrward ɛrliː fɔr toː riːzə
toː taːk uːr wæi ðɛːr as iː juː deːvíːzə
but naːðəlɛ́s hwiːl iː hav tiːm and spaːsə
ɛːr ðat iː fɛrðər in ðis taːle paːsə
meː θiŋkəθ it akɔ́rdaunt toː rəzúːn
toː tɛllə juː al ðə kɔndisiúːn
of ɛːtʃ of hɛm sɔː as it seːməd meː
and hwitʃ ðæi wɛːrən and of hwat deːgréː
and ɛːk in hwat arrǽi ðat ðæi wɛːr innə
and at a kniçt ðan wul iː first bigínnə
a kniçt ðɛːr was and ðat a wurðiː man
ðat frɔ ðə tiːmə ðat (h)eː first bigán
toː riːdən uːt (h)eː luvəd tʃivəlríːə
trouθ and ɔnúːr freːdum and kurtæizíːə
ful wurðiː was (h)eː in (h)is lɔrdəs wɛrrə
and ðɛːrtoː hadd (h)eː ridən nɔː man fɛrrə
as weːl in kristndum as in hɛːðənɛssə
and ɛvr ɔnúːrəd fɔr (h)is wurðinɛssə
at alisaundr (h)eː was hwan it was wunnə

Ful ofte tyme he hadde the bord bigonne
Aboven alle nacions in Pruce;
In Lettow hadde he reysed and in Ruce,
55 No Cristen man so ofte of his degree.
In Gernade at the seege eek hadde he be
Of Algezir, and riden in Belmarye.
At Lyeys was he and at Satalye,
Whan they were wonne; and in the Grete See
60 At many a noble armee hadde he be.
At mortal batailles hadde he been fiftene,
And foughten for oure feith at Tramyssene
In lystes thries, and ay slayn his foo.
This ilke worthy knyght hadde been also
65 Somtyme with the lord of Palatye
Agayn another hethen in Turkye.
And evermoore he hadde a sovereyn prys;
And though that he were worthy, he was wys,
And of his port as meeke as is a mayde.
70 He nevere yet no vileynye ne sayde
In al his lyf unto no maner wight.
He was a verray parfit, gentil knyght.
But, for to tellen yow of his array,
His hors were goode, but he was nat gay.
75 Of fustian he wered a gypoun
Al bismotered with his habergeoun,
For he was late ycome from his viage,
And wente for to doon his pilgrymage.
With hym ther was his sone, a yong SQUIER,

ful ɔftə tiːm (h)eː hadd ðə bɔːrd bigúnnə
abúvən allə naːsiúːns in priusə
in lɛttou hadd (h)eː ræizəd and in riusə
55 nɔː kristən man sɔː ɔft ɔf his deːgréː
in gɛrnaːd at ðə seːdʒ ɛːk hadd (h)eː beː
ɔf aldʒəzíːr and ridn in bɛlmaríːə
at liːæis was (h)eː and sataliːə
hwan ðæi wɛːr wun and in ðə grɛːtə sɛː
60 at manyə nɔːblə armeː hadd (h)eː beː
at mɔrtal batæils hadd (h)eː beːn fiftéːnə
and fɔuxtən fɔr uːr fæiθ at tramisséːnə
in listəs θriːəs and æi slæin (h)is fɔː
ðis ilkə wurðiː kniçt hadd beːn alsóː
65 sumtiːmə wiθ ðə lɔrd ɔf palatíːə
agǽin anóːðər hɛːðən in turkíːə
and ɛvərmɔːr (h)eː hadd a sɔvræin priːs
and ðɔux ðat heː wɛːr wurðiː heː was wiːs
and ɔf (h)is pɔrt as meːk as is a mæidə
70 heː nɛvərj et nɔː vilæiní nə sæidə
in al (h)is liːf untóː nɔː manər wiçt
heː was a vɛrræi parfit dʒentil kniçt
but fɔr toː tɛllən juː ɔf his arrǽi
his hɔrs wɛːr goːdə but (h)eː was nat gæi
75 ɔf fustian (h)eː wɛːrəd a dʒipúːn
al bismútərd wiθ (h)is habərdʒuːn
fɔr (h)eː was laːt ikúm frɔm his viáːdʒə
and wɛntə fɔr toː doːn (h)is pilgrimáːdʒə
    wiθ (h)im ðɛːr was (h)is sun a juŋg skwiːéːr

80   A lovyere and a lusty bacheler,
With lokkes crulle as they were leyd in presse.
Of twenty yeer of age he was, I gesse.
Of his stature he was of evene lengthe,
And wonderly delyvere, and of greet strengthe.
85   And he hadde been somtyme in chyvachie
In Flaundres, in Artoys, and Pycardie,
And born hym weel, as of so litel space,
In hope to stonden in his lady grace.
Embrouded was he, as it were a meede
90   Al ful of fresshe floures, whyte and reede.
Syngynge he was, or floytynge, al the day;
He was as fressh as is the monthe of May.
Short was his gowne, with sleves longe and wyde.
Wel koude he sitte on hors and faire ryde.
95   He koude songes make and wel endite,
Juste and eek daunce, and weel purtreye and write.
So hoote he lovede that by nyghtertale
He slepte namoore than dooth a nyghtyngale.
Curteis he was, lowely, and servysable,
100   And carf biforn his fader at the table.

    A YEMAN hadde he and servantz namo
At that tyme, for hym liste ride so,
And he was clad in cote and hood of grene.
A sheef of pecok arwes, bright and kene,
105   Under his belt he bar ful thriftily—
Wel koude he dresse his takel yemanly:
His arwes drouped noght with fetheres lowe—

80 a luvyər and a lusti: batʃəléːr
wiθ lɔkkəs krul as ðæi wɛːr læid in prɛssə
ɔf twenti jɛːr ɔf aːdʒ (h)eː was iː gɛssə
ɔf his staːtíur (h)eː was ɔf ɛvnə lɛŋgθə
and wundərliː deːlívr and ɔf grɛːt strɛŋgθə
85 and heː hadd beːn sumtíːm in tʃivətʃíːə
in flaundrəs in artɔ́is and pikardíːə
and bɔrn (h)im weːl as ɔf sɔː liːtəl spaːsə
in hɔːp toː stɔːndən in (h)is laːdi graːsə
ɛmbrúːdəd was (h)eː as it wɛːr a mɛːdə
90 al ful ɔf frɛʃə fluːrəs hwiːt and rɛːdə
siŋgiŋg (h)eː was ɔr flɔitiŋg al ðə dæi
heː was as freʃ as is ðə moːnθ ɔf mæi
ʃɔrt was (h)is guːn wiθ sleːvəs lɔːŋg and wiːdə
weːl kuːd (h)eː siːt ɔn hɔrs and fæirə riːdə
95 heː kuːdə sɔːŋgəs maːk and weːl ɛndíːtə
dʒuːst and ɛːk dauns and weːl purtrǽi and wriːtə
sɔː hɔːt (h)eː luvəd ðat biː niçtərtáːlə
heː sleːp namɔ́ːr ðan doːθ a niçtiŋgaːlə
kurtæis heː was lɔuliː and sɛrvisáːblə
100 and karf bifɔrn (h)is fadər at ðə taːblə
   a jeːman hadd (h)eː and sɛrváːnts namɔ́ː
at ðat tiːmə fɔr (h)im listə riːdə sɔː
and heː was klad in kɔːt and hoːd of greːnə
a ʃɛːf ɔf pɛːkɔk arwəs briçt and keːnə
105 undər (h)is bɛlt (h)eː baːr ful θriftiliː
weːl kuːd (h)eː drɛss (h)is taːkəl jeːmanliː
his arwəs druːpəd nɔuxt wiθ fɛðrəs lɔuə

And in his hand he baar a myghty bowe.
A not-heed hadde he, with a broun visage.
110 Of wodecraft wel koude he al the usage.
Upon his arm he baar a gay bracer,
And by his syde a swerd and a bokeler,
And on that oother syde a gay daggere
Harneised wel and sharp as point of spere;
115 A Cristophre on his brest of silver sheene.
An horn he bar, the bawdryk was of grene;
A forster was he, soothly, as I gesse.

   Ther was also a Nonne, a PRIORESSE
That of hir smylyng was ful symple and coy;
120 Hire gretteste ooth was but by Seinte Loy;
And she was cleped madame Eglentyne.
Ful weel she soong the service dyvyne,
Entuned in hir nose ful semely,
And Frenssh she spak ful faire and fetisly,
125 After the scole of Stratford atte Bowe,
For Frenssh of Parys was to hire unknowe.
At mete wel ytaught was she with-alle:
She leet no morsel from hir lippes falle,
Ne wette hir fyngres in hir sauce depe;
130 Wel koude she carie a morsel and wel kepe
That no drope ne fille upon hire brest.
In curteisie was set ful muchel hir lest.
Hir over-lippe wyped she so clene
That in hir coppe ther was no ferthyng sene
135 Of grece, whan she dronken hadde hir draughte.

and in (h)is hand (h)e: ba:r a miçti: bouə
a not hɛ:d hadd (h)e: wiθ a bru:n vizá:ʤə
110 ɔf wo:dəkraft we:l ku:d (h)e: al ð' ju:zá:ʤə
upón (h)is arm (h)e: ba:r a gæi bra:sé:r
and bi: (h)is si:d a swe:rd and a bukəlé:r
and ɔn ðat o:ðər si:d a gæi daggɛ́:rə
harnæisəd we:l and ʃarp as point ɔf spɛ:rə
115 a kristɔfr ɔn (h)is brɛst ɔf silvər ʃe:nə
an hɔrn (h)e: ba:r ðə baudrik was ɔf gre:nə
a fɔrstər was (h)e: so:θli: as i: gɛssə

ðɛ:r was alsó: a nunn a pri:ɔrɛ́ssə
ðat ɔf (h)ir smi:liŋg was ful simpl and koi
120 hir grɛ:ttəst o:θ was but bi: sæintə loi
and ʃe: was klɛ:pəd mada:m ɛgləntí:nə
ful we:l ʃe: sɔ:ŋg ðə sɛrvi:sə diví:nə
ɛntíunəd in (h)ir no:z ful se:məli:
and frɛnʃ ʃe: spak ful fæir and fɛ:ti:sli:
125 aftər ðə sko:l ɔf stratfɔrd attə bouə
fɔr frɛnʃ ɔf paris was to: hir unknóuə
at mɛ:tə we:l itáuxt was ʃe: wiθ allə
ʃe: le:t no: mɔrsəl from (h)ir lippəs fallə
nə wɛtt (h)ir fiŋgrəs in (h)ir sausə de:pə
130 we:l ku:d ʃe: karyə mɔrsəl and we:l ke:pə
ðat no: drɔp nə fill upón (h)ir brɛst
in kurtæizí: was set ful mutʃl (h)ir lɛstə
hir ɔvərlippə wi:pəd ʃe: so: kle:nə
ðat in (h)ir kupp ðɛ:r was no: fɛrðiŋg se:nə
135 ɔf grɛ:sə hwan ʃe: druŋkən hadd (h)ir drauxtə

Ful semely after his mete she raughte.
And sikerly she was of greet desport,
And ful plesaunt, and amyable of port,
And peyned hire to countrefete cheere
140 Of court, and to been estatlich of manere,
And to ben holden digne of reverence.
But, for to speken of hire conscience,
She was so charitable and so pitous
She wolde wepe, if that she saugh a mous
145 Kaught in a trappe, if it were deed or bledde.
Of smale houndes hadde she that she fedde
With rosted flesh, or milk and wastel-breed.
But soore wepte she if oon of hem were deed,
Or if men smoot it with a yerde smerte;
150 And al was conscience and tendre herte.
Ful semyly hir wympul pynched was,
Hir nose tretys, hir eyen greye as glas,
Hir mouth ful smal, and therto softe and reed.
But sikerly she hadde a fair forheed,—
155 It was almoost a spanne brood, I trowe,—
For, hardily, she was nat undergrowe.
Ful fetys was hir cloke, as I was war.
Of smal coral aboute hire arm she bar
A peire of bedes, gauded al with grene,
160 And theron heng a booch of gold ful sheene,
On which ther was first write a crowned A,
And after *Amor vincit omnia*.

  Another NONNE with hire hadde she,

ful seːməliː aftər (h)ir mɛːt ʃeː rauxtə
and sikərliː ʃeː was ɔf grɛːt dispórt
and ful plezáunt and aːmiáːbl ɔf pɔrt
and pæinəd hir toː kuːntrəfɛːtə tʃeːrə
140 ɔf kuːrt and toː beːn ɛstáːtlitʃ ɔf manéːrə
and toː beːn hɔːldən diːn ɔf revərénsə
but fɔr toː spɛːkən ɔf (h)ir kɔnsiénsə
ʃeː was sɔː tʃaritáːbl and sɔː pitúːs
ʃeː wɔldə weːp if ðat ʃeː saux a muːs
145 kauxt in a trapp if it wɛːr dɛːd ɔr blɛddə
ɔf smaːle huːndəs hadd ʃeː ðat ʃeː fɛddə
wiθ rɔːstəd flɛʃ ɔr milk and wastəlbrɛːd
but sɔːrə weptə ʃeː if ɔːn ɔf hɛm wɛːr dɛːd
ɔr if mɛn smɔːt it wiθ a jɛrdə smɛrtə
150 and al was kɔnsiɛns and tɛndrə hɛrtə
ful seːməliː (h)ir wimpəl pintʃəd was
hir nɔːz trɛːtís (h)ir æiən græi as glas
hir muːθ ful smaːl and ðɛːrtoː sɔft and rɛːd
but sikərliː ʃeː hadd a fæir fɔrhéːd
155 it was almɔ́ːst a spannə brɔːd iː trɔuə
fɔr hardiliː ʃeː was nat undərgróuə
ful fɛːtiːs was (h)ir klɔːk as iː was waːr
ɔf smaːl kɔráːl abúːt (h)ir arm ʃeː baːr
a pæir of bɛːdəs gaudəd al wið greːnə
160 and ðɛːrɔn heːŋg a brɔːtʃ ɔf gɔld ful ʃeːnə
ɔn hwitʃ ðɛːr was first writ a kruːnəd aː
and aftər amɔr vinsit omniaː

anóːðər nunnə wiθ (h)ir haddə ʃeː

That was hir chapeleyne, and preestes thre.

165   A MONK ther was, a fair for the maistrie,
An outridere, that lovede venerie,
A manly man, to been an abbot able.
Ful many a deyntee hors hadde he in stable,
And whan he rood, men myghte his brydel heere
170   Gynglen in a whistlynge wynd als cleere
And eek as loude as dooth the chapel belle
Ther as this lord was kepere of the celle.
The reule of seint Maure or of seint Beneit,
By cause that it was old and somdel streit
175   This ilke Monk leet olde thynges pace,
And heeld after the newe world the space.
He yaf nat of that text a pulled hen
That seith that hunters been nat hooly men,
Ne that a monk, whan he is recchelees,
180   Is likned til a fissh that is waterlees,—
This is to seyn, a monk out of his cloystre.
But thilke text heeld he nat worth an oystre;
And I seyde his opinioun was good.
What sholde he studie and make hymselven wood,
185   Upon a book in cloystre alwey to poure,
Or swynken with his handes, and laboure,
As Austyn bit? How shal the world be served?
Lat Austyn have his swynk to hym reverved!
Therefore he was a prikasour aright;
190   Grehoundes he hadde as swift as fowel in flight.
Of prikyng and of huntyng for the hare

ðat was (h)ir tʃapəlæin and preːstəs θreː:
165 a muŋk ðɛːr was a fæir fɔr ðə mæistríːə
a uːtriːdɛr ðat luvəd vɛnəríːə
a manliː man toː beːn an abbɔt aːblə
ful manyə dæinteː hɔrs hadd heː in staːblə
and hwan (h)eː róːd men miçt (h)is briːdəl heːrə
170 dʒiŋglən in a hwistliŋg wiːnd als kleːrə
and ɛːk as luːd as doːθ ðə tʃapəl bɛllə
ðɛːr as ðis lɔrd was keːpər ɔf ðə sɛllə
ðə riul ɔf sæint maur ɔr ɔf sæint bənǽit
biː kauz ðat it was ɔːld and sumdɛːl stræit
175 ðis ilkə muŋk leːt ɔːldə θiŋgas paːsə
and heːld aftər ðə nɛwə wurld ðə spaːsə
heː jaf nat ɔf ðat tɛkst a pulləd hɛn
ðat sæiθ ðat huntərs beːn nat hɔːliː mɛn
nə ðat a muŋk hwan heː is rɛttʃələs
180 is liːknəd til a fiʃ ðat is waːtərlɛs
ðis is toː sæin a muŋk uːt ɔf (h)is klɔistrə
but ðilkə tɛkst heːld heː nat wurθ an ɔistrə
and iː sæid his ɔpiniúːn was gɔːd
hwat ʃɔld (h)eː studiː and maːk (h)imsélvən wɔːd
185 upɔ́n a boːk in klɔistr alwǽi toː puːrə
ɔr swiŋkən wiθ (h)is handəs and labúːrə
as austin bit huː ʃal ðə wurld beː sɛrvəd
lat austin haːv (h)is swiŋk toː him rəsérvəd
ðɛːrfɔːr (h)eː was a prikazúːr aríçt
190 greːhúːndz (h)eː hadd as swift as fuːl in fliçt
ɔf prikiŋ and ɔf huntiŋ fɔr ðə haːrə

Was al his lust; for no cost wolde he spare.
I seigh his sleves ypurfiled at the hond
With grys, and that the fyneste of a lond;
195 And, for to festne his hood under his chyn,
He hadde of gold ywrought a ful curious pyn;
A love-knotte in the gretter ende ther was.
His heed was balled, that shoon as any glas,
And eek his face, as he hadde been enoynt.
200 He was a lord ful fat and in good poynt;
His eyen stepe, and rollynge in his heed,
That stemed as a forneys of a leed;
His bootes souple, his hors in greet estaat.
Now certeinly he was a fair prelaat;
205 He was nat pale as a forpyned goost.
A fat swan loved he best of any roost.
His palfrey was as broun as is a berye.

    A FREERE ther was, a wantowne and a merye,
A limytour, a ful solempne man.
210 In alle the ordres foure is noon that kan
So muchel of daliaunce and fair langage.
He hadde maad ful many a mariage
Of yonge wommen at his owene cost.
Unto his ordre he was a noble post.
215 Ful wel biloved and famulier was he
With frankeleyns over al in his contree,
And eek with worthy wommen of the toun;
For he hadde power of confessioun,
As seyde hymself, moore than a curat,

```
         was al (h)is lust for nɔː kɔst wɔld (h)eː spaːrə
         iː sæiç (h)is sleːvs purfiːləd at ðə hɔːnd
         wiθ griːs and ðat ðə fiːnəst ɔf a lɔːnd
195      and fɔr toː fɛstn (h)is hoːd undər (h)is tʃin
         heː hadd ɔf gɔːld iwrɔ́uxt a ful kiuríuːs pin
         a luvknɔtt in ðə grɛttər ɛnd ðɛːr was
         his hɛːd was baːld ðat ʃɔːn as aniː glas
         and ɛːk (h)is faːs as heː (h)add beːn ɛnɔint
200      heː was a lɔrd ful fat and in goːd pɔint
         his æiən stɛːp and rɔlliŋ in (h)is hɛɜd
         ðat steːməd as a furnæis ɔf a lɛːd
         his boːtəs suːpl his hɔrs in grɛːt ɛstáːt
         nuː sɛrtæinliː (h)eː was a fæir prəláːt
205      heː was nat paːl as a fɔrpíːnəd gɔːst
         a fat swan luvd (h)eː bɛst ɔf aniː rɔːst
         his palfræi was as bruːn as is a bɛryə

         a freːr ðɛːr was a wantuːn and a mɛryə
         a limituːr a ful sɔlɛmpnə man
210      in al ðə ɔrdrəs fuːr is nɔːn ðat kan
         sɔː mutʃl ɔf daliáuns and fæir laŋgáːdʒə
         heː haddə maːd ful manyə marriáːdʒə
         ɔf juŋgə wummən at (h)is ɔunə kɔst
         untóː (h)is ɔrdr (h)eː was a nɔːblə pɔst
215      ful weːl bilúvd and famiulyéːr was heː
         wiθ fraŋklæins ɔvər al in his kuntréː
         and ɛːk wiθ wurðiː wummən ɔf ðə tuːn
         fɔr heː hadd puːər ɔf kɔnfɛssiúːn
         as sæidə himsəlf mɔːr ðan a kiuráːt
```

220 For of his ordre he was licenciat.
Ful swetely herde he confessioun,
And plesaunt was his absolucioun:
He was an esy man to yeve penaunce
Ther as he wiste to have a good pitaunce.
225 For unto a povre ordre for to yive
Is signe that a man is wel yshryve;
For if he yaf, he dorste make avaunt,
He wiste that a man was repentaunt;
For many a man so hard is of his herte,
230 He may nat wepe, althogh hym soore smerte.
Therfore in stede of wepynge and preyeres
Men moote yeve silver to the povre freres.
His typet was ay farsed ful of knyves
And pynnes, for to yeven faire wyves.
235 And certeinly he hadde a murye note;
Wel koude he synge and pleyen on a rote;
Of yeddynges he baar outrely the pris.
His nekke whit was as the flour-de-lys;
Therto he strong was as a champioun.
240 He knew the tavernes wel in every toun
And everich hostiler and tappestere
Bet than a lazar of a beggestere;
For unto swich a worthy man as he
Acorded nat, as by his facultee,
245 To have with sike lazars aqueyntaunce.
It is nat honeste, it may nat avaunce,
For to deelen with no swich poraille,

220 fɔr ɔf (h)is ɔrdr (h)e: was lisənsiá:t
ful swe:təli: hɛrd he: hɔnfɛssiú:n
and plɛzáunt was (h)is absɔlu:siú:n
he: was an ɛ:zi man to: je:v pənáunsə
ðɛ:r as (h)e: wist to: ha:v a go:d pitáunsə
225 fɔr əntó: a pɔvr ɔrdrə fɔr to: ji:və
is si:nə ðat a man is we:l iʃrí:və
fɔr if (h)e: jaf (h)e: durstə ma:k aváunt
he: wistə ðat a man was rɛpəntáunt
fɔr manyə man sɔ: hard is ɔf (h)is hɛrtə
230 he: mæi nat we:p alðɔux (h)im sɔ:rə smɛrtə
ðɛ:rfɔ:r in stɛ:d ɔf we:piŋ and præié:rəs
mɛn mɔ:t jɛ:və silvər to: ðə pɔvrə fre:rəs
his tipət was æi farsəd ful ɔf kni:vəs
and pinnəs fɔr to: je:vən fæirə wi:vəs
235 and sɛrtæinli: (h)e: hadd a miuri nɔ:tə
we:l ku:d (h)e: siŋ and plæiən ɔn a rɔ:tə
ɔf jeddiŋs he: ba:r u:trəli: ðə pri:s
his nɛkkə hwi:t wæs as ðə flu:rdəli:s
ðɛ:rtó: (h)e: strɔ:ŋ was as a tʃampiú:n
240 he: knɛu ðə tavərns we:l in ɛvri: tu:n
and ɛvritʃ ɔstile:r and tappəsté:r
bɛt ðan a laza:r ɔr a bɛggəsté:r
fɔr unto: switʃ a wurði: man as he:
akɔ́rdəd nat as bi: (h)is fakiulté:
245 to: ha:v wiθ si:kə laza:rs akwæintáunsə
it is nat ɔnəst it mæi nat aváunsə
fɔr to: dɛ:lən wiθ nɔ: switʃ pɔrǽillə

But al with riche and selleres of vitaille.
And over al ther as profit sholde arise
250 Curteis he was and lowely of servyse.
Ther nas no man nowher so vertuous.
He was the beste beggere in his hous;
252a [And yaf a certeyn ferme for the graunt;
252b Noon of his bretheren cam ther in his haunt;]
For thogh a wydwe hadde noght a sho,
So plesaunt was his "*In principio*,"
255 Yet wolde he have a ferthyng, er he wente.
His purchas was wel bettre than this rente.
And rage he koude, as it were right a whelpe.
In love-dayes ther koude he muchel helpe,.
For ther he was nat lyk a cloysterer
260 With a thredbare cope, as is a povre scoler,
But he was lyk a maister or a pope.
Of double worstede was his semycope,
That rounded as a belle out of the presse.
Somwhat he lipsed, for his wantownesse,
265 To make his Englissh sweete upon his tonge;
And in his harpyng, whan that he hadde songe,
His eyen twynkled in his heed aryght,
As doon the sterres in the frosty nyght.
This worthy lymytour was cleped Hyberd.
270   A MARCHANT was ther with a forked berd,
In mottelee, and hye on horse he sat;
Upon his heed a Flaundryssh bevere hat,
His bootes clasped faire and fetisly.

	but al wiθ ritʃ and sɛllərs ɔf vitǽillə
	and ɔvr al ðɛːr as prɔfit ʃɔld ariːzə
250	kurtǽis (h)eː was and lɔuliː ɔf sərviːzə
	ðɛːr nas nɔː man nɔːhwɛ́ːr sɔː vɛrtiuúːs
	heː was ðə bɛstə bɛggər in (h)is huːs
252a	[and jaf a sɛrtǽin fɛrmə fɔr ðə graunt
252b	nɔːn ɔf (h)is brɛðrən kam ðɛːr in (h)is haunt]
	fɔr ðɔux a widwə haddə nɔuxt a ʃoː
	sɔː plɛzaunt was (h)is in printʃipioː
255	yɛt wɔld (h)eː haːv a fɛrðiŋg ɛːr (h)eː wɛntə
	his purtʃaːs was weːl bɛttrə ðan (h)is rɛntə
	and raːʤ (h)eː kuːd as it wɛːr riçt a hwɛlpə
	in luvədǽis ðɛːr kuːd (h)eː mutʃel hɛlpə
	fɔr ðɛːr (h)eː was nat liːk a klɔistəréːr
260	wiθ a ðrɛdbaːr kɔːp as is a pɔvr skɔléːr
	but heː was liːk a mǽistər ɔr a pɔːpə
	ɔf duːblə wurstəd was (h)is sɛmikɔːpə
	ðat ruːndəd as a bɛll uːt ɔf ðə prɛssə
	sumhwát (h)eː lipsəd fɔr (h)is wantuːnɛ́ssə
265	toː maːk (h)is ɛŋgliʃ sweːt upɔ́n (h)is tuŋgə
	and in (h)is harpiŋg hwan ðat heː (h)add suŋgə
	his ǽiən twiŋklɔd in (h)is hɛːd aríçt
	as dɔːn ðə stɛrrəs in ðə frɔstiː niçt
	ðis wurðiː limituːr was klɛːpd hiuːbɛ́ːrd
270	a martʃaːnt was ðɛːr wiθ a fɔrkəd bɛːrd
	in mɔttəliː and hiː ɔn hɔrs (h)eː sat
	upɔ́n (h)is hɛːd a flaundriʃ bɛːvər hat
	his bɔːtəs klaspəd fǽir and fɛːtiːsliː

His resons he spak ful solempnely,
275 Sownynge alwey th'encrees of his wynnyng.
He wolde the see were kept for any thyng
Bitwixe Middelburgh and Orewelle.
Wel koude he in eschaunge sheeldes selle.
This worthy man ful wel his wit bisette:
280 Ther wiste no wight that he was in dette,
So estatly was he of his governaunce
With his bargynes and with his chevyssaunce.
For sothe he was a worthy man with-alle,
But, sooth to seyn, I noot how men hym calle.

285   A CLERK ther was of Oxenford also,
That unto logyk hadde longe ygo.
As leene was his hors as is a rake,
And he nas nat right fat, I undertake,
But looked holwe, and therto sobrely.
290 Ful thredbare was his overste courtepy;
For he hadde geten hym yet no benefice,
Ne was so worldly for to have office.
For hym was levere have at his beddes heed
Twenty bookes, clad in blak or reed.
295 Of Aristotle and his philosophie,
Than robes riche, or fithele, or gay sautrie.
But al be that he was a philosophre,
Yet hadde he but litel gold in cofre;
But al that he myghte of his freendes hente,
300 On bookes and on lernynge he it spente,
And bisily gan for the soules preye

his rɛzuːns heː spɑk ful sɔlɛ́mpnəliː
275 suːniŋ alwæi ð'ɛŋkrɛːs ɔf (h)is winniŋ
heː wɔld ðə sɛː wɛːr kɛpt fɔr ɑniː θiŋ
bitwíksə míddəlburx ɑnd ɔrəwɛ́llə
weːl kuːd (h)eː in ɛstʃáundʒə ʃɛːldəs sɛ́llə
ðis wurðiː mɑn ful weːl (h)is wit bisɛ́ttə
280 ðɛːr wist nɔː wiçt ðɑt (h)eː wɑs in dɛ́ttə
sɔː ɛstɑ́ːtliː wɑs (h)eː ɔf (h)is guvərnáunsə
wiθ (h)is bɑrgǽins ɑnd wiθ (h)is tʃɛvizáunsə
fɔr soːθ (h)eː wɑs ɑ wurðiː mɑn wiθ ɑllə
but sɔːθ toː sæin iː nɔːt huː mɛn (h)im kɑllə

285 ɑ klɛrk ðɛːr wɑs ɔf ɔksənfɔrd ɑlsóː
ðɑt untoː lɔdʒik həddə lɔːŋg igóː
ɑs lɛːnə wɑs (h)is hɔrs ɑs is ɑ rɑːkə
ɑnd (h)eː nɑs nɑt riçt fɑt iː undərtɑːkə
but lɔːkəd hɔlw ɑnd ðɛːrtoː sɔːbrəliː
290 ful θrɛdbɑːr wɑs (h)is ɔvrəst kuːrtəpiː
fɔr heː hɑdd gɛtn (h)im jɛt nɔː bɛnəfíːsə
nə wɑs sɔː wurldli fɔr toː hɑːv ɔffíːsə
fɔr him wɑs leːvr (h)ɑːv ɑt (h)is bɛ́ddəs hɛːd
twɛnti bɔːkəs klɑd in blɑk ɔr rɛːd
295 ɔf ɑristɔtl ɑnd his filɔsɔfíːə
ðɑn rɔːbəs ritʃ ɔr fiðl ɔr gæi sautríːə
but ɑl beː ðɑt (h)eː wɑs ɑ filɔsófrə
jɛt həddə heː but liːtəl gɔːld in kɔfrə
but ɑl ðɑt heː miçt ɔf (h)is frɛːndəs hɛntə
300 ɔn bɔːkəs ɑnd ɔn lɛrniŋ heː it spɛntə
ɑnd biziliː gɑn fɔr ðə sɔuləs præiə

Of hem that yaf hym wherwith to scoleye.
Of studie took he moost cure and moost heed.
Noght o word spak he moore than was neede,
305 And that was seyd in forme and reverence,
And short and quyk and ful of hy sentence.
Sownynge in moral vertu was his speche,
And gladly wolde he lerne and gladly teche.

A SERGEANT OF THE LAWE, war and wys,
310 That often hadde been at the Parvys,
Ther was also, ful riche of excellence.
Discreet he was and of greet reverence—
He semed swich, his wordes weren to wise.
Justice he was ful often in assise,
315 By patente and by pleyn commissioun.
For his science and for his heigh renoun,
Of fees and robes hadde he many oon.
So greet a purchasour was nowher noon:
Al was fee symple to hym in effect;
320 His purchasyng myghte nat been infect.
Nowher so bisy a man as he ther nas,
And yet he semed bisier than he was.
In termes hadde he caas and doomes alle
That from the tyme of kyng William were falle.
325 Therto he koude endite, and make a thyng,
Ther koude no wight pynche at his writyng;
And every statut koude he pleyn by rote.
He rood but hoomly in a medlee cote,
Girt with a ceint of silk, with barres smale;

ɔf hɛm ðat jaf (h)im hwɛːrwiθ toː skɔlǽiə
ɔf studiː toːk (h)eː mɔːst kiur and mɔːst heːdə
nɔuxt ɔ wurd spak heː mɔːr ðan was neːdə
305 and ðat was sǽid in fɔrm and rɛvərɛ́nsə
and ʃɔrt and kwik and ful ɔf hiː səntɛ́nsə
suːniŋ in mɔral vɛrtiu was (h)is spɛːtʃə
and gladliː wɔld (h)eː lɛrn and gladliː tɛːtʃə

a sɛrdʒaːnt ɔf ðə lawə waːr and wiːs
310 ðat ɔftən haddə beːn at ðə parvíːs
ðɛːr was alsɔ́ː ful ritʃ ɔf ɛksəllɛ́nsə
diskréːt (h)eː was and ɔf grɛːt rɛvərɛ́nsə
heː seːməd switʃ (h)is wurdəs wɛːrn sɔː wiːsə
dʒustíːs (h)eː was ful ɔftən in assíːzə
315 biː patənt and biː plǽin kɔmmissiúːn
fɔr his siːɛ́ns and fɔr (h)is hǽiç rənúːn
ɔf feːs and rɔːbəs hadd (h)eː mani ɔːn
sɔː grɛːt a purtʃazúːr was nɔːhwɛːr nɔːn
al was feː simplə toː (h)im in əffɛkt
320 his purtʃaːziŋ miçt nat beːn infɛkt
nɔːhwɛ́ːr sɔː bizyə man as heː ðɛːr nas
and jɛt (h)eː seːməd bizyər ðan (h)eː was
in tɛrməs hadd (h)eː kaːs and doːməs allə
ðat frɔm ðə tiːm ɔf kiŋ willyám wɛːr fallə
325 ðɛːrtóː (h)eː kuːd ɛndíːt and maːk a θiŋ
ðɛːr kuːdə nɔː wiçt pintʃən at (h)is wriːtiŋ
and ɛvriː staːtiut kuːd (h)eː plǽin biː rɔːtə
heː rɔːd but hɔːmliː in a mɛdleː kɔːtə
girt wiθ a sǽint ɔf silk wiθ barrəs smaːlə

330   Of his array telle I no lenger tale.
        A FRANKELEYN was in his compaignye.
    Whit was his berd as is the dayesye;
    Of his complexioun he was sangwyn.
    Wel loved he by the morwe a sop in wyn;
335   To lyven in delit was evere his wone,
    For he was Epicurus owene sone,
    That heeld opinioun that pleyn delit
    Was verray felicitee parfit.
    An housholdere, and that a greet, was he;
340   Seint Julian he was in his contree.
    His breed, his ale, was alweys after oon;
    A bettre envyned man was nowher noon.
    Withoute bake mete was nevere his hous,
    Of fissh and flessh, and that so plentevous,
345   In snewed in his hous of mete and drynke,
    Of alle deyntees that men koude thynke.
    After the sondry sesons of the yeer,
    So chaunged he his mete and his soper.
    Ful many a fat partrich hadde he in muwe,
350   And many a breem and many a luce in stuwe.
    Wo was his cook but if his sauce were
    Poynaunt and sharp, and redy al his geere.
    His table dormant in his halle alway
    Stood redy covered al the longe day.
355   At sessiouns ther was he lord and sire;
    Ful ofte tyme he was knyght of the shire.
    And anlaas and a gipser al of silk

330 ɔf his arrǽi tɛll iː nɔː lɛŋgər taːlə

a fraŋkəlæin was in (h)is kumpæiníːə
hwiːt was (h)is bɛːrd as is ðə dæiəzíːə
ɔf his kɔmplɛksiúːn (h)eː was saŋgwíːn
weːl luvd (h)eː biː ðə mɔrw a sɔp in wiːn
335 toː livən in deːlíːt was ɛvr (h)is wunə
fɔr heː was ɛpikíurus ɔunə sunə
ðat heːld ɔpiniúːn ðat plæin deːlíːt
was vɛrræi fɛlisíteː parfíːt
an huːshɔːldər and ðat a grɛːt was heː
340 sæint ʤulíaːn (h)eː was in his kuntréː
his brɛːd (h)is aːl was alwæis aftər ɔːn
a bɛttr ɛnvíːnəd man was nɔːhwɛːr nɔːn
wiðúːtə baːkə mɛːt was nɛvr (h)is huːs
ɔf fiʃ and flɛʃ and ðat sɔː plɛntəvúːs
345 it snɛuəd in (h)is huːs ɔf mɛːt and driŋkə
ɔf allə dæinteːs ðat mɛn kuːdə θiŋkə
aftər ðə sundriː sɛːzuːns ɔf ðə jɛːr
sɔː tʃaunʤəd heː (h)is mɛːt and his supéːr
ful manyə fat partrítʃ (h)add heː in miuə
350 and manyə brɛːm and manyə luːs in stiuə
wɔː was (h)is kɔːk but if (h)is sausə wɛːrə
pɔináunt and ʃarp and rediː al (h)is gɛːrə
his taːblə dɔrmaːnt in (h)is hall alwæi
stoːd rediː kuvrəd al ðə lɔːŋgə dæi
355 at sɛssiúːns ðɛːr was (h)eː lɔrd and siːrə
ful ɔftə tiːmə heː was kniçt ɔf ðə ʃiːrə
and anlaːs and a ʤipsər al ɔf silk

Heeng at his girdel, whit as morne milk.
A shirreve hadde he been, and a contour.
360 Was nowher swich a worthy vavasour.

An HABERDASSHERE and a CARPENTER,
A WEBBE, a DYERE, and a TAPYCER,—
And they were clothed alle in o lyveree
Of a solempne and a greet fraternitee.
365 Ful fressh and newe hir geere apiked was:
Hir knyves were chaped noght with bras
But al with silver; wroght ful clene and weel
Hire girdles and hir pouches everydeel.
Wel semed ech of hem a fair burgeys
370 To sitten in a yeldehalle on a deys.
Everich, for the wisdom that he kan,
Was shaply for to been an alderman.
For catel hadde they ynogh and rente,
And eek hir wyves wolde it wel assente;
375 And elles certeyn were they to blame.
It is ful fair to been ycleped "madame,"
And goon to vigilies al bifore,
And have a mantel roialliche ybore.

A COOK they hadde with hem for the nones
380 To boille the chiknes with the marybones,
And poudre-marchant tart and galyngale.
Wel koude he knowe a draughte of Londoun ale.
He koude rooste, and sethe, and broille, and frye,
Maken mortreux, and wel bake a pye.
385 But greet harm was it, as it thoughte me,

he:ŋg at (h)is girdəl hwi:t as mɔrnə milk
a ʃirre:v hadd (h)e: be:n and a ku:ntú:r
360 was nɔ:hwɛ:r switʃ a wurði: vavazú:r
an habərdaʃe:r and a karpənté:r
a wɛbb a di:ər and a tapisé:r
and ðæi wɛ:r klɔ:ðəd all in ɔ: livré:
ɔf a sɔlémpn and grɛ:t fratərnité:
365 ful freʃ and nɛu (h)ir gɛ:r apí:kəd was
hir kni:vəs wɛ:rə tʃá:pəd nɔuxt wiθ bras
but al wiθ silvər wrɔuxt ful klɛ:n and we:l
hir girdləs and (h)ir pu:tʃəs ɛvri:dɛ:l
we:l se:məd ɛ:tʃ ɔf hɛm a fæir burdʒǽis
370 to: sittən in a jɛldhall ɔn a dæis
ɛvritʃ fɔr ðə wi:sdum ðat (h)e: kan
was ʃa:pli: fɔr to: be:n an aldərman
fɔr katəl haddə ðæi inɔux and rɛntə
and ɛ:k (h)ir wi:vəs wɔld it we:l assɛ́ntə
375 and ɛlləs sɛrtæin wɛ:rə ðæi to: bla:mə
it is ful fæir to: be:n iklɛpt madá:mə
and gɔ:n to: vidʒiliəs al bifɔrə
and ha:v a mantəl rɔialli:tʃ ibɔ́:rə
a kɔ:k ðæi haddə wiθ (h)ɛm fɔr ðə nɔ:nəs
380 to: bɔil ðə tʃiknəs wiθ ðə maribɔ́:nəs
and pu:drəmartʃa:nt tart and galiŋgá:lə
we:l ku:d (h)e: knɔu a drauxt ɔf lɔndu:n a:lə
he: ku:də rɔ:st and se:ð and brɔil and fri:ə
ma:kən mɔrtrɛus and we:l ba:k a pi:ə
385 but grɛ:t harm was it as it θɔuxtə me:

That on his shyne a mormal hadde he.
For blankmanger, that made he with the beste.

    A SHIPMAN was ther, wonynge fer by weste;
For aught I woot, he was of Dertemouthe.
390 He rood upon a rouncy, as he kouthe,
In a gowne of faldyng to the knee.
A daggere hangynge on a laas hadde he
Aboute his nekke, under his arm adoun.
The hoote somer hadde maad his hewe al broun.
395 And certeinly he was a good felawe;
Ful many a draughte of wyn had he ydrawe
Fro Burdeus-ward, whil that the chapman sleep.
Of nyce conscience took he no keep.
If that he faught, and hadde the hyer hond,
400 By water he sente hem hoom to every lond.
But of his craft to rekene wel his tydes,
His stremes, and his daungers hym bisides,
His herberwe, and his moone, his lodemenage,
Ther nas noon swich from Hulle to Cartage.
405 Hardy he was and wys to undertake;
With many a tempest hadde his berd been shake.
He knew alle the havenes, as they were,
Fro Gootlond to the cape of Fynystere,
And every cryke in Britaigne and in Spayne.
410 His barge ycleped was the Maudelayne.

    With us ther was a DOCTOUR OF PHISIK;
In al this world ne was ther noon hym lik,
To speke of phisik and of surgerye,

ðat ɔn (h)is ʃin a mɔrmal haddə heː
fɔr blaŋkmandʒéːr ðat maːd (h)eː wiθ ðə bɛstə
  a ʃipman was ðɛːr wuniŋg fɛr biː wɛstə
fɔr auxt iː wɔːt (h)eː was ɔf dɛrtəmuːðə
390 heː rɔːd upɔ́n a ruːnsiː as (h)eː kuːðə
in a guːn ɔf faldiŋg toː ðə kneː
a daggeːr haŋgiŋg ɔn a laːs (h)add heː
abúːt (h)is nɛk undər (h)is arm ədúːn
ðə hɔːtə sumr (h)add maːd (h)is hiu al bruːn
395 and sɛrtæinliː (h)eː was a goːd fəláuə
ful manyə drauxt ɔf wiːn (h)add heː idráuə
frɔː burduiswɑrd hwiːl ðat ðə tʃapmən sleːp
ɔf niːsə kɔnsiɛ́ns toːk heː nɔː keːp
if ðat (h)eː fauxt and hadd ðə hiːər hɔːnd
400 biː waːtr (h)eː sɛnt (h)em hɔːm toː ɛvriː lɔːnd
but ɔf (h)is kraft toː rɛkən weːl (h)is tiːdəs
his strɛːməs and (h)is daundʒərs him bisíːdəs
his hɛrbərw and (h)is moːn (h)is lɔːdmənáːdʒə
ðɛːr nas nɔːn switʃ frɔm hullə toː kərtáːdʒə
405 hardiː (h)eː was and wiːs toː undərtaːkə
wiθ manya tɛmpəst hadd (h)is bɛːrd beːn ʃaːkə
heː kniu all ðə haːvəns as ðæi wɛːrə
frɔ gɔːtlɔːnd toː ðə kaːp ɔf finistɛ́ːrə
and ɛvriː kriːk in britæin and in spæinə
410 his bardʒ iklɛ́ːpəd was ðə maudəlǽinə
  wiθ uːs ðɛːr was a dɔktuːr ɔf fizíːk
in al ðis wurld nə was ðɛːr nɔːn (h)im liːk
toː spɛːk ɔf fiziːk and ɔf siurdʒəríːə

For he was grounded in astronomye.
415 He kepte his pacient a ful greet deel
In houres by his magyk natureel.
Wel koude he fortunen the ascendent
Of his ymages for his pacient.
He knew the cause of everich maladye,
420 Were it of hoot, or coold, or moyste, or drye,
And where engendred, and of what humour.
He was a verray, parfit praktisour:
The cause yknowe, and of his harm the roote,
Anon he yaf the sike man his boote.
425 Ful redy hadde he his apothecaries
To sende hym drogges and his letuaries,
For ech of hem made oother for to wynne—
Hir frendshipe nas nat newe to bigynne.
Wel knew he the olde Esculapius,
430 And Deyscorides, and eek Rufus,
Olde Ypocras, Haly, and Galyen,
Serapion, Razis, and Avycen,
Averrois, Damascien, and Constantyn,
Bernard, and Gatesden, and Gilbertyn.
435 Of his diete mesurable was he,
For it was of no superfluitee,
But of greet norissyng and digestible.
His studie was but litel on the Bible.
In sangwyn and in pers he clad was al,
440 Lyned with taffata and with sendal;
And yet he was but esy of dispence.

for he: was gru:ndəd in astrɔnəmí:ə
415 he: kɛpt (h)is pa:siént a ful grɛ:t dɛ:l
in u:rəs bi: his madʒik na:tiu:ré:l
we:l ku:də he: fɔrtyú:nən ð'assəndɛnt
ɔf his imá:dʒəs fɔr (h)is pa:siɛnt
he: knɛu ðə kauz ɔf ɛvritʃ maladí:ə
420 wɛ:r it ɔf hɔ:t ɔr kɔ:ld ɔr mɔist ɔr dri:ə
and hwɛ:r ðæi endʒéndrəd and ɔf hwat iumú:r
he: was a vɛrræi parfit praktizú:r
ðə kauz iknóu and ɔf (h)is harm ðə ro:tə
anɔ́:n (h)e: jaf ðə si:kə man (h)is bo:tə
425 ful rɛdi: hadd (h)e: his apɔtəká:riəs
to: sɛnd (h)im druggəs and (h)is lɛtiuá:riəs
fɔr ɛ:tʃ ɔf hɛm ma:d o:ðər fɔr to: winnə
hir frɛ:ndʃip nas nat nɛuə to: bigínnə
we:l knɛu (h)e: ð'ɔ:ldə ɛskyu:la:piú:s
430 and de:iskɔridɛs and ɛ:k riufú:s
ɔ:ld ipókra:s ha:li: and ga:líɛn
sərá:piɔn ra:zí:s and avisɛ́n
avərrɔis damá:ʃiɛn and kɔnstantí:n
bɛrnard and ga:təsdɛn and gilbərtí:n
435 ɔf his di:étə mɛziurá:bl was he:
fɔr it was ɔf nɔ: siupərfliuité:
but ɔf grɛ:t nurissiŋg and di:dʒəstí:blə
his studi: was but li:təl ɔn ðə bi:blə
in saŋgwi:n and in pɛrs (h)e: klad was al
440 li:nəd wiθ taffa:ta: and wiθ səndal
and jɛt (h)e: was but ɛ:zi: ɔf dispénsə

Chaucer · 43

He kepte that he wan in pestilence,
For gold in phisik is a cordial;
Therefore he lovede gold in special.

445   A good WIF was ther OF biside BATHE,
But she was somdel deef, and that was scathe.
Of clooth-makyng she hadde swich an haunt,
She passed hem of Ypres and of Gaunt.
In al the parisshe wif ne was ther noon
450   That to the offrynge bifore hire sholde goon;
And if ther dide, certeyn so wrooth was she,
That she was out of alle charitee.
Hir coverchiefs ful fyne weren of ground;
I dorste swere they weyeden ten pound
455   That on a Sonday were upon hir heed.
Hir hosen weren of fyn scarlet reed,
Ful streite yteyd, and shoes ful moyste and newe.
Boold was hir face, and fair, and reed of hewe.
She was a worthy womman al hir lyve:
460   Housbondes at chirche dore she hadde fyve,
Withouten oother compaignye in youthe,—
But therof nedeth nat to speke as nowthe.
And thries hadde she been at Jerusalem;
She hadde passed many a straunge strem;
465   At Rome she hadde been, and at Boloigne,
In Galice at Seint-Jame, and at Coloigne.
She koude muchel of wandrynge by the weye.
Gat-tothed was she, soothly for to seye.
Upon an amblere esily she sat,

heː kɛptə ðat (h)eː wan in pɛstilɛ́nsə
fɔr gɔːld in fiziːk is a kɔrdiáːl
ðɛːrfɔːr (h)eː luvəd gɔːld in spɛsiáːl

445 a goːd wiːf was ðɛːr ɔf bisíːdə baːðə
but ʃeː was sumdɛːl dɛːf and ðat was skaːðə
ɔf klɔːθmaːkiŋg ʃeː haddə switʃ an haunt
ʃeː passəd hɛm ɔf iprəs and ɔf gaunt
in al ðə pariʃ wiːf nə was ðɛːr nɔːn

450 ðat toː ð'ɔffriŋg bifɔːr (h)ir ʃɔldə gɔːn
and if ðɛːr did sɛrtæin sɔː wrɔːθ was ʃeː
ðat ʃeː was uːt ɔf allə tʃaritéː
hir kuvərtʃiːfs ful fiːnə wɛːr ɔf gruːnd
iː durstə swɛːr ðæi wæiədən tɛn puːnd

455 ðat ɔn a sundæi wɛːrn upɔn (h)ir hɛːd
hir hɔːzən wɛːrən ɔf fiːn skarlət rɛːd
ful stræit itǽid and ʃoːs ful mɔist and nɛuə
bɔːld was (h)ir faːs and fæir and rɛːd ɔf hɛuə
ʃeː was a wurði wummən al (h)ir liːvə

460 huːzbɔ́ːnds at tʃirtʃə dɔːrə ʃeː (h)add fiːvə
wiðúːtən oːðər kumpæiníː in juːðə
but ðɛːrɔf neːdəθ nat toː spɛːk as nuːðə
and θriːs (h)add ʃeː beːn at dʒərsəlɛ́ːm
ʃeː haddə passəd manya straundʒə strɛːm

465 at rɔːmə ʃeː (h)add beːn and at bɔlɔ́ːinə
in galiːs at sæint dʒaːm and at kɔlɔ́ːinə
ʃeː kuːdə mutʃl ɔf wandriŋg biː ðə wæiə
gaːt tóːðəd was ʃeː soːθliː fɔr toː sæiə
upɔ́ːn an amblər ɛːziliː ʃeː sat

470 Ywympled wel, and on hir heed an hat
As brood as is a bokeler or a targe;
A foot-mantel aboute hir hipes large.
And on hir feet a paire of spores sharpe.
In felaweshipe wel knoude she laughe and carpe.
475 Of remedies of love she knew per chaunce,
For she koude of that art the olde daunce.

  A good man was ther of religioun,
And was a povre PERSOUN of a toun,
But riche he was of hooly thoght and werk.
480 He was also a lerned man, a clerk,
That Cristes gospel trewely wolde preche;
His parisshens devoutly wolde he teche.
Benygne he was, and wonder diligent,
And in adversitee ful pacient,
485 And swich he was ypreved ofte sithes.
Ful looth were hym to cursen for his tithes,
But rather wolde he yeven, out of doute,
Unto his povre parisshens aboute
Of his offryng and eek of his substaunce.
490 He koude in litel thyng have suffisaunce.
Wyd was his parisshe, and houses fer asonder,
But he ne lefte nat, for reyn ne thonder,
In siknesse nor in meschief to visite
The ferreste in his parrishe, muche and lite,
495 Upon his feet, and in his hand a staf.
This noble ensample to his sheep he yaf,
That first he wroghte, and afterward he taughte.

470	iwímpləd weːl and ɔn (h)ir hɛːd an hat
	as brɔːd as is a bukleːr ɔr a tarʤə
	a foːtmantəl abúːt (h)ir hipəs larʤə
	and ɔn (h)ir feːt a pæir ɔf spɔːrəs ʃarpə
	in fɛlauʃip weːl kuːd ʃeː laux and karpə
475	ɔf rɛmədiːs ɔf luv ʃeː knɛu pɛr tʃaunsə
	fɔr ʃeː kuːd ɔf ðat art ðə ɔːldə daunsə
	a goːd man was ðɛːr ɔf rəliʤiúːn
	and was a pɔvrə pɛrsuːn ɔf a tuːn
	but ritʃ (h)eː was ɔf hɔːliː θɔuxt and wɛrk
480	heː was alsóː a lɛrnəd man a klɛrk
	ðat kriːstəs gɔspəl trɛuliː wɔldə prɛːtʃə
	his pariʃʃɛ́ːns deːvúːtliː wɔld (h)eː tɛːtʃə
	bəníːn (h)eː was and wundər diliʤɛ́nt
	and in advɛrsitéː ful paːsíɛnt
485	and switʃ heː was prɛːvəd ɔftəsiːðəs
	ful lɔːθ wɛːr him toː kursən fɔr (h)is tiːðəs
	but raːðər wɔld (h)eː jɛːvən uːt ɔf duːtə
	untóː (h)is pɔvrə pariʃʃɛ́ːns abúːtə
	ɔf (h)is ɔffríŋ and ɛːk ɔf (h)is substáunsə
490	heː kuːd in liːtəl θiŋg (h)av suffizáunsə
	wiːd was (h)is parʃ and huːzəs fɛr asúndər
	but heː nə lɛftə nat fɔr ræin nə θundər
	in siːknəs nɔr in mɛstʃiːf toː viziːtə
	ðə fɛrrəst in (h)is pariʃ mutʃ and liːtə
495	upɔ́n (h)is feːt and in (h)is hand a staf
	ðis nɔːbl ɛnsaːmplə toː (h)is ʃeːp (h)eː jaf
	ðat first (h)eː wrɔuxt and aftərward (h)eː tauxtə

Out of the gospel he tho wordes cughte,
And this figure he added eek therto,
That if gold ruste, what shal iren do?
For if a preest be foul, on whom we truste,
No wonder is a lewed man to ruste;
And shame it is, if a preest take keep,
A shiten shepherde and a clene sheep.
Wel oghte a preest ensample for to yive,
By his clennesse, how that his sheep sholde lyve.
He sette nat his benefice to hyre
And leet his sheep encombred in the myre
And ran to Londoun unto Seinte Poules
To seken hym a chaunterie for soules,
Or with a bretherhed to been withholde;
But dwelte at hoom, and kepte wel his folde,
So that the wolf ne made it nat myscarie;
He was a shepherde and noght a mercenarie.
And thogh he hooly were and vertuous,
He was to synful men nat despitous,
Ne of his speche daungerous ne digne,
But in his techyng discreet and benygne.
To drawen folk to hevene by fairnesse,
By good ensample, this was his bisyness.
But it were any persone obstinat,
What so he were, of heigh or lough estat,
Hym wolde he snybben sharply for the nonys.
A bettre preest I trowe that nowher noon ys.
He waited after no pompe and reverence,

uːt ɔf ðə gɔspəl heː ðɔː wurdəs kauxtə
and ðis figíur (h)eː addəd ɛːk ðɛːrtóː
500 ðat if gɔːld rustə hwat ʃal iːrən doː
fɔr if a preːst beː fuːl ɔn hwoːm weː trustə
nɔː wundər is a lɛuəd man toː rustə
and ʃaːm it is if a preːst taːkə keːp
a ʃitən ʃɛphɛrd and a klɛːnə ʃeːp
505 weːl ɔuxt a preːst ɛnsáːmpl fɔr toː jivə
biː (h)is klɛnnəs huː ðat (h)is ʃeːp ʃɔld livə
heː sɛttə nat (h)is bɛnəfiːs toː hiːrə
and leːt (h)is ʃeːp ɛŋkúmbrəd in ðə miːrə
and ran toː lɔnduːn untoː sæintə poulǝs
510 toː seːkən him a tʃauntəriː fɔr soulǝs
ɔr wiθ a breːðərhɛːd toː beːn wiθhɔːldə
but dwɛlt at hɔːm and kɛptə weːl (h)is fɔːldə
sɔː ðat ðə wulf nə maːd it nat miskaryə
heː was a ʃɛːphərd and nɔuxt a mɛrsənáryə
515 and ðɔux (h)eː hɔːliː wɛːr and vɛrtiuúːs
heː was toː sinful mɛn nat despiːtúːs
nə ɔf (h)is spɛːtʃə daundʒəruːs nə diːnə
but in (h)is tɛːtʃiŋg diskreːt and bəníːnə
toː drauən fɔlk toː hɛvən biː fæirnɛ́ssə
520 biː goːd ɛnsáːmpl ðis was (h)is bizinɛ́ssə
but it wɛːr ani pɛrsuːn ɔbstináːt
hwat sɔː (h)eː wɛːr ɔf hæiç ɔr lou ɛstáːt
him wɔld (h)eː snibbən ʃarpliː fɔr ðə nɔːnis
a bɛttrə preːst iː trou ðat nɔːhwɛːr nɔːn is
525 heː wæitəd aftr nɔː pɔmp and rɛvərɛ́nsə

Ne maked hym a spiced conscience,
But Cristes loore and his apostles twelve
He taughte, but first he folwed it hymselve.
    With hym ther was a PLOWMAN, was his brother,
530 That hadde ylad of dong ful many a fother;
A trewe swynkere and a good was he,
Lyvynge in pees and parfit charitee.
God loved he best with al his hoole herte
At alle tymes, thogh him gamed or smerte,
535 And thanne his neighebore right as hymselve.
He wolde thresshe, and therto dyke and delve,
For Cristes sake, for every povre wight,
Withouten hire, if it lay in his myght.
His tithes payde he ful faire and wel,
540 Bothe of his propre swynk and his catel.
In a tabard he rood upon a mere.
    Ther was also a REVE, and a MILLERE,
A SOMNOUR, and a PARDONER also,
A MAUNCIPLE, and myself—ther were namo.
545   The MILLERE was a stout carl for the nones;
Ful byg he was of brawn, and eek of bones.
That proved wel, for over al ther he cam,
At wrastlynge he wolde have alwey the ram.
He was short-sholdred, brood, a thikke knarre;
550 Ther was no dore that he nolde heve of harre,
Or breke it at a rennyng with his heed.
His berd as any sowe or fox was reed,
And therto brood, as though it were a spade.

nə mɑːkəd him ɑ spiːsəd kɔnsiɛ́nsə
but kriːstəs lɔːr ɑnd his apɔ́stləs twɛlvə
heː tauxt but first (h)eː fɔlwəd it (h)imsɛ́lvə
    wiθ him ðɛːr was ɑ pluːman was (h)is broːðər
530 ðat (h)add iĺad ɔf duŋg ful manyə foːðər
ɑ trɛuə swinkər and ɑ goːd was heː
living in pɛːs ɑnd parfit tʃarité
gɔd luvd (h)eː bɛst wiθ al (h)is hɔːlə hɛrtə
at allə tiːməs ðɔux (h)im gaːmd ɔr smɛrtə
535 and ðann (h)is næiçəbuːr riçt as (h)imsɛ́lvə
heː wɔldə θrɛʃ and ðɛːtoː diːk and dɛlvə
fɔr kriːstəs saːk fɔr ɛvriː pɔvrə wiçt
wiðúːtən hiːr if it læi in (h)is miçt
his tiːðəs pæidə heː ful fæir and weːl
540 bɔːθ ɔf (h)is prɔprə swink and his katéːl
in ɑ tabard (h)eː rɔːd upɔ́n ɑ mɛːrə
    ðɛːr was alsɔ́ ɑ rɛːv and ɑ millɛ́ːrə
ɑ sumnuːr and ɑ pardɔnɛːr alsɔ́
ɑ maunsipl and miːsɛ́lf ðɛːr wɛːr namɔ́
545 ðə millɛːr was stuːt karl fɔr ðə nɔːnəs
ful big (h)eː was ɔf braun and ɛːk ɔf bɔːnəs
ðat prɔːvəd weːl fɔr ɔːvr al ðɛːr (h)eː kam
at wrastliŋg (h)eː wɔld haːv alwæi ðə ram
heː was ʃɔrtsuldrəd brɔːd ɑ θikkə knarrə
550 ðɛːr nas nɔː dɔːr ðat heː nɔld hɛːv ɔf harrə
ɔr brɛːk it at ɑ rɛnniŋg wiθ (h)is hɛːd
his bɛːrd as ani suː ɔr fɔks was rɛːd
and ðɛːtoː brɔːd as ðɔux it wɛːr ɑ spaːdə

Upon the cop right of his nose he hade
555 A werte, and theron stood a toft of herys,
Reed as the brustles of a sowes erys;
His nosethirles blake were and wyde.
A swerd and bokeler bar he by his syde.
His mouth as greet was as a greet forneys.
560 He was a janglere and a goliardeys,
And that was moost of synne and harlotries.
Wel koude he stelen corn and tollen thries;
And yet he hadde a thombe of gold, pardee.
A whit cote and a blew hood wered he.
565 A baggepipe wel koude he blowe and sowne,
And therwithal he broghte us out of towne.

    A gentl MAUNCIPLE was ther of a temple,
Of which achatours myghte take exemple
For to be wise in byynge of vitaille;
570 For wheither that he payde or took by taille,
Algate he wayted so in his achaat
That he was ay biforn and in good staat.
Now is nat that of God a ful fair grace
That swich a lewed mannes wit shal pace
575 The wisdom of an heep of lerned men?
Of maistres hadde he mo than thries ten,
That weren of lawe expert and curious,
Of which ther were a duszeyne in that hous
Worthy to been stywardes of rente and lond
580 Of any lord that is in Engelond,
To make hym lyve by his propre good

upɔ́n ðə kɔp riçt ɔf (h)is nɔːz (h)eː haːdə
555 a wɛrt and ðɛːrɔn stoːd a tuft ɔf hɛːris
rɛːd as ðə brustls ɔf a suːəs ɛːris
his nɔːzəθirləs blaːkə wɛːr and wiːdə
a swɛːrd and bukleːr baːr (h)eː biː (h)is siːdə
his muːθ as grɛːt was as a grɛːt furnǽis
560 heː was a dʒanglɛ́ːr and a gɔliardǽis
and ðat was mɔːst ɔf sinn and harlətríːəs
weːl kuːd (h)eː stɛːlən kɔrn and tɔllən θriːəs
and jet (h)eː hadd a θumb ɔf gɔːld pardéː
a hwiːt kɔːt and a blɛu hoːd wɛːrəd heː
565 a baggəpiːp weːl kuːd (h)eː blɔu and suːnə
and ðɛːwiðal (h)eː brɔuxt uːs uːt ɔf tuːnə

a dʒɛntil maunsipl was ðɛːr ɔf a tɛmplə
ɔf hwitʃ atʃaːtuːrs miçtə taːk ɛksɛ́mplə
fɔr toː beː wiːs in biːiŋ ɔf vitǽillə
570 fɔr hwæiðər ðat (h)eː pæid ɔr toːk biː tǽillə
algáːt (h)eː wæitəd sɔː in his atʃáːt
ðat heː was æi bifɔrn and in goːd staːt
nuː is nat ðat ɔf gɔd a ful fæir graːsə
ðat switʃ a lɛuwəd mannəs wit ʃal paːsə
575 ðə wiːsduːm ɔf an hɛːp ɔf lɛrnəd mɛn
ɔf mæistrəs hadd (h)eː mɔː ðan θriːəs tɛn
ðat wɛːr ɔf lau ɛkspɛ́rt and kiuriúːs
ɔf hwitʃ ðɛːr wɛːr a duzæin in ðat huːs
wurðiː toː beːn stiːwardəs ɔf rɛnt and lɔːnd
580 ɔf aniː lɔrd ðat is in ɛŋgəlɔːnd
toː maːk (h)im livə biː (h)is prɔprə goːd

In honour detteless (but if he were wood),
Or lyve as scarsly as hym list desire;
And able for to helpen al a shire
585   In any caas that myghte falle or happe;
And yet this Manciple sette hir aller cappe.

The REVE was a sclendre colerik man.
His berd was shave as ny as ever he kan;
His heer was by his erys ful round yshorn;
590   His top was dokked lyk a preest biforn.
Ful longe were his legges and ful lene,
Ylyk a staf; ther was no calf ysene.
Wel koude he kepe a gerner and a bynne;
Ther was noon auditour koude on him wynne.
595   Wel wiste he by the droghte and by the reyn
The yeldynge of his seed and of his greyn.
His lordes sheep, his neet, his dayerye,
His swyn, his hors, his stoor, and his pultrye
Was hoolly in this Reves governynge,
600   And by his covenant yaf the rekenynge,
Syn that his lord was twenty yeer of age.
Ther koude no man brynge hym in arrerage.
Ther nas baillif, ne hierde, nor oother hyne,
That he ne knew his sleighte and his covyne;
605   They were adrad of hym as of the deeth.
His wonyng was ful faire upon an heeth;
With grene treës shadwed was his place.
He koude bettre than his lord purchace.
Ful riche he was astored pryvely:

in ɔnuːr dɛttəlɛ́ːs but if (h)eː wɛːrə woːd
ɔr liv as skarsliː as (h)im list dəzíːrə
and aːblə fɔr toː hɛlpən al a ʃiːrə
585 in aniː kaːs ðat miçtə fall ɔr happə
and jɛt ðis maːnsipl sɛtt (h)ir allər kappə
   ðə reːvə was a slɛndrə kɔlrik man
his bɛrd was ʃaːv as niː as ɛvr (h)eː kan
his hɛːr was biː (h)is ɛːrs ful ruːnd iʃɔrn
590 his tɔp was dɔkkəd liːk a preːst bifɔrn
ful lɔːŋgə wɛːr (h)is lɛggəs and ful lɛːnə
iliːk a staf ðɛːr was nɔː kalf iséːnə
weːl kuːd (h)eː keːp a gɛrnər and a binnə
ðɛːr was nɔːn audituːr kuːd ɔn (h)im winnə
595 weːl wist (h)eː biː ðə drɔuxt and biː ðə ræin
ðə jɛldiŋ ɔf (h)is seːd and ɔf (h)is græin
his lɔrdəs ʃeːp (h)is nɛːt (h)is dæiəríːə
his swiːn (h)is hɔrs (h)is stɔːr and his pultríːə
was hɔːlliː in ðis reːvəs guvərniŋgə
600 and biː (h)is kɔvnaːnt jaf ðə rɛkəniŋgə
sin ðat (h)is lɔrd was twɛntiː jɛːr ɔf aːdʒə
ðɛːr kuːd nɔː man briŋ him in arrəráːdʒə
ðɛːr nas bæillíf nə hiːrd nɔr oːðər hiːnə
ðat heː nə knɛu (h)is slæiçt and his kuvíːnə
605 ðæi wɛːr adráːd ɔf him as ɔf ðə dɛːθ
his wuniŋ was ful fæir upɔ́n an hɛːθ
wiθ greːnə treːs iʃádwəd was (h)is plaːsə
heː kuːdə bɛttrə ðan (h)is lɔrd purtʃáːsə
ful ritʃ (h)eː was astɔ́ːrəd priːvəliː

610 His lord wel koude he plesen subtilly,
To yeve and lene hym of his owene good,
And have a thank, and yet a cote and hood.
In youthe he hadde lerned a good myster;
He was a wel good wrighte, a carpenter.
615 This Reve sat upon a ful good stot,
That was al pomely grey and highte Scot.
A long surcote of pers upon he hade,
And by his syde he baar a rusty blade.
On Northfolk was this Reve of which I telle,
620 Biside a toun men clepen Baldeswell.
Tukked he was as is a frere aboute,
And evere he rood the hyndreste of oure route.

  A SOMONOUR was ther with us in that place,
That hadde a fyr-reed cherubynnes face,
625 For saucefleem he was, with eyen narwe.
As hoot he was and lecherous as a sparwe,
With scalled browes blake and piled berd.
Of his visage children were aferd.
Ther nas quyksilver, lytarge, ne brymstoon,
630 Boras, ceruce, ne oille of tartre noon,
Ne oynement that wolde clense and byte,
That hym myghte helpen of his whelkes white,
Nor of the knobbes sittynge on his chekes.
Wel loved he garleek, onyons, and eeek lekes,
635 And for to drynken strong wyn, reed as blood;
Thanne wolde he speke and crie as he were wood.
And whan that he wel dronken hadde the wyn,

610 his lɔrd we:l ku:d (h)e: plɛ:zən subtilli:
to: jɛ:v and lɛ:n (h)im ɔf (h)is ɔunə go:d
and ha:v a θaŋk and jɛt a kɔ:t and ho:d
in ju:θ (h)e: haddə lɛrnd a go:d mistéːr
he: was a we:l go:d wriçt a karpəntéːr
615 ðis re:və sat upɔ́n a ful go:d stɔt
ðat was al pɔmli græi and hiçtə skɔt
a lɔ:ŋg siurkɔ:t ɔf pers upɔ́n (h)e: ha:də
and bi: (h)is si:d (h)e: ba:r a rusti: bla:də
ɔf nɔrθfɔlk was ðis re:v ɔf hwitʃ i: tɛllə
620 bisí:d a tu:n mɛn klɛ:pən baldəswɛllə
tukkəd (h)e: was as is a fre:r abúːtə
and ɛvr (h)e: rɔ:d ðə hindrəst ɔf u:r ru:tə
a sumnu:r was ðɛ:r wiθ u:s in ðat pla:sə
ðat hadd a fi:rrɛ:d tʃeru:bínnəs fa:sə
625 fɔr sausəflɛe:m (h)e: was wiθ æien narwə
as ho:t (h)e: was and lɛtʃru:s as a sparwə
wiθ skallə́d bru:əs bla:k and pi:lə́d bɛːrd
ɔf his vizá:ʤə tʃildrən wɛ:r afɛ:rd
ðɛ:r nas kwiksílvər litarʤ nə brimstɔ́:n
630 bɔra:s sɛru:s nə ɔill ɔf tartrə nɔ:n
nə ɔinəmɛnt ðat wɔldə klenz and bi:tə
ðat (h)im miçtə hɛlpən ɔf (h)is hwɛlkəs hwi:tə
nɔr ɔf ðə knɔbbəs sittiŋ ɔn (h)is tʃe:kəs
we:l luvd (h)e: garle:k ɔinəns and ɛ:k le:kəs
635 and fɔr to: driŋkən strɔ:ŋg wi:n rɛ:d as blo:d
ðan wɔld (h)e: spɛ:k and kri: as he: wɛ:r wo:d
and hwan ðat (h)e: we:l druŋkən hadd ðə wi:n

Chaucer · 57

Thanne wolde he speke no word but Latyn.
A fewe termes hadde he, two or thre,
640 That he had lerned out of som decree;
No wonder is—he herde it al the day;
And eek ye knowen wel how that a jay
Kan clepen "Watte" as wel as kan the pope.
But whoso koude in ooher thyng hym grope,
645 Thanne hadde he spent al his philosophie;
Ay "*Questio quid iuris*" wolde he crie.
He was a gentil harlot and kynde;
A bettre felawe sholde men noght fynde.
He wolde suffre for a quart of wyn
650 A good felawe to have his concubyn
A twelf-monthe, and excuse hym atte fulle;
Ful prively a fynch eek koude he pulle.
And if he foond owher a good felawe,
He wolde techen hym to have noon awe
655 In swich caas of the ercedekenes curs,
But if a mannes soule were in his purs;
For in his purs he sholde ypunysshed be.
"Purs is the ercedekenes helle," seyde he.
But wel I woot he lyed right in dede;
660 Of cursyng oghte ech gilty man him drede,
For curs wol slee right at assoillyng savith,
And also war hymn of a *Significavit*.
In daunger hadde he at his owene gise
The yonge girles of the diocise,
665 And knew hir conseil, and was al hir reed.

ðann wɔld (h)e: spɛ:kə nɔ: wurd but latí:n
a fɛuə tɛrməs hadd (h)e: two: ɔr θre:
640 ðat he: (h)add lɛrnəd u:t ɔf sum de:kré:
nɔ: wundər is (h)e: hɛrd it al ðə dæi
and ɛ:k je: knouən we:l hu: ðat a dʒæi
kan klɛ:pən watt as we:l as kan ðə pɔ:pə
but hwo:sɔ ku:d in o:ðər θiŋg (h)im grɔ:pə
645 ðann hadd (h)e: spɛnt al his filɔsɔfí:ə
æi kwɛstio kwid ju:ris wɔld (h)e: krí:ə
he: was a dʒɛntil harlət and a kí:ndə
a bɛttrə fɛlau ʃɔldə mɛn nouxt fí:ndə
he: wɔldə suffrə fɔr a kwart of wí:n
650 a go:d fɛláu to: ha:v (h)is kɔnkiubí:n
a twɛlf mɔnθ and ɛkskíuz (h)im attə fullə
ful pri:vəli: a fintʃ ɛ:k ku:d (h)e: pullə
and if (h)e: fɔ:nd ɔ:hwɛ́:r a go:d fəláuə
he: wɔldə tɛ:tʃən him to: ha:v no:n auə
655 in switʃ ka:s ɔf ðə ɛrtʃədɛ:knəs kurs
but íf a mannəs soul wɛ:r in (h)is purs
fɔr in (h)is purs (h)e: ʃɔld ipúniʃd be:
purs is ðɛrtʃədɛ́:knəs hɛllə sæidə he:
but we:l i: wɔ:t (h)e: li:əd riçt in de:də
660 ɔf kursiŋg ouxt ɛ:tʃ gilti: man (h)im drɛ:də
fɔr kurs wul slɛ: riçt as assóilliŋg sa:viθ
and alsó wa:r (h)im ɔf a signifiká:vit
in daundʒər hadd (h)e: at (h)is ounə gi:zə
ðə juŋgə girləs ɔf ðə di:ɔsí:zə
665 and knɛu (h)ir ku:nsæil and was al (h)ir rɛ:d

A gerland hadde he set upon his heed
As greet as it were for an alestake.
A bokeleer hadde he maad hym of a cake.
    With hym ther rood a gentil PARDONER
670 Of Rouncivale, his freend and his compeer,
That streight was comen from the court of Rome.
Ful loude he soong "Com hider, love, to me!"
This Somonour bar to hym a stif burdoun;
Was nevere trompe of half so greet a soun.
675 This Pardoner hadde heer as yelow as wex,
But smothe it heeng as dooth a strike of flex;
By ounces henge his lokkes that he hadde,
And therwith he his shuldres overspradde;
But thynne it lay, by colpons oon and oon.
680 But hood, for jolitee, wered he noon,
For it was trussed up in his walet.
Hym thoughte he rood al of the newe jet;
Dischevelee, save his cappe, he rood al bare.
Swiche glarynge eyen hadde he as an hare.
685 A vernycle hadde he sowed upon his cappe.
His walet lay biforn hym in his lappe,
Bretful of pardoun, comen from Rome al hoot.
A voys he hadde as smal as hath a goot.
No berd hadde he, ne nevere sholde have;
690 As smother it was as it were late shave.
I trowe he were a geldyng or a mare.
But of his craft, fro Berwyk into Ware,
Ne was ther swich another pardoner;

a gɛrland hadd (h)eː sɛt upɔ́n (h)is hɛeːd
as grɛːt as it wɛːr fɔr an aːləstáːkə
a buklɛːr hadd (h)eː maːd (h)im ɔf a kaːkə
wiθ him ðɛːr rɔːd a dʒɛntil pardɔnéːr

670 ɔf ruːnsival (h)is frɛːnd and his kumpéːr
ðat stræiçt was kumən frɔ ðə kuːrt ɔf roːmə
ful luːd (h)eː sɔːŋg kum hidər luvə toː mə
ðis sumnuːr baːr toː him a stif burdúːn
was nɛvər trɔmp ɔf half sɔː grɛːt a suːn

675 ðis pardɔneːr (h)add heːr as jɛlɔu as wɛks
but smoːð it heːŋg as doːθ a striːk of flɛks
biː uːnsəs heːŋg (h)is lɔkkəs ðat (h)eː haddə
and ðɛːrwiθ heː (h)is ʃuldrəs ɔvərsprádə
but θin it læi bi kulpɔns ɔːn and ɔːn

680 but hoːd fɔr dʒɔliteː wɛːrəd (h)eː nɔːn
fɔr it was trussəd up in his walɛ́t
him θɔuxt (h)eː rɔːd al ɔf ðə nɛuə dʒɛt
diʃévleː saːv (h)is kapp (h)eː rɔːd al baːrə
switʃ glaːriŋg æiən hadd (h)eː as an haːrə

685 a vɛrnikl hadd (h)eː soud upɔ́n (h)is kappə
his walət læi bifɔrn (h)im in (h)is lappə
brɛtful ɔf pardúːn kumn frɔm roːm al hɔːt
a vɔis (h)eː hadd as smaːl as haθ a gɔːt
nɔː bɛːrd (h)add heː nə nɛvər ʃɔldə haːvə

690 as smoːð it was as it wɛːr latə ʃaːvə
iː trɔu (h)eː wɛːr a gɛldiŋg ɔr a maːrə
but ɔf (h)is kraft frɔ bɛrwik intoː waːrə
nɛ was ðɛːr switʃ anóːðər pardɔneːr

For in his male he hadde a pilwe-beer,
695 Which that he seyde was Oure Lady veyl:
He seyde he hadde a gobet of the seyl
That Seint Peter hadde, whan that he wente
Upon the see, til Jhesu Crist hym hente.
He hadde a croys of latoun ful of stones,
700 And in a glas he hadde pigges bones.
But with thise relikes, whan that he fond
A povre person dwellynge upon lond,
Upon a day he gat hym moore moneye
Than that the person gat in monthes tweye;
705 And thus, with feyned flaterye and japes,
He made the person and the peple his apes.
But trewely to tellen atte laste,
He was in chirche a noble ecclesiaste.
Wel koude he rede a lessoun or a storie,
710 But alderbest he song an offertorie;
For wel he wiste, whan that song was songe,
He moste preche and wel affile his tonge
To wynne silver, as he ful wel koude;
Therefore he song the murierly and loude.

715   Now have I toold you shortly, in a clause,
Th'estaat, th'array, the nombre, and eek the cause
Why that assembled was this compaignye
In Southwerk at this gentil hostelrye
That highte the Tabard, faste by the Belle.
720 But now is tyme to yow for to telle
How that we baren us that ilke nyght,

for in (h)is maːs (h)eː hadd a pilwəbeːr
695 hwitʃ ðat (h)eː sæid was uːrə laːdi væil
heː sæid (h)eː hadd a gɔbət of ðə sæil
ðat sæint peːtər hadd hwan ðat (h)eː wɛntə
upɔ́n ðə sɛː til ʤeːzuː kriːst (h)im hɛntə
heː hadd a krɔis of latuːn ful ɔf stɔːnəs
700 and in a glaːs (h)eː haddə piggəs bɔːnəs
but wiθ ðiz rɛlikəs hwan ðat (h)eː fɔːnd
a pɔvrə pɛrsun dwɛlliŋ upɔn lɔːnd
upɔ́n a dæi (h)eː gat (h)im mɔːr munǽiə
ðan ðat ðə pɛrsən gat in moːnθəs twǽiə
705 and ðus wiθ fæinəd flatəriː and ʤaːpəs
heː maːd ðə pɛrsun and ðə peːpl (h)is aːpəs
but trɛuəliː toː tellən attə lastə
heː was in tʃirtʃ a nɔːbl ɛkkleːziástə
weːl kuːd (h)eː rɛːd a lɛssuːn ɔr a stɔːryə
710 but aldərbɛst (h)eː sɔːŋg an ɔffərtɔ́ːryə
fɔr weː (h)eː wistə hwan ðat sɔːŋg was sunŋgə
heː mɔːstə prɛːtʃ and weːl affiːl (h)is tuŋgə
toː winnə silvər as (h)eː ful weːl kuːdə
ðɛːrfɔːr (h)eː sɔːŋg ðə miuryərliː and luːdə
715 nuː haːv iː tɔːld juː soːθliː in a klauzə
ð'ɛstáːt ð'arrǽi ðə numbr and ɛːk ðə kauzə
hwiː ðat assɛmbləd was ðis kumpæiniːə
in suːðwɛrk at ðis ʤɛntil ɔstərliːə
ðat hiçt ðə taːbard fastə biː ðə bɛllə
720 but nuː is tiːmə toː juː for toː tɛllə
huː ðat weː baːrən uːs ðat ilkə niçt

Whan we were in that hostelrie alyght;
And after wol I telle of oure viage
And al the remenaunt of oure pilgrimage.
725 But first I pray yow, of youre courteisye,
That ye n'arette it nat my vileynye,
Thogh that I pleynly speke in this mateere,
To telle yow hir wordes and hir cheere,
Ne thogh I speke hir wordes proprely.
730 For this ye knowen al so wel as I,
Whoso shal telle a tale after a man,
He moot recherce as ny as evere he kan
Everich a word, if it be in his charge,
Al speke he never so rudeliche and large,
735 Or ellis he moot telle his tale untrewe,
Of feyne thyng, or fynde wordes newe.
He may nat spare, althogh he were his brother;
He moot as wel seye o word as another.
Crist spak hymself ful brode in hooly writ,
740 And wel ye woot no vileynye is it.
Eek Plato seith, whoso kan hym rede,
The wordes moote be cosyn to the dede.
Also I prey yow to foryeve it me,
Al have I nat set folk in hir degree
745 Heere in this tale, as that they sholde stonde,
My wit is short, ye may wel understonde.

    Greet chiere made oure Hoost us everichon,
And to the soper sette he us anon.
He served us with vitaille at the beste;

hwɑn we: wɛ:r in ðat ɔstərlí: ɑliçt
and aftər wul i: tɛll ɔf u:r viá:ʤə
and al ðə rɛmnaunt ɔf u:r pilgrimá:ʤə
725 but first i: præi ju: ɔf ju:r kurtæizí:ə
ðat je: narétt it nat mi: vilæiní:ə
ðoux ðat i: plæinli: spɛ:k in ðis maté:rə
to: tɛllə ju: (h)ir wurdəs ənd (h)ir tʃe:rə
ne ðoux i: spɛ:k (h)ir wurdəs prɔprəli:
730 fɔr ðis je: knouən al sɔ: we:l ɑs i:
hwo:sɔ́: ʃal tɛll a tɑ:l aftər a man
he: mo:t rəhérs as ni: as ɛvr (h)e: kan
ɛvritʃ a wurd if it be: in (h)is tʃarʤə
al spɛ:k (h)e: nɛvr sɔ: ru:dəlitʃ and larʤə
735 ɔr ɛllis (h)e: mo:t tɛll (h)is tɑ:l untrɛuə
ɔr fæinə θiŋg ɔr fi:ndə wurdəs nɛuə
he: mæi nat spɑ:r alðóux (h)e: wɛ:r (h)is bro:ðər
he: mo:t as we:l sæi ɔ wurd as anó:ðər
kri:st spak (h)imsélf ful brɔ:d in hɔ:li: writ
740 and we:l je: wɔ:t nɔ: vilæini: is it
ɛ:k plɑ:tɔ: sæiθ hwo:sɔ́: ðat kan (h)im rɛ:də
ðə wurdəs mo:t be: kuzin to: ðə de:də
alsɔ́: i: præi ju: to: fɔryɛ:v it me:
al hɑ:v i: nat sɛt fɔlk in hir de:gré:
745 he:r in ðis tɑ:l as ðat ðæi ʃɔldə stɔ:ndə
mi: wit is ʃɔrt je: mæi we:l undərstɔ:ndə
  grɛ:t tʃe:rə mɑ:d u:r hɔ:st u:s ɛvritʃɔ:n
and to: ðə supe:r sɛt (h)e: u:s anɔ́:n
he: sɛrvəd u:s wiθ vitæill at ðə bɛstə

750 Strong was the wyn, and wel to drynke us leste.
A semely man OURE-HOOST was withalle
For to been a marchal in an halle.
A large man he was with eyen stepe—
A fairer burgeys was ther noon in Chepe—
755 Boold of his speche, and wys, and wel ytaught,
And of manhod hym lakkede right naught.
Eek therto he was right a myrie man,
And after soper pleyen he bigan,
And spak of myrthe amonges othere thynges,
760 Whan that we hadde maad our rekenynges,
And seyde thus: "Now, lordynges, trewely,
Ye been to my right welcome, hertely;
For by my trouthe, if that I shal nat lye,
I saugh nat this yeer so myrie a compaignye
765 Atones in this herberwe as is now.
Fayn wolde I doon yow myrthe, wiste I how.
And of a myrthe I am right now bythoght,
To doon yow ese, and it shal coste noght.
  Ye goon to Caunterbury—God yow speede!
770 The blisful martir quite yow youre meede!
And wel I woot, as ye goon by the weye,
Ye shapen yow to talen and to pleye;
For trewely, confort ne myrthe is noon
To ride by the weye doumb as a stoon;
775 And therfore wol I maken yow disport,
As I seyde erst, and doon yow som confort.
And if yow liketh alle by oon assent

750	strɔːŋg was ðə wiːn and weːl toː drink uːs lɛstə
	a seːmli man uːr hɔːstə was wiðállə
	fɔr toː (h)aːn beːn a marʃəl in an hallə
	a lardʒə man (h)eː was wiθ æiən stɛːpə
	a fæirər burdʒæis is ðɛːr nɔːn in tʃɛːpə
755	bɔːld of (h)is spɛːtʃ and wiːs and weːl itáuxt
	and ɔf manhoːd (h)im lakkədə riçt nauxt
	ɛːk ðɛːrtoː heː was riçt a miuri man
	and aftər supeːr plæiən heː bigan
	and spak ɔf miurð amúŋgəs oːðər θiŋgəs
760	hwan ðat weː (h)ad maːd uːr rɛkəniŋgəs
	and sæidə ðus nuː lɔrdiŋgs trɛuəliː
	yeː beːn toː meː riçt weːlkum hɛrtəliː
	fɔr biː miː truːθ if ðat iː ʃal nat liːə
	iː saux nat ðis jeːr sɔː miryə kumpæiniːə
765	atɔ́nəs in ðis hɛrbərw as is nuː
	fæin wɔld iː doːn juː mirðə wist iː huː
	and ɔf a mirð iː am riçt nuː biθɔ́uxt
	toː doːn juː ɛːz and it ʃal kɔstə nɔuxt
	jeː gɔːn toː kauntərbiuriː gɔd juː speːdə
770	ðə blisful martir kwiːt juː juːrə meːdə
	and weːl iː wɔːt as jeː gɔːn biː ðə wæiə
	yeː ʃaːpən juː toː taːlən and toː plæiə
	fɔr trɛuəliː kɔnfɔrt nə mirð is nɔːn
	toː riːdə biː ðə wæi duːmb as a stɔːn
775	and ðɛːfɔːr wul iː maːkən juː dispɔ́rt
	as iː sæid ɛrst and doːn juː sum kɔnfɔrt
	and if juː liːkəθ all biː ɔːn assént

> For to stonden at my juggement,
> And for to werken as I shal yow seye,
> To-morwe, whan ye riden by the weye,
> Now, by my fader soule that is deed,
> But ye be myrie, I wol yeve yow myn heed!
> Hoold up youre hondes, withouten moore speche."
> Oure conseil was nat longe for to seche.
> Us thoughte it was noght worth to make it wys,
> And graunted hym withouten moore avys,
> And bad him seye his voirdit as hym leste.
> "Lordynges," quod he, "now herkneth for the beste;
> But taak it nought, I prey yow, in desdeyn.
> This is the poynt, to speken short and pleyn,
> That ech of yow, to shorte with oure weye,
> In this viage shal telle tales tweye
> To Caunterbury-ward, I mene it so,
> And homward he shal tellen othere two,
> Of aventures that whilom han bifalle.
> And which of yow that bereth hym best of alle,
> That is to seyn, that telleth in this caas
> Tales of best sentence and moost solaas,
> Shal have a soper at oure aller cost
> Heere in this place, sittynge by this post,
> What that we come agayn fro Caunterbury.
> And for to make yow the moore mury,
> I wol myselven goodly with yow ryde,
> Right at myn owene cost, and be youre gyde;
> And whoso wole my juggement withseye

for to: stɔːndən at miː ʤuːʤəmént
and for to: wɛrkən as iː ʃal juː sæiə
780 to:mórwə hwan jeː riːdən biː ðə wæiə
nuː biː miː fadər sɔulə ðat is dɛːd
but jeː beː miri iː wul jɛːvə juː miːn hɛːd
hɔːld up juːr hɔːndz wiðúːtən mɔːrə spɛːtʃə
uːr kunsæil was nat lɔːŋgə for toː seːtʃə
785 uːs θɔuxt it was nɔuxt wurθ toː maːk it wiːs
and grauntəd him wiðúːtən mɔːr avíːs
and bad (h)im sæi (h)is vɔirdit as (h)im lɛstə
lɔrdiŋgəs kwɔd heː nuː hɛrknəθ for ðə bɛstə
but taːk it nɔuxt iː præi juː in disdǽin
790 ðis is ðə pɔint toː spɛːkən ʃɔrt and plǽin
ðat ɛːtʃ ɔf juː toː ʃɔrtə wiθ uːr wæiə
in ðis viáːʤ ʃal tɛllə taːləs twæiə
toː kauntərbiuriward iː mɛːn it sɔː
and hɔːmward (h)eː ʃal tɛllən oːðər twɔː
795 ɔf aːvəntiurəs ðat hwiːlum han bifallə
and hwitʃ ɔf juː ðat bɛːrθ (h)im bɛst ɔf allə
ðat is toː sæin ðat tɛlləθ in ðis kaːs
taːlz ɔf bɛst səntɛ́ns and mɔːst sɔláːs
ʃal haːv a supɛːr at uːr allər kɔst
800 hɛːr in ðis plaːsə sitting biː ðis pɔst
hwan ðat weː kum agǽin frɔ kauntərbiuriː
and for toː maːkə juː ðə mɔːrə miuːriː
iː wul miːsɛlvən gɔːdliː wiθ juː riːdə
riçt at miːn ɔunə kɔst and beː juːr giːdə
805 and hwɔːsɔː wul miː ʤuːʤəmɛnt wiθsǽiə

Shal paye al that we spenden by the weye.
And if ye vouchesauf that it be so,
Tel me anon withouten wordes mo,
And I wol erly shape me therfore."

810   This thyng was graunted, and oure othes swore
With ful glad herte, and preyden hym also
That he wolde vouchesauf for to do so,
And that he wolde been oure governour,
And of our tales juge and reportour,
815   And sette a soper at a certeyn pris,
And we wol reuled been at his devys
In heigh and lough; and thus by oon assent
We been acorded to his juggement.
And therupon the wyn was fet anon;
820   We dronken, and to reste wente echon,
Withouten any lenger taryynge.

A-morwe, whan that day bigan to sprynge,
Up roos oure Hoost, and was oure aller cok,
And gadrede us togidre alle in a flok,
825   And forth we riden a litel moore than paas
Unto the wateryng of seint Thomas;
And there oure Hoost bigan his hors areste
And seyde, "Lordynges, herkneth, if yow leste.
Ye woot youre foreward, and I it yow recorde.
830   If even-song and morwe-song accorde,
Lat se now who shal telle the firste tale.
As evere mote I drynke wyn or ale,
Whoso be rebel to my juggement

ʃal pæi al ðat weː spɛndən biː ðə wæiə
and if jeː vuːtʃə sauf ðat it beː sɔː
tɛl meː anɔːn wiðúːtən wurdəs mɔː
and iː wul ɛrliː ʃaːpə meː ðɛːfɔːrə
810   ðis θiŋg was grauntəd and uːr ɔːðəs swɔːrə
wiθ ful glad hɛrt and præidən him alsɔ́ː
ðat (h)eː wɔld vuːtʃ sauf fɔr toː doː sɔː
and ðat (h)eː wɔldə beːn uːr guvərnúːr
and ɔf uːr taːləs ʤuːʤ and rɛpɔrtúːr
815   and sɛt a supeːr at a sɛrtæin priːs
and weː wul riuləd beːn at his deːvíːs
in hæiç and lɔux and ðus biː ɔːn assɛ́nt
weː beːn akɔ́rdəd toː (h)is ʤuːʤəmɛ́nt
and ðɛːrupɔ́n ðə wiːn was fɛt anɔ́ːn
weː druŋkən and toː rɛstə wɛnt ɛːtʃɔ́ːn
820   wiðúːtən aniː lˑɛŋgər tariiŋgə
amɔ́rwə hwan ðat dæi bigán toː spriŋgə
up roːs uːr hɔːst and was uːr allər kɔk
and gadrəd uːs toːgídrə allə in a flɔk
825   and fɔrθ weː ridn a liːtəl mɔːr ðan paːs
untóː ðə watəriŋg ɔf sæint tomáːs
and ðɛːr uːr hɔːst bigán (h)is hɔrs arɛstə
and sæidə lɔrdiŋgs hɛrknəθ if juː lɛstə
yeː wɔːt juːr fɔrward and it juː rəkɔ́rdə
830   if ɛːvən sɔːŋg and mɔrwəsɔːŋg akkɔ́rdə
lat seː nuː hwoː ʃal tɛl ðə firstə taːlə
and ɛvər moːt iː driŋkə wiːn ɔr aːlə
hwoːsɔ́ː beː rɛbəl toː miː ʤuːʤəmɛ́nt

Shal paye for al that by the wey is spent.
835 Now draweth cut, er that we ferrer twynne;
He which that hath the shorteste shal bigynne.
Sire Knyght," quod he, "my mayster and my lord,
Now draweth cut, for that is myn accord.
Cometh neer," quod he, "my lady Prioresse.
840 And ye, sire Clerk, lat be youre shamefastnesse,
Ne studieth noght; ley hont to, every man!"
Anon to drawen every wight bigan,
And shortly for to tellen as it was,
Were it by aventure, or sort, or cas,
845 The sothe is this, the cut fil to the Knyght,
Of which ful blithe and glad was every wyght,
And telle he moste his tale, as was resoun,
By foreward and by composicioun,
As ye han herd; what nedeth wordes mo?
850 And whan this goode man saugh that it was so,
As he that wys was and obedient
To kepe his foreward by his free assent,
He seyde, "Syn I shal bigynne the game,
What, welcome be the cut, a Goddes name!
855 Now lat us ryde, and herkneth what I seye."
And with that word we ryden forth oure weye,
And he bigan with right a myrie cheere
His tale anon, and seyde as ye may heere.

ʃal pæi fɔr al ðat biː ðə wæi is spɛnt
835 nuː drauəθ kut ɛːr ðat weː fɛrrər twinnə
heː hwitʃ ðat haθ ðə ʃortəst ʃal bigínnə
siːr kniçt kwɔd heː miː mæistər and miː lɔrd
nuː drauəθ kut fɔr ðat is miːn akkɔ́rd
kuməθ neːr kwɔd heː miː laːdi priːɔréssə
840 and jeː siːr klɛrk lat beː juːr ʃaːmfastnéssə
nə studiːθ nɔuxt læi hoːnd toː ɛvriː man
anɔ́ːn toː drauən ɛvriː wiçt bigán
and ʃɔrtliː fɔr toː tɛllːən as it was
wɛːr it biː aːvəntiur ɔr sɔrt ɔr kaːs
845 ðə soːθ is ðis ðə kut fil toː ðə kniçt
ɔf hwitʃ ful bliːð and glad was ɛvriː wiçt
and tɛll (h)eː mɔːst (h)is taːl as was rəzúːn
biː fɔrward and biː kɔmpɔzisiúːn
as jeː han (h)eːrd hwat neːdəθ wurdəs mɔː
850 and hwan ðis goːd man saux ðat it was sɔː
and heː ðat wiːs was and ɔbeːdiént
toː keːp (h)is fɔrward biː (h)is freː assɛ́nt
heː sæidə sin iː ʃal bigínn ðə gaːmə
hwat wellkum beː tə kut a gɔddəs naːmə
855 nuː lat uːs riːd and hɛrknəθ hwat iː sæiə
and wiθ ðat wurd weː riːdən fɔrθ uːr wæiə
and heː bigán wiθ riçt a miri tʃeːrə
his taːl anɔ́ːn and sæid as jeː mæi heːrə

General Prologue

1-18   구문 상 1행에서 18행까지가 하나의 절이다. Whan(=when)으로 시작하는 1행과 5행 이하가 부사절이며, Thanne(=then)으로 시작하는 12행 이하 18행까지가 주절이다. 내용은 4월이 오면 사람들이 Canterbury 사원으로 순례를 가고 싶어 한다는 것인데, 영국의 4월이 생명력 넘치는 정경으로 묘사되고 있다. 영국의 봄이라고 특별히 아름다울 것은 없지만 영국의 겨울이 워낙 암울하여 봄이 더욱 아름답게 느껴졌을 것으로 짐작된다. 여기에서처럼 도입부를 봄에 관한 묘사로 시작하는 것은 중세 구라파 시의 하나의 관행으로서, 특히 이태리나 라틴어 시에서 흔히 발견된다. Guido delle Golonne, Boccaccio, Petrarch, Virgil 등을 예로 들 수 있다.

1   **Whan that**=When. when의 뜻으로 whan that이 흔히 쓰이는데, 여기서 that은 별 뜻이 없는 허사로서 이 경우 강세는 whan에 놓인다. **his**=its. 당시 its의 뜻으로는 his가 보통이었으며, its는 17세기 후반에 들어서서야 쓰이기 시작했다. **shoures soote**=sweet showers. sweet의 뜻인 soote는 5행에서는 sweete로 쓰이고 있다. 이것은 당시 철자가 확정되지 않았음을 보여주는 좋은 예이다.

2   **droght**=dryness, drought(가뭄). **perced**=pierced. **roote**=root.

3   **veyne**=vessel of sap, vein(수맥의 잎맥). **swich licour**=such moisture.

4   **Of which vertu**=by the power of which. **vertu**=efficacy(효험). **engendred**=produced, generated. **flour**=flower.

5   **Zephirus**=the west wind(봄바람). **eek**=also.

6   **Inspired**=breathed life into, breathed upon. **holt**=woodland. **heeth**=field.

7   **croppes**=shoots, sprouts(새싹). **the yonge sonne**=the young sun. 당시는 새해가 춘분(equinox)으로 잘못 알려진 3월12일에 시작되었다. (춘분은 1582년에 지금처럼 3월21일로 정정되었다.) 이 시의

배경이 4월이므로 아직 새해가 시작 된지 얼마 되지 않아 이런 표현을 사용하고 있다.

8 **Ram**=일명 Aries[éəri:z](백양궁白羊宮)라고도 불리며 Zodiac(12궁도)의 첫 번째이므로 쉽게 말해 정월에 해당한다. **halve cours yronne**=have run the half course(s). **yronne**의 y-는 고대영어의 ġe-나 현대 독일어의 ge-에 해당하는 것으로서, 주어진 동사가 과거분사임을 나타낸다. 뒤에 나오는 *The Man of Law's Tale*의 *Prologue*(5-6)에서 작자는 순례를 떠난 지 이틀 째되는 날이 4월 18일이라고 말하고 있으므로 순례를 떠난 것은 4월17이리고, 그 전날인 '오늘'은 4월16일이 된다. 3월12일에 백양궁에 들어선 '젊은' 태양은 4월11일에 백양궁의 전후반 과정(course)를 모두 지나게 되며, 지금은 두 번째 자리인 Taurus(금우궁金牛宮)의 전반에 들어서 있다. 한편 cours는 단수와 복수형이 동일하므로 단수인 경우에는 the second half course의 뜻으로, 그리고 복수인 경우에는 both of the half courses의 뜻이 될 것이다. 여기서는 후자의 뜻으로 해석하는 것이 무난할 것이다.

9 **foweles**=birds. foweles는 현대영어의 fouls(가금)의 옛날 모습이지만 현대영어와는 달리 조류 전반을 가리킨다. 여기 등장하는 새는 짐작컨대 nightingale일 것이라고 몇몇 주석자들이 지적하고 있다. **maken melodye**=sing.

10 **open yë**=open eye. Baugh(237)는 실제로 새들은 밤새 뜬눈으로 자지는 않지만 워낙 잠이 얕아서 사람들이 보면 늘 눈을 뜨고 자는 것처럼 보일 것이라는 점을 들어 Chaucer가 대단한 관찰자란 점을 지적하고 있다.

11 **So priketh hem nature in hir corages**=so much does Nature prick them in their hearts. **priketh**=spurred, pricked. **hem**=them. **nature**=priketh의 주어. Robinson(651)은 nature가 Chaucer가 즐겨 사용하는 여신 Nature를 가리킬 것이기 때문에 대문자로 시작하는 것이 옳다고 말한다. **hir**=their. 3인칭 복수의 경우 Chaucer는 주격에서는 they를 사용하지만 소유격과 대격에서는 통상적으로 hir와 hem을 사용하고 있다. **corages**=hearts.

12　　　**Thanne**=then. 여기서부터 whan이 이끄는 부사절에 대한 주절이 시작된다. **longen folk to goon**=people long to go. **longen**=long, desire, yearn. **goon**=go. **pilgrimages**=journeys to worship at a holy shrine.

13　　　**palmeres**=pilgrims(순례자들). 본래는 성지(Holy Land)인 Jerusalem에로의 순례자를 뜻했으나 뒤에 가서는 직업적인 순례자(professional pilgrim)나 단순한 관광객의 뜻으로 사용되었다. '직업적'이라는 것은 속죄(penance)를 목적으로 사람을 사서 대신 순례를 보내는 일을 뜻한다. 1361년에 Canterbury까지 걸어서 갔다오는 데 20쉴링을 받았다. 이들이 돌아오는 길에 야자나무 잎(palm leaf)을 가져오는 일이 많은데서 pilgrim이라는 이름이 붙었다. **seken**=seek. **straunge**=foreign, strange. **strondes**=strands, shores.

14　　　**ferne halwes**=far-off shrines. **kouthe**=well-known. **sondry londes**= various lands. **sondry**=sundry.

15　　　**shire**=행정 구역 중의 하나.

16　　　**Canterbury**=우리나라의 부산에 해당하는 위치에 있다. 런던에서 56마일 떨어진 거리에 있으며 도바 해협을 향하고 있다. **wende**=go.

17　　　**The hooly blisful martir**=the holy blessed martyr. Canterbury 사원에 모셔놓은 St. Thomas à Becket를 뜻한다. Canterbury의 archbishop(대주교)였던 그는 당시 국왕인 Henry II세와의 불화 때문에 왕이 보낸 자객에 의해 1170년 12월 29일에 살해된다. 그 뒤 1173년에 시성(諡聖, canonize)된 그는 그 뒤 오랫동안 영국 사람들의 사랑과 존경을 받았으며, 그가 살해된 장소인 Canterbury 사원은 영국과 구라파 순례자들이 즐겨 찾는 성지가 되었다. **seke**=seek.

18　　　**That hem hath holpen whan that they were seeke**=who helped them when they were sick. **that**=who. **holpen**=helped. **seeke**=sick, ill. 당시 사람들은 성자들마다 특정한 '효험'이 있다고 믿었으며, Thomas à Becket는 사람들의 건강을 돌보는 것으로 생각되었다. 한편 seeke는 앞줄의 seke와 발음이 동일[séːkə]하며, 이른바 동일

	압운(identical rhyme)이라고 불리는 것으로서 Chaucer는 심심치 않게 사용하고 있다.
19	**Befil**=it befell, it happened. 비인칭 구문이다. **seson**=season.
20	**Southwerk**=런던 템즈 강의 London Bridge 남쪽에 있는 구역. **Tabard**=여관 이름으로 당시 실제로 존재했다고 한다. 이 여관은 그 뒤 1676년의 화재 때 불탔다가 다시 Talbot라는 이름으로 재건축 되었으나 지금은 그 자리에 Tabard라는 옛날 이름의 pub이 들어서 있다. 한편 tabard는 중세에 갑옷 위에 입던 짧은 겉옷으로서, 당시는 여관에 간판 대신 물건(예를 들어 마차 바퀴 따위)이나 물건(tabard 따위)의 그림을 걸어두는 것이 관행이었다. **lay**=lodged, was stopping overnight.
21	**wenden**=go.
22	**ful devout corage**=fully devout heart. Chaucer를 읽을 때 조심해야 하는 것은 corage처럼 현대와 철자는 같으면서 뜻이 다른 경우이다.
23	**was come**=had come. Chaucer 시대에는 자동사는 be동사와 결합하여 완료형을 이루는 것이 보통이었으며, have동사와 결합하게 된 것은 Shakespeare 시대를 거쳐 현대영어에 들어서면서이다. **hostelrye**=inn.
24	**Wel**=fully, as many as. 자그마치. **nyne and twenty**=twenty-nine. Chaucer의 본래 의도는 자기를 포함하여 총 30명으로 일행을 구성하는 것이었으나 만약에 priest가 한 명뿐이라면 Chaucer외에 28명만이 있게 되어 한 사람이 부족하게 된다. 여관집 주인까지 포함하면 30명이 되지만 그는 이야기에는 참가하지 않고 심판 자격으로 남겠다고 했으므로 그는 열외이다. Chaucer도 이 잘못을 뒤에 발견하고 나중에 일행이 Boughton-under-Blee에서 canon(사제)과 yeoman(부하)을 만나게 하고 이 중 yeoman이 동참하게 함으로써 30명을 채우고 있다.
25	**sondry**=sundry, various. **by aventure**=by chance. **yfalle**=fallen. 8행의 yronne의 경우와 마찬가지로 y-는 과거분사의 표시.
26	**felaweshipe**=companionship.
27	**wolden**=would, wished. **ryde**=ride.

28 **chambres**=bedrooms. **wyde**=wide, spacious, roomy.

29 **weren esed**=were accommodated, were entertained. **atte beste**=in the best way, most excellently. **atte**=at the의 축약형.

30 **shortly**=briefly, in short, to cut a long story short. **was to reste**=had set. 여기서 to는 현대영어의 at의 뜻.

31 **so**=in such a manner. **hem everichon**=every one of them. **hem**=them. **everichon**=(ever+each one)=everyone.

32 **anon**=at once, soon.

33 **made forward**=(we) made agreement. 여기서 보듯 Chaucer는 주어가 분명한 경우 종종 생략한다. **erly for to ryse**=to rise early. *Reeve's Tale*의 *Prologue*(3906)를 보면 미적거리고 이야기를 하지 않는 Reeve에게 사람들이 이야기를 재촉하느라 "Lo Depeford! and it is half-wey pryme" (Look there's Deptford, and it's half-past seven!)라고 말한다. 이때는 이미 Knight의 이야기와 Miller의 이야기가 끝난 뒤이고, 이 두 이야기의 낭송을 위해 각기 55분과 35분가량, 도합 한 시간 반이 걸린다는 것을 생각하면 일행은 상당히 일찍 떠났을 것으로 짐작된다.

34 **ther as I yow devyse**=in the way I shall recount to you. **ther**=there. **yow devyse**=describe to you. 현재형으로 미래시를 나타내는 것은 고대영어 때부터의 관행이다.

35 **nathelees**=nevertheless. **while**=while. **tyme**=time. **space**=time, opportunity.

36 **Er**=ere, before. **ferther**=further. **pace**=pass.

37 **Me thynketh**=it seems to me. thynken은 비인칭 동사. **accordaunt to resoun**=reasonable. **resoun**=order, suitable arrangement.

38 **condicioun**=status (social, economic, etc.), circumstances.

39 **hem**=them. **semed me**=seemed to me.

40 **whiche**=what. 여기서는 직업을 말한다. **degree**=social rank.

41 **eek**=also. **array**=dress.

42 **wol**=will.

The Knight

43 **worthy**=distinguished, honorable.
44 **fro**=from.
45 **riden out**=go on campaign, go on military expeditions. **chivalrye**=knighthood.
46 **Trouthe**=integrity, fidelity to obligation. **fredom**=nobility, liberality. **curteisie**= courtesy(공손함)이라는 뜻 외에 '궁정(court)의 예절'이라는 뜻도 함축돼 있다. chivalrie, troughe, honour, fredom, curteisie의 다섯 가지 미덕은 기사가 기사답기 위해서는 꼭 갖춰야 할 품격이다.

⟨The Knight⟩

47 **lord**=the person (here the king) to whom he owed feudal homage and military service. **werre**=war.
48 **therto**=moreover. **ferre**=farther.
49 **As wel in cristendom as in hethenesse**=as much in Christian as in nonChristian lands. **hethenesse**=non-Christian territory, heathendom.
50 **honoured**=(had been) honored.
51 **Alisaundre**=Alexandria (Egypt), captured by King Peter of Cyprus in 1365. 여기 열거한 전투들은 Knight의 광범위한 전투 경력을 나타내기 위한 것인데, 이 전투들은 사라센이나 터기, 혹은 러시아나 리투아니아 등 모두 이교도들에 대한 싸움이긴 하나 이른바 십자군 원정은 아니다. 여기 Chaucer가 열거한 전투들은 1342년에서 1362년에 걸쳐 일어난 것들이라는 점을 생각하면 Knight는 지금 50대에 들어서 있다. 당시 기사들은 독자적인 자격(free-lancer)으로나, 혹은 자기가 속한 대군주(overlord)의 통솔 하에 이런 전투에 많이 참전하였다.
52 **Ful ofte tyme**=many a time. **he hadde the bord bigonne**=he had sat at the head of the table as a mark of honor.

53 **Pruce**=Prussia.
54 **Lettow**=Lithuania. **reysed**=made a military expedition. **Ruce**=Russia.
55 **degree**=rank.
56 **Gernade**=남부 스페인에 있는 Granada 왕국. **seege**=siege. **be**=been.
57 **Algezir**=Algeciras. 1344년에 Grenada의 왕으로부터 점령. **Belmarye**=Benmarin, Morocco. 스페인 맞은 편의 아프리카 서북부에 있다.
58 **Lyeys**=Ayas. 소 아세아의 Antioch 근처에 있다. 1367년에 터키로부터 점령. **Satalye**=Adalia. 소 아세아에 있으며, 1361년에 Cyprus 왕에 의해 점령.
59 **Whan**=when. **Grete See**=Mediterranean.
60 **armee**=armed expedition.
62 **oure feith**=Christianity. **Tramyssene**=Algeria의 Tlemcen.
63 **lystes**=lists (마상 창시합). 각각의 진영을 대표하는 선수가 겨루는 시합. 짐작컨대 상대는 사라센 인이었을 것이다. **ay**=always. **foo**=foe.
64 **ilke**=same.
65 **Sometyme**=at one time. **Palatye**=Balat, Turkey.
66 **Agayn**=against.
67 **everemoore**=always, evermore. **a sovereyn prys**=the highest reputation.
68 **though that**=though. that는 허사이다. **were**=가정법의 동사로서 여기서는 단순양보(simple concession)를 나타낸다. **worthy**=full of worth, of high rank or prominence. **wys**=prudent. wise, discreet.
69 **port**=bearing, demeanor.
70 **vileynye**=what is characteristic of a villain, lack of courtesy, rudeness. 여기서는 천한 말. **ne**=the negative particle.
71 **no maner wight**=no man whatever.
72 **verray**=true (*not* very). **parfit**=perfect, ideal, supreme. Chaucer는 verray를 강조사, 즉 truly의 뜻으로 쓰는 경우가 없다. 따라서 verray parfit는 true and perfect로 읽어야 한다. **gentil**=of noble rank or birth, belonging to the gentry, noble. 이른바 '양반'. 14세기의 기사도는 몰락 단계에 있었고, 또 지저분한(sordid) 면도 있

었으나 여기서 Chaucer는 기사의 이상형을 그리고 있다.

73 **array**=dress.
74 **hors**=horses. 당시 기사들은 여분의 말을 끌고 여행을 다녔다. **he**=the Knight. **gay**=dressed up, gaily dressed.
75 **fustian**=thick coarse cotton cloth. **gypon**=a tight-fitting vest, tunic.
76 **bismotered**=stained, soiled. **habergeon**=coat of chain mail.
77 **was late ycome**=had come back lately. was ycome는 완료형. **late**=recently, lately. **viage**=journey, expedition, campaign.
78 **doon**=do, make.

The Squire

79 **Squier**=esquire, a candidate for knighthood who serves in attendance upon a knight. 기사 후보생. 신분 상 기사 바로 밑이며, 본래는 마술과 창술이 특히 뛰어나야 했다. 그러나 후세에 오면서 궁정인으로서의 수행이 중요시되면서 음악과 춤, 그림에 이르기까지 전반적인 교양을 갖출 필요가 생겼다. 그리하여 여기 등장하는 Squire도 이 방면에 조예가 있을 뿐만 아니라 귀부인(his lady)에 잘 보이기 위해 복장도 화려하다. squire를 묘사함에 있어 Chaucer는 자기의 젊은 날을 머리에 두고 있었을 것이라는 지적도 있다.

⟨The Squire⟩

80 **lovyere**=lover. lovere의 남부 사투리이다. **lusty**=vigorous, lively, zestful(*not* lustful). **bacheler**=a young man으로 해석하는 사람과 a probationer in knighthood로 해석하는 사람이 있다.
81 **lokkes crulle**=locks of curled hair. **crulle**=curly. curl은 crul의 음위전환(metathesis)에 의해 생긴 것임. **as they were leyd in presse**=as if they had been pressed in a curling iron.

82   **twenty yeer**=twenty years. yeer는 단수와 복수가 같은 모양이다. **gesse**=guess. guess의 이와 같은 용법은 지금의 영국에서는 볼 수 없으나 미국영어에서는 흔히 볼 수 있는 용법이다.

83   **Of his stature**=in respect of his stature. **evene lenthe**=average or moderate height, well-proportioned.

84   **wonderly delyvere**=wonderfully agile.

85   **chivachie**=expedition, especially with a body of cavalry.

86   1383년에 있었던 전투들이다. 여기 거명된 지명들은 영불해협 맞은 편의 현대의 프랑스와 벨기에에 속하는 땅으로서, 1338년에 시작된 100년 전쟁 당시 영국이 자국의 영토라고 주장했던 곳이다. Chaucer도 1359년에 프랑스에서 싸운 적이 있다.

87   **born hym weel**=behaved well. **hym**은 재귀대명사이다. **as of so litel space**=considering the short time of his service.

88   **stondon in his lady grace**=enjoy his lady's favor. **stonden**=stand. **lady**=lady's.

89   **Embrouded**=embroidered. 당시 부유층에서는 수놓은 doublet을 입는 것이 보통이었다. 1363년에 반포된 법령에 의하면 수입이 200 파운드에 미치지 않는 경우 기사 이하의 직급의 사람들은 수놓은 옷을 일체 입지 못하게 되어 있긴 하였으나, 이 법령은 잘 지켜지지 않았다. **meede**=meadow.

91   **floytynge**=playing the flute or, possibly, whistling. 지금도 구라파 일부에서는 그렇거니와, 공공장소에서 휘파람을 부는 것은 예절 바르지 못한 것으로 간주될 수 있었다.

92   **fressh**=fresh, bright.

94   **koude**=could. **faire**=fairly.

95   **songes make**=compose music. **endite**=compose words to songs.

96   **Juste**=joust([dʒaust]) (마상 창시합). **purtreye**=draw, portray.

97   **hoote**=hotly, fervently. **nyghtertale**=nighttime.

98   **sleep**=slept. **nyghtyngale**=the nightingale, whose sweet night-song is associated with lovers. 짝짓기 계절이 오면 나이팅게일 들은 밤새 운다.

99   **Curteis**=respectful. **lowely**=moderate in demeanor.
100   **carf**=carved. 원형은 kerven(=to carve (meat) at the table and serve it and other food). 기사가 먹기 좋게 고기를 썰어 놓는 것도 squire의 중요한 임무 가운데 하나였다. **bifore**=in front of.

The Yeoman

101   **Yeman**=yeoman, a servant ranking above a groom(garson) and below a sergeant. 여기에 등장하는 Yeoman은 기사의 foresters(산림감시원) 가운데 한 사람이었던 것 같다. **he**=the Knight. **namo**=no more. 기사가 여행할 때에는 위신을 세우기 위해 squire와 servant를 동반하게 되어 있었기 때문에 이 기사는 그 최소한의 조건을 갖춘 셈이다. 한편 이와 같은 표현에서 우리는 여기 등장하는 Yeoman이 기사가 거느린 유일한 하인이 아니라는 것을 알 수 있다.

102   **hym liste ride so**=it pleased him to ride in such a manner. **liste**는 비인칭동사 listen의 과거형. 전통적으로 forester는 녹색 옷을 입고 있었다.

104   **pecok arwes**=arrows feathered with peacock feathers. 공작 깃털이 활촉 만들기에 좋은 것으로 알려져 있었다. 그러나 가장 좋은 것은 거위 깃털이고, 백조나 공작의 깃털은 그 다음으로 좋은 것이었다고 한다. Lydgate의 *Hors Goose and Sheep*(l. 21ff.)에 다음과 같은 대목이 있다.

      Goos is the best
      Except fetheris of Pekok or of Swan.

여기에 대해 궁술에 밝은 사람들은 공작의 깃털은 보기에만 좋을 뿐 실제로는 거위 깃털보다 훨씬 못하다고 한다.

105   **Under**=below. **bar**=bore. **thriftily**=carefully.
106   **koude**=could. **dresse his takel**=care for his gear. **takel**=bow and arrow. **yemanly**=as a good yeoman should.
107   **noght**=not. **fetheres lowe**=the feathers stood out firmly and

uncrushed. 화살촉의 깃털이 빳빳이 서지 않고 늘어지면 날라 가는 도중에 실속하여 목표물에 도달하지 못하게 된다.

109 **not-heed**=close-cropped crewcut head.

110 **koude**=knew, understood. **usage**=practice.

111 **gay**=ornamented, fancy. **bracer**=leather shield used by archers to prevent the arm from being struck by the string when the arrow was loosed.

112 **bokeler**=small shield, buckler.

114 **Harneised**=fitted, mounted, ornamented. 가죽으로 된 칼집 끝은 예쁘고 반짝이는 쇠 장식이 있었다.

115 **Cristophre**=St. Christopher를 색인 메달로서 일종의 부적(talisman) 삼아 패용했었다. Christopher는 foresters의 patron saint였다. 그러나 Christopher의 조각상은 모든 이에게 행운을 가져다주는 것으로 생각되었다. **sheene**=bright.

116 **bawdryk**=a belt or girdle usually of leather and richly ornamented, worn pendant from one shoulder across the breast and under the opposite arm, and used to support the wearer's sword, bugle, etc., a baldric. 그러나 여기 등장하는 Yeoman은 horn 하나만을 차고 있으므로 그의 baldric은 끈으로 된 것일 수도 있다.

117 **forster**=forester, a game keeper. **soothly**=truly.

The Prioress

118 **Prioresse**=a nun who is the superior of a priory.

119 **of hyr smylyng**=그녀의 미소에 대해 말하자면. **symple and coy**=modest and quiet. 현대의 coquetry (요염)라는 함축은 전혀 없다. 한편 symple과 coy는 동의어이다. 이처럼 중세 영시에서는 같은 뜻의 단어를 겹쳐 쓰는 것이 흔히 있던 일이다. 한편 symple and coy는 당시 여인을 수식하는 낭만시의 상투적 표현이었다.

120 **ooth**=oath. **but**=only. **Seinte Loy**=프랑스의 성자 St. Eligius (프랑스 명 St. Eloi). Seinte는 보통은 seint로 쓰이나 여기서는 운(meter)을

맞추기 위해 두 음절([sæintə])로 읽혀야 한다. 그래야 후속하는 Loy와 함께 -tĕ Lóy라는 약강음보(iambic meter)가 생기기 때문이다. Seinte Loy는 금은세공업자의 견습공으로 시작하여 왕의 고문을 거쳐 마침내는 주교가 된 사람이다. 그는 금은세공업자들의 patron saint이다. 사람들은 욕을 할 때 Jesus Christ라고 하듯

⟨The Prioress⟩

성자의 이름으로 욕하는 경우가 많다. 그런데 하필 많은 성자들 가운데 왜 그의 이름을 사용하였는가에 대해 신빙성이 없는 몇 가지 설들이 있다. 이를테면 그 이름의 느낌이 내우 여성스럽다(ladylike sound)든지, 그가 언젠가 한번은 욕하기를 거부한 일이 있다는 점, 따라서 Prioress가 한번도 욕을 한 일이 없다는 것, 또는 여기 등장하는 깔끔한 수녀원장처럼 그가 매우 예의 바른(courtly) 사람이었다는 점, 혹은 그가 여행자들의 patron saint였다는 점 등등. 그러나 가장 중요한 이유는 그의 이름(Loy)이 앞줄 마지막 단어(coy)와 압운이 맞는다는 사실일 것이다.

121 **cleped**=called. **madame**=모든 수녀들에게 madame이라는 칭호가 주어졌다. **Eglentyne**=그 뜻은 briar rose(들장미)로서 madame Eglentyne은 Lady Sweetbriar 정도로 옮길 수 있다. Stratford atte Bowe에 St. Leonard's Priory라는 여자수도원이 있었고 거기에 실제로 Argentyn이라는 이름의 수녀님이 계셨는데, Eglentyne은 Argentyn의 한 변형이다. 그러나 이야기에 등장하는 인물들을 역사적으로 존재했던 실제 인물에서 일일이 그 모델을 찾는 것은 바람직하지 않다. 사람들의 이같은 노력은 Chaucer의 인물묘사가 그만큼 리얼하기 때문일 것이다.

122 **service dyvyne**=divine worship. 성무일과서(Breviary, 聖務日課書)에 정해진 입정시과(canonical hours, 入定時課)로서 음악에 맞춰 이루어진다. 입정시과에는 Matins, (Lauds), Prime, Terce, Sext,

Nones, Vesper, Compline이 있다.

123 **Entuned in hir nose**=intoned in her nose. 콧소리를 내는 것이 제대로 된 낭송법이었다. 이것은 낭송이 음악적으로 들리게 한다는 목적 외에도 성대의 부담을 줄인다는 또 다른 목적이 있었다. 그러나 Chaucer가 이와 같은 객관적 사실만을 기술하고 있는지 아니면 Prioress에 대해 부드러운 조롱을 하고 있는지는 분명치 않다. **semely**=in a seemly manner, becomingly. 기사에겐 worthy라는 형용사가 늘 붙어 다녔듯이 수녀님에게는 항용 semely라는 부사가 사용되고 있다.

124 **spak**=spoke. **faire and fetisly**=둘 다 elegantly의 뜻. 흔히 있던 동의어의 중첩인데, 여기서는 f-라는 동일 자음으로 시작함으로써 두운(alliteration)도 맞추고 있다. faire and fetisly는 273행에서도 사용되고 있다.

125 **After the scole of Stratford atte Bowe**=Stradford 식으로. 런던에서 동쪽으로 2마일 떨어진 근교에 있던 Stradford에는 베네딕트 수녀원(Benedictine convent)이 있었으며, 여기에서는 표준어인 Parisian French(Central French)가 아니라 사투리인 Norman French가 사용되고 있었다. 이것은 1066년에 영국을 침략하여 지배하게 된 Norman족이 사용하던 언어였으나, 당시 파리의 프랑스어가 표준어로 여겨졌다. Norman 왕조가 3대에 끝나자 궁정에서는 Central French가 공용어가 되었고, 물론 Chaucer 시대에는 영어가 공용어이긴 하나 프랑스어는 아직도 널리 사용되고 있었다. **After**=according to. **scole**=fashion.

126 **unknowe**=unknown. 파리의 프랑스어(Parisian French)가 노르만 프랑스어(Norman French)보다 더 상위의 것으로 여겨졌다.

127 **At mete**=at table. **mete**=meals (*not* meat). **wel ytaught**=well taught. y-는 과거분사를 나타내는 접두사. 여기 묘사된 Prioress의 식탁 예절은 대부분이 *Roman de la Rose*에(14178-99)에서 그대로 가져온 것이다. **with alle**=moreover.

128 **leet**=let.

129 **ne**=nor. **sauce**=sauce, gravy. **depe**=deeply. 당시는 포크와 나이프를

사용하지 않고 손가락으로 집어먹었다.

130 **kepe**=take care.
131 **That no drope ne fille upon hire brest**=that no drop might fall upon her breast. ne…ne는 이른바 2중부정으로서 단순 부정을 나타낸다. **fille**=가정법 과거형.
132 **In curteisie was set ful muchel hir lest**=she took a particular pleasure in courtly behavior. **curteisie**=etiquette. **lest**=delight.
133 **over-lippe**=upper lip.
134 **coppe**=cup. **no ferthyng**=nothing at all. **ferthying**=small spot, like the tiny English coin. **sene**=visible. 15세기 젊은이들을 위한 예절 교과서에는 다음과 같이 기록되어 있다. Wype thi mouthe when thou wyll drinke, Lest it foule thi copys brinke.
135 **grece**=grease. **draughte**=drink.
136 **after hir mete she raughte**=reached for her food. **mete**=food.
137 **sikerly**=certainly. **desport**=agreeableness, charm. of greet desport를 dignified in manner, fine deportment로 해석하는 사람도 있다.
138 **port**=bearing, behavior.
139 **peyned**=took pains. **hire**=재귀대명사. **countrefete**=copy, imitate. 현대의 나쁜 뜻(implication of dishonesty)은 없다. **cheere of court**=courtly manners. **cheere**=behavior, bearing.
140 **been**=be. **estatlich**=stately, dignified.
141 **holden digne**=considered worthy. Prioress는 작품 전편을 통해 다른 순례자들의 존경을 받는 존재로 묘사돼 있다.
142 **for to speken of**=to tell you of. **conscience**=tender feeling, sensitiveness. 현대의 moral conscience(양심)의 뜻은 없다.
143 **pitous**=merciful, tenderhearted.
144 **if that she saugh**…=if she should see… that는 허사이다. **mous**=mouse.
145 **deed**=dead. **bledde**=was bleeding.
146 **Of smale houndes**=some small dogs. **Of**는 전체 가운데 일부분을 나타내는 부분속격(partitive). **houdes**=dogs. 당시 수녀원에서 강아

지를 키우는 것은 원칙적으로 금지되어 있었으며, 경우에 따라서는 위해서는 특별허가증(dispensation)이 필요했으므로 Prioress가 강아지들을 데리고 있었다는 것은 그녀가 유력한 집안 출신이라는 것을 말해준다.

147 **flessh**=meat. **wastel-breed**=fine white bread. 당시 네 등급의 빵이 있었으며, wastel-breed는 payndemayn 다음으로 좋은 빵이고, 평상시 먹는 빵으로는 가장 좋은 빵이었다. 서민들이 먹는 빵은 barley-bread였다. Prioress가 강아지에게 wastel-breed를 먹였다는 것으로 보아 St. Leonard 수녀원에서는 가장 좋은 빵만을 먹었다고 생각할 수 있다.

148 **soore**=sorely. **oon**=one. **hem**=them.
149 **men**=someone. **smoot**=struck. **yerde**=stick, rod. **smerte**=smartly, sharply.
150 **conscience**=tenderness.
151 **semely**=seemly. **wympel**=wimple, a nun's prescribed neck-covering. 머리와 얼굴 좌우 옆, 그리고 목을 가리는 일종의 두건. **pynched**=pleated(=아코디언처럼 주름을 넣은). 당시 수녀원에서는 두건에 주름 장식을 넣는 것(fluted)이 허용되지 않다.
152 **tretys**=slender, well-shaped. 중세의 미인들의 코는 항상 tretys했다. **hir eyen greye as glas**=유리처럼 반짝이는 눈. **greye**=blue(?). grey eyes는 중세 미인들을 묘사할 때의 상투적인 표현.
153 **therto**=also, moreover. **reed**=red.
154 **fair forheed**=fair forhead. **sikerly**=certainly, indeed.
155 **spanne**=한 뼘. 엄지손가락에서 새끼손가락까지의 거리. 넓은 이마는 당시의 관상학(physiognomy)에 의하면 어리석음의 표시(sign of stupidity and folly)로 여겨졌다. 그러나 Chaucer는 금방 다음 줄에서 Prioress가 몸이 작은 사람(undergrowe)이 아니라는 점을 들어 넓은 이마가 꼭 보기 싫지만은 않다는 점을 강조하고 있다. 이와 같은 묘사들이 전형적인 인물의 등장으로 끝날 수 있는 순례자 묘사를 보다 실감나게 하고 있으며, 그런 까닭에 많은 사람들이 등장인물들에 대해 실존하는 인물을 찾으려는 노력을 하게 되는 것 같다. **trowe**=believe.

156　**hardily**=surely, assuredly. **undergrowe**=undergrown, short. 먹을 것이 넉넉지 못했던 중세 영국에서 몸이 크다는 것은 부자라는 것을 함축한다.

157　**fetys**=well-made, neat, elegant. **was war**=perceived, noticed, was aware.

158　**Of smal coral**은 다음 줄의 A peire of bedes와 연결된다. coral은 부적으로 많이 사용되었다. **bar**=bore.

159　**peire of bedes**=a string of beads, a rosary. peire는 pair의 뜻보다는 set의 뜻. **gauded al with grene**=adorned with large, ornamental beads in the set, all in green. **gauded**=divided into groups by "gauds," beads of distinct size, material, color, or ornamentation, the purpose of which in Chaucer's day is still not certain. 묵주는 열 개의 작은 bead와 한 개의 큰 bead가 한 조를 이르며, 작은 bead는 Ave Maria를 칭송(Hail Ave)하기 위한 것으로서 Ave라고 부르며, 열 한번째는 gaud라고 불리는 큰 것으로, 이 때마다 주기도문(Paternoster)을 외우는 데서 이것을 Paternoster라고도 부른다. 그러나 이와 같은 관례는 15세기 이후의 것이므로 Chaucer 시대의 gaud의 역할은 불분명하다. 묵주는 대개 50개의 Ave와 5개의 Paternosters로 이루어져 있으나, 15세기 이전에는 150개의 Ave와 15개의 Paternosters로 도합 165개의 beads로 이루어져 있었다고 한다.

160　**heng**=hung. **brooch**는 반드시 현대의 broach만을 가리키지 않고 pendant, amulet, bracelet, necklace 등 일체의 장신구를 가리킨다. 당시 수녀들이 이런 장신구를 부착하는 것은 금지되어 있었다. 이러고 보면 Prioress는 장신구를 패용하고 있다는 것 말고도 주름잡은 모자를 쓰고 있다는 것, 이마를 가리지 않았다는 것, 애완견을 기르고 있었다는 것, 그리고 무엇보다도 Prioress가 관광 성격의 순례에 참가하는 것 자체가 규칙 위반(breaches of discipline)이다. 그러나 이와 같은 규칙들은 당시 엄하게 지켜지지도 않았으며, Prioress에 대한 Chaucer의 시선도 매우 동정적이라는 것을 알 수 있다. **sheene**=bright.

161　**write**=engraved, cut. **crowned**=surmounted by the figure of a crown.

대문자 A 위에 왕관이 새겨져 있었을 것이다.

162 **Amor vincit omnia**=Love conquers all. Virgil, *Eclogue* 10:60.

The Prioress's Chaplain, or Second Nun

The Nun's Priest

164 **chapeleyne**=a kind of private secretary, assistant. Prioress가 혼자 나다니는 일은 없었다. preestes thre가 three priests(사제)의 뜻이라면 순례자의 수는 32명이 되어 24행의 29명(Wel nyne and twenty in a compaignye)과 맞지 않게 된다. thre를 there의 잘못이라고 해도 문제가 풀리지 않는 것은 preetes가 복수형이기 때문이다. 또 다른 해석은 three가 Prioress와 another Nonne(chapeleyne)와 preest 모두를 포함한다는 것인데, 이것도 preests라는 복수형 때문에 매끄러운 해석이라고 할 수 없다. *Canterbury Tales*가 미완성의 작품이고, Chaucer가 뒤에 다시 손볼 기회를 예기했었다면 크게 문제 삼지 않아도 될 것이다.

The Monk

⟨The Monk⟩

165 **a fair**=a splendid person. 형용사가 명사로 사용된 경우. **for the maistrie**=surpassing all others, to a well-nigh unequalled degree, extremely.

166 **outridere**=an officer in a monastery whose duty it was to look after the manors belonging to it. 원래 수도사는 수도원에서 오로지 수도에만 전념하도록 되어 있었다. 하루의 일과도 자세히 정해져 있어 수도원 제도의 창시자인 St. Benedict가 만든 Benedictine Rule에 의하면 수도사들은 매일 네 시간은 기도, 네 시간은 독서, 그리고 적어도 여섯 시간은 노동을 하게 되어 있었다. 그러나 신자들의 땅 기증이 늘어나면서 수도사만으로는 땅을 경작할 수 없게 되자 전문적인 농부들에게 경작을 맡기게 되었다. 땅이 여러 곳에 분산되어 있었기 때문에 여러 곳에 celle를 두게 되며, 이를 관리하는 outridere의 일을 수도사들이 맡게 되었다. 수도사들이 수도원을 떠나게 되면서 이들의 타락이 시작된다. **venerie**= hunting. 이 수도사는 수도원을 떠날 수 있게 된 것을 기화로 말을 타고 사냥을 하고 다니는데, 당시 수도사들의 사냥은 사람들의 빈축을 샀다.

167 **to been an abbot able**=worthy to have been head of an abbey. **able**=worthy.

168 **deyntee**=valuable, fine.

169 **heere**=hear.

170 **Gynglen**=jingle. 당시 말에 작은 방울을 다는 것이 유행이었다. **cleere**=clearly.

172 **Ther as**=where. **lord**=라틴어의 dominus(=lord)를 본받아 수도사를

lord라고 높여 불렸다. **kepere**=head. **celle**=a small dependent monastery, a priory. 요양소(convalescent house) 구실도 했다.

173　**reule**=rule. St. Benedict와 St. Maurus가 제정한 수도원(benedictine order)의 수도사들이 지켜야 할 규칙들. St. Benedict(480?-?543)는 이태리의 Nursia 태생으로서 수도원 운동을 일으켰으며, 529년에 최초의 수도원을 Monte Cassino(Rome과 Naples 중간)에 세웠다. St. Maurus는 St. Benedict의 제자로서 프랑스에 Benedictine rule을 소개했다.

174　**somdel streit**=somewhat strict.

175　**ilke**=same. **leet olde thynges pace**=allowed old things (such as Rules) to pass away. **pace**=pass by. Chaucer는 이 Monk가 전통적인 수도원의 규칙들을 어긴 것에 대해 날카로운 비판을 하기보다 그가 옛날 것을 좋아하지 않는다는 말로 Monk를 감싸주고 있다.

176　**heeld after the newe world the space**=observed the freedom of modern times. **heeld after**=followed the customs of. **the space**=course, custom. the space를 meanwhile을 뜻하는 부사로 해석하는 사람들도 있다.

177　**yaf nat of that text a pulled hen**=didn't give a plucked hen for the text, care nothing about. **yaf**=gave. **that text**=saying, quotation. 다음 줄의 That seith… 이하를 받는다. **a pulled hen**=a plucked hen. worthless thing을 나타내는 정해진 표현.

178　**hunters been nat hooly men**=이 구절의 정확한 전거는 알 수 없으나 Gratian이 쓴 *Decretum*에 나오는 Essau venator erat, quoniam pecator erat…(=Essau was a hunter, therefore he was a sinner…)에서 나온 말이라는 주장이 있다. 그러나 14세기에 hunters are sinful이라는 생각이 일반적이었으므로 Chaucer가 특정한 대목을 마음에 두고 있지 않았다고 보는 것이 마땅하다.

179　**recchelees**=neglectful of duty and rules.

180　**likned**=compared. **til**=to. **a fissh that is waterlees**=수도원을 떠난 수도사(cloisterless monk)를 물 없는 물고기에 비유하는 것은 당시 작품 여러 곳에서 볼 수 있다. **waterlees**=out of water.

181　**seyn**=say. **cloystre**=cloister.

182	**thilke**=that. **nat worth an oystre**=worth nothing at all. a pulled hen 이나 an oystre는 쓸모없는 것을 나타내기 위해 중세영어에서 흔히 쓰이던 정해진 표현.
184	**What**=why. **wood**=mad, crazy.
185	**Upon a book…to poure**=by reading a book intently. **poure**=pore.
186	**swynken**=work, toil.
187	**Austyn**=St. Augustine of Hippo(354-430). **bit**=commands. biddeth의 축약형. St. Augustine(354-430)은 그의 글 *De Opere Monachorum*에서 몸이 건강한 수도사는 St. Paul을 본받아 육체노동을 해야 한다고 강조하고 있다. 그러나 14세기 수도원에서는 이 규칙이 잘 지켜지지 않았다. **How shal…**="How shall the world's work be done if monks spend all their time on religious duties?" An ironic question.
188	**Lat Austyn have his swynk to hym reverved!**=Let Austin keep his hard work to himself!
189	**he**=the Monk. **prikasour**=hunter on horseback. **aright**=truly, indeed, assuredly.
190	**grehoundes**=greyhounds. **fowel**=bird.
191	**prikyng**=following the tracks (of a hare). **prick**=a hare's track or footprint.
192	**lust**=pleasure. **cost**=expense or effort. **wolde**=would.
193	**seigh**=saw. **ypurfiled**=trimmed at the edges. **hond**=hand.
194	**grys**=an expensive gray fur. 다람쥐 털이었을 듯. 수도사가 털옷을 입는 것은 허용되지 않았다. **of a lond**=in the country.
195	**festne**=fasten.
196	**of gold ywroght**=made of gold. **curious**=carefully or beautifully made, elaborate.
197	**love-knotte**=an ornamental knot. 수도사가 금장식을 갖는 것은 금지되어 있었으며, 더욱이 love-knot(사랑 매듭) 따위를 갖는 것은 수도사에게 합당치 않은 장식이다. **gretter**=greater.
198	**balled**=bald.

199   **eek**=also. **as**=as if. **enoynt**=anointed.

200   **in good poynt**=in good (physical) condition.

201   **eyen**=eyes. **stepe**=projecting, prominent. bright, glaring with passion 으로 해석하는 사람도 있다. **heed**=head.

202   **stemed**=glowed. **forneys of a leed**=fire under a cauldron. **leed**=auldron. 옛날엔 솥을 납의 합금으로 만들었다.

203   **souple**=supple. **estaat**=condition.

204   **prelaat**=senior cleric, prelate.

205   **forpyned**=tormented. **goost**=ghost. 수도사가 네발짐승(quadrupeds)을 먹는 것은 금기 사항이었다.

206   **fat swan**=중세의 별미 음식이었다. **roost**=roast.

207   **palfrey**=saddle horse. **berye**=berry. 여기 등장하는 수도사는 어느 모로 보나 정상적인 수도사는 아니다. 비싼 말과 사냥개를 가지고 있다는 점, 비싸고 사치스러운 옷을 좋아한다는 점, 종래의 규칙 따위는 우습게 안다는 것, 돈이 많이 드는 사냥을 좋아한다던가, 자기가 좋아하는 것을 위해서는 돈을 아끼지 않는다던가, 기름진 백조 고기만 먹어 얼굴에는 기름이 흐르고 있다는 점등, 어느 하나를 보아도 수도사의 모습은 아니다. 그러나 늘 그렇듯이 이와 같은 수도사를 묘사하는 Chaucer의 붓끝은 날카롭지 않다.

The Friar

208   **Frere**=friar. **a wantowne**=a person given to pleasure. 형용사가 명사로 쓰인 경우. friar(탁발 수도사)는 세상과 등지고 수도에만 몰두하는 monk(수도사)와는 달리 세상 속으로 들어와 세상을 바꿔놓는 것을 그 임무로 삼는다. 그러나 그들의 문란한 생활 때문에 인기가 없었다. **a wantowne and a merye**=a jovial

⟨The Friar⟩

	and merry person. 형용사가 명사로 사용된 경우.
209	**lymytour**=a begging friar having the exclusive right to beg within an assigned district or limit. **solempne**=cheerful, gay, festive. solempne 는 이 밖에도 grand, imposing, important, pompous, solemn 등의 뜻이 있다.
210	**ordres foure**=the four orders of friars: Dominican, Franciscan, Carmelite, Augustinian. **kan**=knows.
211	**daliaunce**=polite, leisurely, intimate conversation or entertainment. 잡담뿐만 아니라 행위도 나타낸다.
212	**maad**=arranged.
213	**at his owene cost**=i.e. possibly because they had been his mistresses.
214	**post**=pillar, support, i.e., he was "a pillar of his society."
216	**frankeleyns**=country gentlemen, franklins. 지방의 지주계급으로서 귀족 바로 다음 신분으로서 이른바 gentry에 속하는 사람들이다. **over al**=everywhere. **contree**=region, country
217	**worthy**=respectable. 여기서는 well-to-do의 뜻도 있다.
218-20	**power of confessioun**=he was licensed (a *licenciat*) by his order to hear confessions and give absolution in cases beyond the jurisdiction of a parish priest (*curat*). friar들이 고해를 들을 수 있게 함으로써 priest들의 수입이 줄게 되고, 이것이 당시 두 부류 사이의 마찰의 한 원인이 되었다.
219	**moore than a curat**=경우에 따라서는 friar가 더 심각한 잘못에 대한 사면권(absolution)이 있었다. **curat**=parish priest, parson.
220	**licenciat**=adj. having an official ecclesiastical license to preach and hear confession. 1330년에 반포된 교황청의 칙서(papal bull)에 의해 탁발수도원(mendicant order)에서 몇몇 사람을 지정해 고해를 받을 수 있도록 면허장을 주었다.
221	**swetely**=sweetly. **herde**=heard.
222	**absolucion**=absolution.
223	**esy**=easy. **yeve penaunce**=impose penance.
224	**Ther as he wiste to have**=where he knew he would have. **ther as**=

	there where. **wiste**=knew. **pitaunce**=a pious donation, often probably a good dinner.
225	**povre**=poor. **yive**=give.
226	**yshryve**=shriven.
227	**if he**=if the penitent. **yaf**=gave. **he dorste make avaunt**=he. i.e., the Friar, dared make a boast. **avaunt**=boast.
227-8	**For…repentaunt**=For if a man gave, the Friar dared to assert he knew the man was repentant.
228	**wiste**=knew.
230	**althogh hym soore smerte**=though it (his heart) may sorely hurt him. The passage is an ironic statement of the Friar's cynical attitude toward penance.
232	**Men moote**=one ought to.
233	**typet**=a broad black scarf, capable of being wound round the head and neck as a hood. 짐작컨대 Friar의 typet의 좌우 끝엔 호주머니가 있어 거기에 칼 따위를 넣고 다녔을 것이다. **farsed**=stuffed.
234	**yeven**=give.
235	**murye note**=a pleasant singing voice. **murye**=merry. **note**=tune.
236	**koude**=could. **rote**=a stringed instrument resembling lyre. 대개 다섯 내지 여덟 개의 줄이 있다.
237	**of yeddynges**=for songs. **baar outrely the pris**=absolutely took the prize (문제없이 상을 받았다).
238	**nekke**=neck. **whit**=white. 중세의 관상학(physiognomy)에서는 흰 목과 264행의 lisping(혀 짧은소리)은 호색(sensuality)의 표시로 생각되었다. 하루의 대부분을 밖에서 살아야 하는 탁발 수도사의 목이 희다는 것부터가 특이하다. **flour-de-lys**=lily.
239	**therto**=moreover. **champioun**=champion wrestler or athlete.
241	**hostiler**=innkeeper. **tappestere**=barmaid. 문맥으로 보아 여기서는 분명히 여성을 가리킬 것이나 본래 여성을 가리키던 -ster는 (예 spinster) 다음 줄의 beggestere에서 보듯 반드시 그렇지도 않다.
242	**Bet**=better. **lazar**=leper, but here probably any poor or diseased

	person. **beggestere**=beggar.
243	**swich**=such.
244	**Acorded nat**=it was not befitting. accorded는 비인칭 동사. **as by**⋯ =considering his position. **facultee**=profession, occupation.
245	**sike**=sick.
246	**honeste**=befitting one's social status or office. **avaunce**=be profitable.
247	**deelen**=deal. **poraille**=poor people.
248	**riche**=rich people. **selleres of vitaille**=sellers of foodstuff. 당시 식료품 상인은 런던에서는 유력층에 속했다.
249	**over al ther as**=everywhere where. **over al**=everywhere. **ther as**=there where.
250	**Curteis he was and lowely of servyse**=he was humble in offering his services. **Curteis**=courteous. **lowely**=modest in demeanor. **servyse**=service.
251	**vertuous**=capable, effective. 강조를 위해 3중부정이 사용되었다. vertuous를 showing moral rectitude로 해석하는 사람도 있으나 문맥으로 보아 맞지 않는다.
252a	Chaucer의 글이 분명한 이 행은 몇몇 원고에서만 보인다. **ferme**=rent paid by the friar for the privilege of begging within assigned limits.
252b	**haunt**=a friar's territory in which he is privileged to beg.
253	**wydwe**=widow. **sho**=shoe.
254	**In principio** (*erat verbum*)="in the beginning was the word" (*John* 1:1), quoted as a greeting. 탁발 수도사들이 남의 집에 들어설 때에는 요한복음의 처음 14절을 읊는 것이 관례였다.
255	**wolde**=would. **ferthyng**=a coin=1/4 penny. **ere**=ere, before.
256	**purchas**=(illegal) profit (from begging). **rente**=regular income의 뜻도 있으나 탁발 수도사들은 정규적인 수입이 없었으므로 여기서는 rente를 특정 구역에서의 동냥할 수 있는 세나 권리금(ferme)으로 해석하는 것이 문맥상으로는 맞다. Robinson은 이 부분을 What he picked up amounted to more than his income. 즉 '부수입

(purchas)이 월급(rente)보다 많았다'라고 해석하고 있다.

257   **rage**=flirt or play amorously, behave wantonly or foolishly. **as**=as if. **whelpe**=young dog, puppy.

258   **love-dayes**=days for settling suits out of court. 법정 밖에서 중재 (arbitration)에 의해 분쟁을 해결하는 것. **koude he muchel helpe**= could give much help (and also enrich himself).

259   **cloysterer**=a poor brother who remained in the cloister.

260   **cope**=a priest's vestment.

261   **maister**=Master of Arts. 당시는 대단한 권위가 있었으며, 또 많은 돈을 드려야 얻을 수 있었다. 여기서는 '대학자' 정도의 뜻으로 해석될 수 있다.

262   **double worstede**=a stout worsted cloth 45 inches wide. **semycope**= short cloak.

263   **rounded**=stood out in a rounded form. **presse**=the round mold in which a bells is cast. **presse**를 clothespress, wardrobe(옷장)로 해석 하는 사람도 있다. 한편 Aldgate에 있던 Chaucer의 집은 런던에서 종 만드는 중심지에 있었다.

264   **lipsed**=lisped. 이 또한 white neck와 더불어 sensuality를 나타내는 하나의 특징이다. **for wantownesse**=as an affectation.

266   **songe**=sung.

268   **doon**=do. **sterres**=stars.

269   **cleped**=called. Huberd는 14세기 영국에서는 흔하지 않은 이름이 다. *Prologue*에 등장하는 인물들이 정형화하는 것을 피하기 위해 Chaucer가 종종 사용하는 테크닉 가운데 하나이다. 흔하지 않은 이름을 부여함으로써 그가 실존했던 인물 같은 인상을 준다. 그런 이유 때문에 Friar를 특정 인물과 연관 지으려는 노력이 생겨 났다. 소설에 등장하는 소년과 소녀의 이름을 가령 '철수', '영희'라고 한다면 그것은 고유명사가 아니고 추상명사가 된다. 여기서는 그것을 거꾸로 이용한 것이다.

The Merchant

270 **forked berd**=forked beard. 좌우로 갈라진 수염. 당시 유행하던 수염 모양 중 하나다.

271 **mottelee**=cloth woven with a parti-colored figured design. 상인 조합의 조합복이었을 것이다. **hye**=high. 그는 남의 눈을 끌기 위해 높은 안장의 말을 탔다.

272 **Flaundryssh**=of Flemish style. **bevere**=beaver.

273 **clasped**=fastened with clasps. **fetisly**=neatly.

⟨The Merchant⟩

274 **resons**=opinions. **spak**=spoke. **solempnely**=importantly, pompously.

275 **Sownynge**=conducing to, tending to. 대개는 뒤에 to나 into와 같은 전치사가 온다. **encrees**=increase. **wynnyng**=profits. Merchant는 정치에 대해 이런 저런 의견을 내놓지만 그것은 항상 자기 사업의 이익을 증대시키려는 것에 귀착된다.

276 **wolde**=wished. **see**=sea. **kept**=guarded. **for any thyng**=under all circumstance, at all costs (against pirates). 당시 해적의 출몰이 빈번하였으므로 Merchant에게는 어떤 일이 있더라도 바다를 지켜주기를 바랬다. 영국과 프랑스가 전쟁을 할 때면 각각의 사략선 (privateers)들이 상대방 배들을 공격하고는 했다.

277 **Middelburgh**=Netherland에서 떨어진 섬에 있는 항구. **Orewelle**=영국의 Suffolk에 있는 강. 모두 양모 무역의 중심지들이다.

278 **eschaunge**=exchange. **sheeld**=a French coin. 외환 장사하는 것은 위법이었다.

279 **wit besette**=employed his wit.

Chaucer · 99

280   **wiste**=knew. **wight**=person. **dette**=debt.
281   **So estatly was he of his governaunce**=so dignified was he in the conduct of his business. **governaunce**=management.
282   **bargayes**=bargainings. **chevyssaunce**=borrowing money, usury. 다른 사람의 물건을 외상으로 받아다 판 다음에 값을 치르는 상거래 방식을 말하는 데, 이 때는 정상적인 값보다 비싸게 받는다.
283   **For sothe**=forsooth, truly. **with-alle**=after all.
284   **sooth**=truth. **noot**=know not (his name). 이처럼 내놓고 Merchant의 이름을 모르겠다고 하는 것은 시민(city-people) 계급에 대한 양반(courtier) 계급의 무시라고도 말할 수 있으나 그보다는 Merchant의 부정직함에 대한 Chaucer의 경멸을 나타내기 위함이라고 보는 것이 타당할 것이다.

The Clerk

285   **Clerk**=an ecclesiastical student (at Oxford). 신부가 되기 위해 공부하고 있는 학생. **Oxenford**=Oxford. 12세기 이래로 Oxford 대학의 요람이다.
286   **logyk**=logic. 인문과학 중 가장 중요한 과목이다. **ygo**=gone, betaken himself.
287   **leene**=lean.
288   **he nas nat right fat**=he himself was not very fat. **I undertake**=I swear.
289   **holwe**=hollow (cheeked). **therto**=moreover. **sobrely**=gravely.
290   **overeste courtepy**=outermost short cloak.
291   **geten hym**=obtained himself. **benefice**=appointment to the rectorship of a parish church.
292   **office**=secular employment. 학생들이 정부 관계 일에 종사하는 일이 잦았다.

⟨The Clerk⟩

293 **hym was levere**=it was preferable to him, he preferred. **heed**=head.
294 **Twenty bookes**=당시 책들은 필사본이었으므로 20권은 당시 학생으로서는 상당히 많은 책이었다. **clad in black or reed**=bound in red or black. 까만색은 소가죽이고, 빨강색은 양가죽이다.
295 **Aristotle**=(384-322BC) 희랍의 철학가로서 12세기에 아랍 철학가들에 의해 파리에 소개되면서 서양 철학에 대 변혁을 가져왔다.
296 **fithele**=fiddle. **sautrie**=psaltery, a kind of harp. 삼각형이거나 능형의 악기로서 8~20개의 현이 있었으며, 세워 놓거나 무릎 위에 놓고 연주했다. fithele와 sautrie는 당시 학생들에게 인기 있는 악기였다.
297 **at be**=though. **philosphre**=a pun on the secondary meaning "alchemist." philosophre가 '철학자' 와 '연금술사'라는 뜻을 모두 가지고 있는 것을 가지고 말장난을 한 것.
298 **cofre**=coffer, chest, money box.
299 **freendes**=friends. **hente**=get.
301 **gan**=did. **bisily**=earnestly. **gan**=began.
302 **Of hem that yaf hym wherwith to scoleye**=those who gave him the means to study. **hem**=them. **yaf**=gave. **scoleye**=study, attend school.
303 **took cure**=gave attention. **cure**=care.
304 **o**=one. **neede**=needful.
305 **in forme and reverence**=with propriety and respect.
306 **quyk**=lively, sharp. **hy sentence**=elevated thought, weighty significance.
307 **Sownynge in**=conducing to, tending to.
308 **lerne**=learn. **teche**=teach.

The Sergeant of Law

⟨The Sergeant of Law⟩

309 **Sergeant**=a barrister of the highest degree, chosen from among the most eminent senior members of the bar. 14세기 영국의 법률가는 barrister와 solicitor로 나누어지며, 이들 사이의 계급차는 엄연한 것이었다. 후자는 대중과 barrister 사이의 사무적 연락의 책임을 맡았으며, 법정에서의 변호는 전자의 임무였다. Sergeant of the Lawe는 16년 이상의 경력을 가진 barrister 가운데서 왕이 임명하는 상급법정 변호사로서 Richard III세 때에 전국에 15명이 있었다고 한다. 현재 우리 나라의 대법관에 해당하는 지위로서 왕 앞에서 두건(coif)을 벗지 않아도 되었다. **war**=wary, cautious. **wys**=wise.

310 **Parvys**=a place where clients met lawyers for consultation. 당시 자주 이용되던 장소는 St. Paul's Cathedral의 입구였다.

312 **reverence**=respect.

313 **He semed swich**=he seemed to be so. **swich**=such. **his wordes weren to wise**=his words were so wise. 이 말을 더함으로써 Chaucer는 He semed swich(Discreet he was and of greet reverence)가 Lawyer의 말에만 해당될 뿐 그의 인격에 대한 평가는 아니라는 점을 암시하고 있다.

314 **Justice**=judge. **assise**=the country court, held periodically, to which justices were sent on temporary appointment by the king, assize; the justices of which were usually sergeants.

315 **patente**=letter of appointment from the king. **a pleyn commissiuon**=a letter addressed to the appointee giving him jurisdiction over all

kinds of cases.
316　**for**=on account of. **science**=knowledge, learning. **renoun**=reputation.
317　**fees and robes**=representing payment by his clients. 중세의 변호사들은 정규적인 보수 외에 옷도 선물로 받았다. **many oon**=many a one.
318　**purchasour**=buyer of land.
319　**Al**=all. **fee symple**=a title without restriction. 중세 봉건사회의 영토의 소유권(fee)에는 두 가지가 있는데, 상속인이 한정되는 것을 fee taille이라고 하면, 무조건의 한정이 없는 것을 fee simple이라고 한다. **in effect**=in the end result.
320　**infect**=legally invalidated.
321　**nas**=ne+was=was not.
322　**And yet he semed bisier than he was**=i.e. to make clients think more of him.
323　**In termes hadde he**=he could recite. **termes**=probably the Year Books, which were compiled from notes taken at trials and were valuable to lawyers and students as a record of precedents. **caas**=cases. English common law is 'case law', based on preceding decisions in similar cases. **doomes**=judgments, i.e., legal precedents.

The Franklin

324　**from the tyme of kyng William**=Year Books reaching back to William the Conqueror. 이 부분은 과장이다. 가장 오래된 것이 Edward I세(1239-1307) 때 것이다. **were falle**=had happened.
325　**therto**=moreover. **endite**=write. **make a thyng**=draw up a document.
326　**wight**=person. **pynche**=find fault with, pick holes in.

⟨The Franklin⟩

327   **statut**=statute, Act of Parliament. **koude**=knew, understood. **pleyn**=fully. **by rote**=by heart.

328   **rood**=rode. **hoomly**=unpretentiously, dressed informally. **medlee**=cloth made of wool dyed before weaving, motley. 단색이거나 얼룩무늬, 혹은 줄무늬였다.

329   **ceint**=girdle, belt. **barres**=ornamental bands to keep the silk spread. 띠는 허리가 아니라 엉덩이에 묶었었다.

330   **array**=dress. **telle I no lenger tale**=I say no more.

331   **Frankeleyn**=franklin, a landowner and member of the gentry immediately below the nobility. Baugh는 Sergeant of the Law가 돈 많은 Frankleleyn과 같이 여행한다는 것은 눈여겨볼 일이라고 말한다.

332   **dayesye**=daisy.

333   **complexioun**=temperament(기질). 중세 의학은 인간의 기질(temperament)을 네 가지 체액(humor), 즉 피(blood), 담(phlegm), 황담즙(choler), 흑담즙(black choler) 중 어느 것이 승한가에 따라 네 가지로 분류하였다. 피가 승한 사람은 다혈질(sanguine)이며, 담이 승한 사람은 냉담(phlegmatic)하고, 황담즙이 승한 사람은 신경질적(cholelic)이며, 흑담즙이 승한 사람은 우울(melancholic)하다. **sangwyn**=다혈질. 대개 몸이 크고, 얼굴은 불그스레하고, 대담한데다가 쾌락을 좋아한다. 사상한의학(四象韓醫學)의 입장에서 보면 태음인(太陰人)에 가깝다.

334   **by the morwe**=in the morning. **sop in wyn**=pieces of toasted bread or cake soaked in wine (a common light breakfast).

335   **delit**=pleasure. **wone**=custom.

336   **Epicurus**=최고의 선은 향락이라고 말했던 희랍의 철학가(341-270 B.C.). 그가 말하는 향락은 '영혼의 향락'으로서 번뇌로부터의 해방을 의미했다. 이것이 후세에 가서 그의 도덕철학은 잊어버린 채 그를 마치 쾌락주의의 시조처럼 생각하게 되었다.

337   **that**=who, i.e., Epicurus. **pleyn**=full. **pleyn delit**=purely sensual pleasure.

338   **verray felicitee parfit**=true and perfect happiness. truly perfect happiness로 해석하는 사람도 있다. **verray**=true. **felicitee**=felicity.

339	**a greet**=형용사에 부정관사가 붙어 명사로 사용된 예.
340	**Seint Julian**=patron saint of hospitality. **contree**=region, country.
341	**after oon**=according to a single standard, of uniform quality, presumably the best.
342	**envyned**=stocked with wine.
343	**bake mete**=baked food (i.e., meat pies), a pie in which meat or fish is baked with fruit, spices, etc.
344	**flessh**=meat. **plentevous**=plentiful, plenteous.
345	**It snewed in his hous of mete and drynke**=His house was abundant in mat and drink. **snewed**=snowed. **mete**=food.
346	**deyntees**=delicacies.
347	**After**=according to. **sondry**=various, sundry.
348	**chaunged he his mete and his soper**=It was customary to change one's diet according to the season. **mete**=dinner.
349	**partrich**=partridge. **muwe**=cage, coop.
350	**breem**=bream. **luce**=pike. **stuwe**=fish pond. 해안으로부터의 생선의 수송이 여의치 않았던 중세에는 개인용 낚시터가 흔했다.
351	**Wo was his cook**=Woe was to his cook. **wo**=woeful. **but if**=unless.
352	**Poynaunt**=pungent, piquant. **redy**=ready. **geere**=utensils for the table (knives, cups, plates, etc.).
353	**table dormant**=table fixed permanently in place. 당시 테이블과 의자는 받침(trestle) 위에 올려놓는 이동식인 것이 많았는데 이 집은 손님이 많아 고정식 테이블을 쓰고 있다. **halle**=the main room of the house, also used for meals.
355	**sessiouns**=meetings of the Justices of the Peace, at which he presided. 1년에 네 번 행해진다. Chaucer 자신도 Kent의 Justice of Peace였다. **lord**=one who presides at a judicial sessions. **sire**=종종 lord와 함께 사용되었다.
356	**knyght of the shire**=a member of Parliament for his country.
357	**anlaas**=short, two-edged dagger. **gipser**=purse, pouch.
358	**Heeng**=hung. **morne**=morning.

359   **shirreve**=sheriff, the administrative officer of a country. The sheriff is responsible for keeping the king's peace, and carrying out all legal judgements. Lord Lieutenant(주지사) 바로 다음 직책이다. **contour**=an official who oversees the collecting and auditing of taxes for a shire, an auditor. 회계 감사.

360   **vavasour**=sub-vassal, large landholder. 남작(baron) 바로 아래 신분.

361   **Haberdasher**=a seller of hats or of needles, button, etc.

362   **Webbe**=weaver. **Dyere**=dyer of cloth. **Tapycer**=upholsterer or tapestry maker.

363   **o lyveree**=one (the same) livery. 중세에는 친목이 주 목적인 종교, 사회적(religious and social)적일 조합(gild)과 특정 직업의 두 가지 종류의 gild(조합)가 있었다. 여기 등장하는 다섯 조합원들이 동일한 조합복(livery)을 입었다는 것은 각각의 직업에 따른 복장이 아니라 당시 유행한 구역 조합(parish gild)이나 종교적인 친목 단체(religious and fraternal organization)의 복장을 했다는 것을 의미한다.

364   **solempne**=distinguished. **fraternitee**=a group of persons associated by some common aim or interest; a secular society or company, a gild. **greet**=important.

365   **hir**=their. **geere**=gear, equipment. **apiked**=polished, adorned.

366   **chaped**=ornamented with metal on the scabbard. 사치금지법(sumptuary law)에 의해 상인이나 장인들은 원칙적으로 은장식이 된 칼을 갖고 다니는 것이 금지되어 있었으나, 재산이 £500 이상인 경우에는 허용되었다.

367   **wroght**=made. **weel**=well.

368   **everydeel**=every bit.

369   **ech**=each. **hem**=them. **burgeys**=burgess, established citizen.

370   **yeldehalle**=gildhall. **deys**=dais or platform where the mayor and aldermen sat.

371   **Everich**=everyone. **for**=because of. **kan**=knows.

372   **shaply**=suited, fit. **alderman**=the head of the gild and hence a

373 　member of the Common Council of the town. 지금의 시의원 격. **catel**=property. **ynogh**=enough. **rente**=income. burgess가 alderman이 되기 위해서는 일정한 재산과 수입이 있어야 했다.

374 　**assente**=agree to.

375 　**And elles**=otherwise. **certeyn**=certainly. **to blame**=blameworthy.

376 　**ycleped**=called.

377 　**goon**=to go. **vigilies**=vigils, ceremonies on the eve of gild festivals. **al bifore**=at the head of the procession. 부인들의 순서는 남편의 순위를 따랐다.

378 　**mantel**…=a mantle borne by a servant in the manner of royalty.

The Cook

379 　**Cook**=다섯 guildmen이 데리고 온 이 요리사는 대단해 보이지 않는다. 그가 할 수 있는 요리 품목도 그렇거니와 정강이에 종기(on his shyne a mormal hadde he)가 있다는 사실하며, 그가 나중에 하는 천한 이야기, 그리고 순례 끝에 가서 술에 취해 낙마하는 일 따위가 그렇다. **nones**=occasion. for the nones는 문자 그대로 번역하면 for the occasion이 되지만 실제로는 별 뜻 없이 사용되곤 했다.

〈The Cook〉

380 　**chiknes**=chickens. **marybones**= marrowbones. 중세 요리 책에는 사골(marrow)이 흔하게 등장한다.

381 　**powdre-marchant**=맛이 신 일종의 양념이었다는 것 말고는 그 뜻을 정확히 알 수 없다. **tart**=tart, sharp-tasting. **galyngale**=생강 맛이 나는 일종의 향신료.

382　**knowe**=distinguished. **Londoun ale**=the best-quality ale.
383　**rooste**=roast. **sethe**=boil.
384　**mortreux**=a stew. **pye**=meat (or fish) pie.
385　**thoughte me**=seemed to me.
386　**shyne**=shin. **mormal**=an open sore, ulcer.
387　**For**=as for. **blankmanger**=a dish of capon, rice, milk, sugar, almonds. 오늘날의 blancmange와 다르다. **with the beste**=as well as anyone.

The Shipman

388　**Shipman**=a ship owner. **wonynge fer by weste**=dwelling far to the west. **wonynge**=dwelling. **by weste**=westward.

389　**For aught I woot**=for all I know. **Dartmouth**=서남부에 있는 당시의 중요한 항구로서 선주들의 해적들의 출몰이 잦은 곳으로 알려져 있기도 했다.

390　**rouncy**=a horse of small size, originally a pack horse, often used for riding. **as he knouthe**=as best he could (that is, poorly).

〈The Shipman〉

391　**faldyng**=coarse woolen cloth.
392　**laas**=lace, cord.
394　**hote**=hot. **somer**=summer(sun). **hewe**=color.
395　**a good felawe**=a good fellow. 그러나 여기서처럼 종종 rascal의 뜻으로 쓰였다.
396　**draughte**=a drink or a quantity drawn off. **ydrawe**=drawn (from the cask).
397　**Burdeux-ward**=while carrying wine from Bordeaux. Bordeaux는 예나 지금이나 포두주의 중요한 산지이다. **chapman**=merchant, who

	was traveling with his cargo. **sleep**=slept.
398	**nyce**=foolish. **conscience**=conscience. 이 밖에도 compassion이나 tender feeling의 뜻도 있다. **keep**=heed.
399	**faught**=fought (with pirates). **hyer hond**=upper hand, victory.
400	**By water he sente hem hoom to every lond**=made the enemy sailors walk the plank blindfolded. 직역하면 '물길로 각각의 고향으로 보내주었다'는 뜻인데, 당시 해적이 포로를 처리하는 하나의 방법으로 포로의 눈을 가린 채 널빤지를 위를 걷게 해서 바다에 빠뜨려 죽였다.
401	**craft**=skill. **rekene**=calculate.
402	**stremes**=currents. **his daungers hym bisides**=dangers all around him. **hym bisides**=that beset him.
403	**herberwe**=harbor. **lodemenage**=pilotage(수로 안내).
404	**nas**=was not. **noon swich**=none such, none like him. **from Hull to Cartage**=from Hull in Yorkshire to Cartagena in Spain. 모르는 곳 없이 전부 다 라는 뜻.
405	**Hardy**=bold. **wys to undertake**=wise in undertakings.
406	**berd been shake**=beard been shaken.
407	**havenes**=harbors.
408	**Gootlond**=Sweden 근처의 섬. **Fynystere**=스페인 서북부에 있는 곶 (cape).
409	**cryke**=creek, harbor, inlet. **Britaigne**=Brittany.
410	**barge**=a sailing vessel of medium size (between 100 and 200 tons). **ycleped**=called.

The Doctor of Physic

411 **Doctour of Phisik**=여기 등장하는 의사는 대학교의 정규 과정을 마친 의사로서 의사 자격을 받기 위해서는 대개 8, 9년이 걸렸다. 폭 넓은 공부를 해야 했으며 특히 astronomy (정확히는 astrology(점성술))에 정통할 필요가 있었다. 그럼에도 불구하고 의사의 사회적 신분은 높지 않았다.

〈The Doctor of Physic〉

412 **noon hym lik**=none like him.

413 **To speke of**=in the matter of, with regard to, if we consider.

414 **for**=because. **grounded**=well instructed. **astronomye**=astrology. 중세 의학에서는 인간이 태어날 때의 별자리(constellation)가 그의 체질을 결정하는 데 중요한 요소일 뿐만 아니라 시술에 미치는 별자리의 영향도 큰 것으로 여겨졌다. 예를 들어 Cancer(6.21-7.22 巨蟹宮, 게 달)에 태어난 사람은 cold and dry, Capricorn (12.21-1.19 磨葛宮, 염소 달)에 태어난 사람은 cold and moist하다는 등이다. 우수한 의사는 이 치료에 임할 때 이 모든 것을 고려해야 했다.

415-6 **kepte his pacient a ful greet deel In houres**=kept his patient under favorable planetary influence. 의사는 환자를 면밀히 관찰하여 치료에 가장 적절한 천문학적 시간과 부적(ymage=talisman)을 만들 시간을 알아내야 한다. **kepte**=watched over, cared for. **a ful greet deel**=very closely.

416 **in houres**=according to the astrological hours favorable to the treatment. **magyk natureel**=natural magic, the knowledge of hidden natural forces (e.g. magnetism, stellar influence), and the art of using these in calculating future events, curing diseases, etc.

417 **Well koude he fortunen the ascendent**=he knew well how to find the Ascendent in favorable position, i.e. determine the favorable time for using images, or talismans, in medicine. **fortunen**=calculate. **ascendent**=the zodiacal sign rising above the eastern horizon; whether or not it is 'fortunate' depends upon the conjunction of the planets, which the Doctor foresees. 각각의 12궁도(zodiac) 안에 있는 중요한 별을 lord of the ascendent라고 한다.

418 **ymages**=a figure made for purposes of magic or divination; also a talisman marked with a Zodiacal figure. 흙으로 빚거나 칼로 새겨 만들었다.

419 **everich maladye**=every illness.

420 **Were**=whether it were. **of**=from. **hoot, or coold, or moyste, or drye**=중세에서는 모든 물질은 earth, water, fire, air의 네 원소(four elements)로 이루어졌다고 생각했으며, 이들은 각기 다음과 같은 네 자질(four qualities)의 배합으로 이루어졌다고 생각했다.

    earth = cold and dry
    water = cold and moist
    fire = hot and dry
    air = hot and moist

한편 인간을 구성하고 있는 것은 다음의 네 체액(four humors)이라고 생각되었으며, 인간의 체질은 이들 체액들의 배합 상태에 따라 결정된다고 생각되었다. 한편 주어진 체액이 승할 때 나타나는 체질적 특성을 괄호 안에 표시하였다.

    cold and dry = melancholy or black bile (melancholic)
    cold and moist = phlegm (phlegmatic)
    hot and dry = choler or yellow bile (choleric)
    hot and moist = blood (sanguinary)

이 배합에 문제가 생길 때 인간은 병을 얻는다고 생각했다. 333행과 587행 참조.

421 **engendred**=originated.

422 **verray, parfit**=true and perfect. **praktisour**=practitioner.

423	**The cause yknowe, and of his harm the roote**=once the cause and the root of his disease known. **yknowe**=known. **harm**=illness.
424	**Anon**=at once. **yaf**=gave. **boote**=remedy.
425	**apothecaries**=pharmacists.
426	**drogges**=drugs. **letuaries**=electuaries, medicines mixed with syrup.
427	**For ech of hem made oother for to wynne**=for each of them made the other to gain. 의사와 약제사가 서로 누이 좋고 매부 좋은 관계라는 것은 예나 지금이나 다름이 없다. **wynne**=profit.
428	**newe to bigynne**=newly begun.
429-34	**Esculapius**=legendary father of medicine, Aesculapius, a Greek god, supposed in the middle Ages to be the author of severl books. 이 뒤에 거명된 14명은 모두 중세에 잘 알려진 의학계의 권위들로서 대체로 보아 시대순으로 나열되어 있으며 다음 세 그룹으로 나눌 수 있다. 첫째, 희랍의 대가들: Ypocras, Deyscorides, Rufus, Galyen. 둘째, 아랍(페르샤)의 대가들: Razis, Haly, Avycen, Averrois, Damascien, Serapion, Constantyn. 셋째, 그라파(영국)의 대가들: Geilbertyn, Bernard, Gatesden.
431	**Ypocras**=Hippocrates. Socrates와 동시대 사람으로서 기원전 5세기에 활약한 희랍 의학의 창시자.
435	**measurable**=moderate.
436	**superfluitee**=excess.
437	**of greet norissyng**=greatly nourishing.
438	**His studie was but litel on the Bible**=Physicians were commonly regarded as skeptical. 성경이 아직 영어로 번역되기 이전이긴 했으나 많은 사람들이 라틴어를 읽을 수 있었고, 더구나 의사들은 유식했으므로 성경을 읽지 못해 성경 공부가 부족했다고 할 수는 없다.
439	**sangwyn**=blood red (cloth). **pers**=blue or bluish gray (cloth).
440	**taffata**=taffeta. **sendal**=a rich silk. taffata와 sendal 모두 얇고 비싼 명주 옷감이다.
441	**esy of dispence**=slow to spend money, careful about spending,

442 **that he wan in pestilence**=what he made during the plague. **that**= what. **pestilence**=1349년의 흑사병(Black Death). 영국 인구의 3분의 1내지 반이 죽었다. 이 난리 통에도 돈을 벌었다는 것은 이 의사가 보통 사람이 아니라는 것을 말해준다.

443 **For gold in phisik is a cordial**=because gold was considered an excellent medicine, he specially loved it. 풍자적인 표현이다. **cordial**= a medicine good for the heart. 당시에는 약값을 올리기 위해 실제로 약에다 금가루를 섞는 일도 있었다.

The Wife of Bath

445 **biside**=near. **ă góod Wĭf**=the mistress of a household. 강세로 보아 good Wif가 gentleman처럼 하나의 합성어였을 것으로 생각된다. Wife에 대한 보다 자세한 기술은 그녀의 이야기 앞의 Prologue에서 볼 수 있다. 다른 서문들과는 달리 거기서 Wife는 자기가 살아온 과정을 길게 이야기하고 있다.

⟨The Wife of Bath⟩

446 **somdel deef**=somewhat deaf. 뒤에 Wife of Bath는 다섯 번째 남편의 책장을 찢은 탓에 매를 맞아 귀가 먹었다고 말한다. (*The Wife of Bath's Prologue*, 667-8. Why that I rente out of his book a leef, For which he smoot me so that I was deef=why I tore that leaf from his book, for which he hit me and made me deaf.) **scathe**=a pity, a matter for regret.

447 **hadde swich an haunt**=was so skilful. **haunt**=skill.

448 **passed**=surpassed. **hem of Ypres and of Gaunt**=those of Ypres and

Ghent. Ypres와 Ghent는 Flemish에 있는 방직의 중심지였다. 따라서 이 문장은 She beat the Dutch의 뜻이 된다. 당시만 해도 옷감 만드는 기술은 네덜란드가 한 수 위였다.

449 **In al the parisshe wife ne was ther noon**=not a woman in the whole parish.

450 **offrynge**=offertory(봉헌). 지금은 주로 돈을 내지만 중세에는 스스로가 만든 소출이나 선물을 들고 사회적 신분 순서에 따라 제단으로 걸어갔다. **bifore**=in front of.

451 **if ther dide**=if any woman were to do so. **wrooth**=angry.

452 **out of alle charitee**=beyond thought of being charitable, angry.

453 **coverchiefs**=kerchiefs, scarfs for covering head. **fyne weren of ground**= finely woven. **ground**=texture.

454 **dorste**=dare. **weyeden ten pound**=weighed ten pounds (5킬로 정도). 모자는 종종 크고 무겁기는 했으나 5킬로라면 조금은 과장된 것이다.

455 **weren**=were.

456 **hosen**=stockings. **fyn**=fine.

457 **streite yteyd**=tightly fastened. **moyste**=soft, not dried out.

458 **fair**=pleasing. **hewe**=hue.

459 **worthy**=여기서는 comfortable economic and social position의 뜻. **lyve**=life.

460 **at chirche dore**=in front of the church door. 모든 결혼은 교회 문 앞에서 이루어졌는데, 주례를 맡은 사제가 이 결혼에 이의가 없는가를 물어보고, 없다면 신혼부부와 그 친구들이 안으로 들어가서 미사를 드리는 것이 관례였다. **fyve**=five. 성경의 Samaritan 여인의 남편의 수이기도 하다 (*John*, 4:6-26). cf. *The Wife of Bath's Prologue*, 17-9, 'Thou hast yhad fyve housbondes,' quod he, 'And that ilke man that now hath thee Is noght thyn housbonde,…' (='You have had five husbands,' he said, 'and that man whom you now have is not your husband,'…). The Wife of Bath는 남편은 여섯 이래도 마다하지 않겠다고 말한다. (*The Wife of Bath's*

Prologue, 45, Welcome the sixte, whan that evere he shal(=The sixth, whenever he comes, shall be welcome.) 그러나 당시 과부가 수절한다는 것은 어려웠을 것이고 또 위험하기도 했다. 실제로 Chaucer 자신의 어머니, 이모, 할머니에 이르기까지 적어도 세 번 이상 남편을 바꾼 경력이 있다. 그녀가 처음 결혼한 것은 12세 때이고 다섯 번째 남편을 만난 것은 그녀가 40세일 때이다.

461 **Withouten**=not counting, in addition to. **compaignye**=sexual union, intercourse.

462 **nedeth nat**=it is not necessary. **as nowthe**=at present, for now.

463 **thries**=thrice. 당시 성지 순례는 드문 일이 아니었으나 Jerusalem에 세 번씩이나 갔다는 것은 좀 지나치다. **Jerusalem**=three syllables, Jer-sa-lem.

464 **passed**=crossed. **straunge strem**=foreign river.

465-6 **Rome, Boloigne, Seint-Jame, Coloigne**는 모두 유명한 사원들이 있는 곳이다. Boulogne는 Virgin Mary의 조각상으로 유명하며, 스페인 서북부 Galicia 지방의 Compostella에 있는 St. James는 4대 사도 중의 한 사람인 St. James를 모신 곳으로, 그리고 Cologne에는 동방의 세 박사(Three Magi)의 뼈가 묻혀있는 곳으로 알려져 있다.

467 **koude**=knew. **wandrynge by the weye**=wandering along the road, traveling. 사람에 따라서는 이 대목을 '옆길로 새는 것'으로 해석하는 경우도 있다.

468 **Gat-tothe**=gate-toothed, with teeth widely spaced, gap-toothed. 당시의 관상학으로 볼 때 이것은 허영(vanity), 대담(boldness), 거짓(falseness), 식탐(gluttony), 음탕(lasciviousness) 등을 나타내는 것으로 알려졌었다. **soothly for to seye**=to tell the truth.

469 **amblere**=an ambling saddle horse. **esily**=in a relaxed way.

470 **Ywympled**=covered with wimple. 151행 참조.

471 **brood**=broad. **bokeler or a targe**=buckler or a shield.

472 **foot-mantel**=a riding skirt, or outer skirt. 앞치마처럼 생겼다.

473 **spores**=spurs.

474   **felaweshipe**=company. **carpe**=joke.
475   **remedies of love**=means of relief for lovers; means of contraception or abortion이라는 두 가지 해석이 있다. **remedies**=cures. **per chaunce**=doubtless.
476   **koude**=knew. **olde daunce**=all the tricks of the game, i.e., of love.

The Poor Parson

478   **povre**=poor. **Person**=parson or parish priest. 여기 등장하는 목사님은 앞서 등장한 기사(Knight), 대학생(Clerk)과 더불어 어디 하나 흠 잡을 데 없는 모범적인 인물이다. 어떤 이는 이것을 이 세 직종에 대한 Chaucer의 평상시의 존경심의 표출이라고 해석하는 이도 있으나, Miller's Tale에 등장하는 대학생은 말할 수 없는 엉터리 학생이며, 여기서도 주인공 목사님 말고 다른 목사님들은 별로 존경받을 존재가 아니라는 점을 생각하면 이 가난한 목사님도 하나의 등장인물일 뿐이라고 해석하는 것이 좋을 듯하다. 그보다는 당시 쇠락해가고 있던 기사도나 타락한 성직자들에 대한 하나의 경고로 보는 것이 좋을 듯하다. **toun**=village.

⟨The Poor Parson⟩

479   **werk**=work, deeds.
480   **He was also a lerned man**=사제들이 뇌물에 의해 서품 받는 일이 많았으며, 일단 서품을 받고 나면 공부를 하지 않는 경향이 있었다. 그러나 이 목사님은 선한 목자인 동시에 유식한 선생님이기도 했다.
482   **parisshens**=parishioners, inhabitants of his parish.
483   **Benygne**=benign, kind, gracious. **wonder**=wonderfully, marvelously.
484   **pacient**=patient.

485	**And swich he was ypreved ofte sithes**=often proven. **swich**=such. **ypreved**=proved, i.e., by circumstances. **ofte sithes**=many times, oftentimes.
486	**looth were hym**=it would be full loathful for him, it would be displeasing to him. **cursen**=excommunicate, i.e., in order to force payment of tithes.
487	**But rather wolde he yeven**=but he would rather give. **yeven**=give. **out of doute**=without doubt, certainly.
488	**aboute**=round about, in the parish.
489	**offryng**=the church offering. 법으로 정해진 십일조 외에도 자발적인 헌금이 이루어졌다. 일종의 감사헌금이다. **substaunce**=fixed income, derived from him benefice, property.
490	**koude**=could, knew how to. **suffisaunce**=enough to live on.
491	**wyd**=wide. **fer asonder**=far apart.
492	**ne lefte nat**=ceased not (to visit). **lefte**=left. **for**=in spite of, notwithstanding.
493	**meschief**=misfortune, trouble.
494	**ferreste**=those who lived farthest away. **muche and lite**=person of high and low estate, all people.
495	**Upon his feet, and in his hand a staf**=초기 기독교 사제의 모습이다.
496	**ensample**=example. **sheep**=parishioners. **yaf**=gave.
497	**wroghte**=practiced, i.e., he practiced what he preached.
498	**gospel**=cf. *Matthew* 5:19. **tho wordes caughte**=took those words, i.e., the above. **tho**=those.
499	**figure**=figure of speech, analogy, a parable. **eek**=also.
500	i.e., if the highest should weaken, what can be expected of the lowest.
502	**no wonder is**=it is no wonder. **lewed**=ignorant, uneducated, unlearned. **ruste**=rust, tarnish.
503	**if a prest take keep**=if a priest were to take heed. **keep**=notice.
504	**shiten**=fouled with dung, covered in excrement. 당시 타락하고 위

선적인 목사들은 많은 비판의 대상이었다. **clene**=clean.

505 **Wel oghte a preest ensample for to yive**=it well becomes a priest to set an example. **ensample…yive**=to give, or set, an example.

507 **sette nat his benefice to hyre**=did not rent out his parish appointment. Absentee parsons appointed vicars (대리 목사)and curates(부 목사).

508 **and leet**=nor left. **cncombred**=stuck fast (in the mire of sin).

509 **Seinte Poules**=당시 St. Paul's Cathedral 근처에만도 35개의 기도실에 54명의 사제들이 있었다.

510 **To seken hym a chaunterie for soules**=to get himself a chantry for souls. chantry는 망자의 명복을 빌기 위한 기도실로서, 사제들은 자기 교구에 대리 목사나 부 목사를 두고 자기는 런던에 가서 부유한 사람들의 헌금으로 별로 하는 일없이 기도실에서 편하게 지내는 경우가 많았다. 동시에 수입도 배로 늘었다. 그러나 당시 목사님들의 수당이 매우 작았다는 사실을 감안하면 나무라기만 할 일은 아닐는지 모른다.

511 **Or with a bretherhede to been withholde**=to be retained by a guild as chaplain. 이 또한 편하고 돈이 생기는 생활이었다. **whithholde** =supported.

512 **kepte wel his folde**=kept watch over his sheepfold.

513 **myscarie**=go amiss, come to destruction.

514 **mercenarie**=a hireling. cf. *John* 10:12. A hired hand will run when he sees a wolf coming. He will leave the sheep because they aren't his and isn't their shepherd. 여기서 wolf는 Devil을 뜻한다.

516 **despitous**=scornful, contemptuous.

517 **ne of**=nor in. **daungerous ne digne**=neither domineering nor disdainful. **daungerous**=haughty, overbearing. **ne**=nor. **digne**=dignified, superior.

518 **discreet**=courteous.

519 **fairnesse**=living a good life.

520 **bisynesse**=what he worked for, constant endeavor, concern.

521 **But it were**=but if it happeneed that any person was obstinate.

522 **What so**=whatsoever. **lough estat**=low position.

523 **snybben**=reprimand, rebuke. **for the nonys**=for the particular occasion.
524 **trowe**=believe. **nowher noon ys**=is none anywhere.
525 **waited after**=looked for, expected.
526 **spiced conscience**=overscrupulous nature, fastidiousness. **spiced**=seasoned, hence highly refined, overscrupulous.
527 **loore**=teaching, i.e., of Christ and his apostles.
528 **He taughte, but first he folwed it hymselve**=the parson practised what he preached.

The Plowman

529 **a Plowman, was his brother**=a plowman who was his brother. **Plowman**=자기 형인 Parson 못지않게 건실한 사람이다. 하나님과 이웃을 사랑하고, 11조를 꼬박꼬박 내면서 열심히 살아가는 사람으로 묘사되어 있다. 그러나 당시는 Black Death 이후의 어려운 사회적 여건과 인두세(人頭稅)를 비롯한 갖가지 혹독한 가렴주구에 시달리던 농민들이 봉기를 일으켜 방화와 약탈, 파괴가 한바탕 휩쓸고 지난 다음이다. 모든 농민이 여기 등상하는 인물처럼 착하게만 살 수 없었던 시대이다. 그럼에도 불구하고 이처럼 모범적이고 선량한 농민을 등장시켰다는 것은 그를 따르고 배워야할 하나의 모델로 삼으려고 한 듯하다. *Canterbury Tales*가 미완으로 끝나 Plowman은 이야기를 할 기회를 갖지 못한다.

530 **ylad of dong ful many fa fother**=pulled many a cart-load of dung. **ylad**=led, carried, carted. **dong**=dung. **fother**=cart load.
531 **trewe**=true, honest. **swynkere**=worker.
532 **pees**=peace.
533 **hoole**=whole.
534 **thogh him gamed or smerte**=whether it was pleasant or painful to him, in pleasure or pain. gamed와 smerte 모두 비인칭 동사이다.
535 **thanne**=i.e., he love God best and then (i.e., next) his neighbor just as much as himself. cf. *Matthew* 22:37-39. Jesus replied, "'You

must love the Lord your God with all your heart, all your soul, and all your mind.' This is the first and greatest commandment. A second is equally important: 'Love your neighbor as yourself.' "

536   **thresshe**=thresh. **dyke and delve**=make ditches and cultivate. 결국 밭일을 한다는 뜻.

537   **povre**=poor. **wight**=person.

538   **hire**=payment. **myght**=power.

539   **tithe**=십일조. **faire and wel**=completely. 동의어의 중첩에 대해서는 124행의 주 참조. **faire**=fairly.

540   **of his propre swynk and his catel**=with his own labor and his goods. **of**=with. **propre swynk**=own labor. **catel**=property, possession (*not* cows).

541   **tabard**=a kind of smock, often confined at the waist by a belt, a loose upper coat. **mere**=mare. 가난한 사람들만 탔다.

542   **Reeve**=reeve, estate-manager. 587행 이하 참조.

543   **Somnour**=summoner (to the church court). 623행 이하 참조.

544   **Maunciple**=manciple, college servant. 567행 이하 참조. **namo**=no more.

The Miller

545   **Miller**=중세의 장원제도(莊園制度) 하에서는 영내의 모든 토지 보유자(tenant)들은 장원 안의 방앗간을 사용하도록 되어 있었다. 따라서 방앗간은 일종의 독점 기업이 되고, 그 주인은 각가지 부정을 저질러 사복을 채우게 된다. **stout**=sturdy. **carl**=churl, fellow. **for the nones**=for the occasion. **for the nones**=for then ones=for them ones. cf, **atte nale**=atten ale=at the

〈The Miller〉

alehouse. **The Miller was a stout carl for the nones**=The Miller for the nones was a stout carl=The Miller we had with us, our particular Miller.

546   **brawn**=muscle. **eek**=also.

547   **That proved wel**=that proved to be true, that was certain. **over al ther he cam**=everywhere where he went.

548   **have alwey**=always win. **ram**=the traditional prize at wrestling match.

549   **short-sholdred**=broad-shouldered, short in the upper arm, stocky. **brood**=broad. **a thikke knarre**=a fellow thickly knotted with muscle, knotty fellow. **knarre**=knot.

550   **dore**=door. **no doore that he nolde heve of harre**=no door that he could not heave off its hinge. **nolde**=ne wold=would not. **of harre**=off its hinges.

551   **breke**=break. **at a rennyng**=with a single charge.

552   **berd**=beard. **as any sowe or fox was reed**=was as red as any sow or fox.

553   **therto**=also.

554   **cop right**=right (on the) top. **cop**=top.

555   **werte**=wart. **toft of herys**=tuft of hairs. His short-shouldered, stocky figure, his fat face with red bushy beard, his flat nose with a wart on top—these variously denoted a shameless, loquacious, quarrelsome, and lecherous fellow.

556   **Reed**=red. **brustles**=bristles. **erys**=ears.

557   **nosethirles**=nostrils. **blake**=black. 콧구멍이 크고 까맣다는 것은 관상학적으로 보아 lustfulness, desire for coition, and love of things Venerian의 표시라고 한다.

558   **bokeler**=a small shield. **bar**=bor, carried.

559   **forneys**=furnace, cauldron.

560   **janglere**=loud talker, teller of dirty stories. **goliardeys**=a teller of ribald tales, a coarse buffoon.

561　　**that**=his talk. **harlotries**=ribaldries, vulgarities, dirty jokes.

562　　**stelen**=steal. **tollen thries**=charge three times over. **tollen**=take his toll or percentage of the grain which he ground. 규정상(statue)으로는 20분의 1에서 24분의 1이었으나 실제로는 16분의 1, 심할 때는 13분의 1까지 받았다. 대개는 방앗간을 세내서 운영했으므로 요금을 올리려는 유혹은 컸을 것이다.

563　　**he hadde a thombe of gold**=방앗간 주인은 손바닥 위에 밀가루를 펼쳐놓고 엄지손가락으로 가루의 곱기를 측정했다. 따라서 그가 thombe of gold를 가졌다는 것은 문자 그대로는 그의 능력이 뛰어나다는 뜻이 된다. 그런데 방앗간 주인에 관해서는 다음과 같은 속담이 있다. Every honest miller has a thumb of gold." 다시 말해 정직한 방앗간 주인은 없다는 뜻. 따라서 이 문구는 이상과 같은 두 뜻을 함축하는 pun이 된다. **pardee**=by God, indeed.

565　　**sowne**=sound, play upon.

566　　**therwithal he broghte us out of towne**=with the music of the pipe he conducted us out of town.

The Manciple

567　　**gentl**=pleasant, friendly. **Manciple**= a minor employee of an institution, such as a college or one of the Inns of Court, whose principal function was to purchase provisions under the direction of the cook and the steward. **temple**=one of the Inns of Court. Inns of Court는 일종의 법률학원으로서 당시 런던에는 Lincoln's Inn, Gray's Inn, the Inner Temple, the Middle Temple의 네 곳이 있었으며, 이

〈The Manciple〉

들 학원은 각기 200명가량의 학생들이 있었다. 학생들은 대개 부유하거나 높은 신분의 자제들로서 이들은 변호사가 되기보다는 자기 재산을 지키기 위한 목적으로 법률 공부를 했다. 직제로 보아 Manciple은 steward나 cook의 지시에 따라 식량 조달을 해야 할 터이지만 여기 등장하는 Manciple은 거의 steward의 역할도 담당했던 것 같다. 참고로 당시 steward의 연봉은 53s. 4d., chief cook의 연봉은 40s, 그리고 manciple의 연봉은 26s. 8d였다.

568 **Of which**=from whom. **achatours**=caterers, purchasers of food. **take exemple**=take as model.

569 **vitaille**=victuals.

570 **by taille**=by tally, on credit. 외상 거래를 할 때에는 나무 조각에 칼로 값이나 수량을 새긴 다음 나무 조각을 반으로 갈라 판 사람과 산 사람이 하나씩 보관했다가 지불할 때에는 서로 맞춰보고 확인했다.

571 **Algate**=always. **wayted**=watched, paid attention, took precautions. **achaat**=buying, purchase.

572 **ay biforn**=always ahead. **ay**=ever. **biforn**=ahead. **staat**=financial condition.

573 **grace**=grace, favor.

574 **swich**=such. **lewed**=uneducated, unlearned (*not* lewd). **wit**=intelligence. **pace**=surpass.

575 **heep**=heap.

576 **maistres**=masters. **mo than thries ten**=more than thirty.

577 **curious**=skillful.

578 **duszeyne**=dozen.

579 **stywardes**=managers of an estate of lords, stewards. **rente**=income.

581 **him**=the lord. **lyeve by**=sustain himself upon. **by his propre good**=by his own income.

582 **dettelees**=without debt. **but if he were wood**=unless he were mad.

583 **scarsly**=economically. **as hym list desire**=as he would desire.

584 **al a shire**=a whole shire, a whole country.

585 **caas**=circumstance, situation. **falle**=befall, come about.

586   **sette hir aller cappe**=made a fool of them all.

The Reeve

587   **Reve**=an official assisting in the management of an estate. 중세 장원은 lord—steward—bailiff-reeve의 직제로 이루어져 있다. 그러나 여기 등장하는 Reve는 lord와 직접 상대했고 분명히 baillif 보다 한 등급 위이며, 심지어는 steward급의 실세에 속한 듯하다. Reve는 농노(serf) 출신들이었으므로 농노들의 잔꾀에 도통해 있어 두려움의 대상이기도 했다. 보

〈The Reeve〉

통 1년 단위로 고용되었으나 대개는 재임명되었다. 문맹이기는 하였으나 놀라운 기억력으로 빈틈없이 일 처리를 했다. 연봉은 5실링이었으나 팁(perquisites)이 있었다. 여기 등장하는 목수이기도 하다. **sclendre**=slender. **colerik**=a choleric man was slender, keen-witted, irritable, wanton. 333행과 420행의 주 참조. 여기 등장하는 것과 같이 생긴 사람이라면 관상학적으로 보아 choleric complexion, sharpness of wit, irascibility, wantonness의 소유자일 가능성이 높다.

588   **as ny as he kan**=as closely as he can. **shave**=shaved. **neigh**=close.

589   **His heer was by his erys ful round yshorn**=his hair was cut round his head at the height of his ears. cf. tonsure. 신분이 낮은 사람의 모습이다. **erys**=ears. **yshorn**=cut.

590   **dokked**=cut short (across the forehead). 짧은 머리가 점차 유행되기 시작했으나 역시 낮은 신분의 표시였다. **biforn**=in front.

591   **lene**=lean.

592	**Ylik**=like. **staf**=staff, stick. **ysene**=visible, to be seen. **ysene**의 y-는 고대영어의 ġe-의 잔재로서 과거분사를 나타내는 표시이다. 다리가 희고 가는 것은 당시 골상학으로 보아 lustful and intemperate in their sensual desire의 소유자로 알려져 있다.
593	**Wel koude he kepe a gerner and a bynne**=he knows how to take care of a granary and corn-bin. **kepe**=guard. **gerner**=granary. **bynne**=뚜껑이 달린 나무 상자로서 곡물이나 밀가루, 빵 등을 담아두었다.
594	**noon auditour koude on him wynne**=no auditor(=accountant) who could get the better of him.
595	**wiste**=knew. **droghte and by the reyn**=drought and rain.
596	**yelding**=yield.
597	**neet**=milch cows, cattle. **dayerye**=dairy.
598	**swyn**=swine. **stoor**=livestock. **pultrye**=poultry.
599	**hoolly**=wholly. **governynge**=control.
600	**covenant**=terms of his appointment, contract. **yaf the rekenynge**=gave the reckoning.
601	**Syn that**=since.
602	**koude no man brynge hym in arrerage**=no one could find him short in accounts, no one could prove him in arrears.
603	**nas**=was not. **baillif**=bailiff, steward, foreman. **hierde**=herdsman, shepherd. **hyne**=hind, farm laborer.
604	**That···his**=whose. **his**=of the above men. **sleighte**=trickery. **covyne**=fraud, deceit.
605	**adrad**=afraid, in dread, terrified. **the deeth**=death. the pestilence나 the plague는 지나친 해석이라는 의견이 있다.
606	**wonyng**=dwelling, habitation. **heeth**=a piece of uncultivated land.
608	**purchace**=make gains, become rich, increase his possessions.
609	**astored**=provided with supplies. **pryvely**=privately.
610	**plesen**=please. **subtilly**=craftily.
611-2	**To yeve and lene hym of his owene good**=to give and lend him from out of the lord's own goods. 주인한테서 훔친 것을 주인에

게 빌려줌으로써 주인을 기쁘게 해준다.

612   **cote and hood**=coat and hood. 일종의 prequisite(=tip)로 받은 것.
613   **myster**=trade, craft, occupation.
614   **wrighte**=workman or artisan.
615   **stot**=horse, stallion, cob.
616   **pomely**=dappled. **highte**=was called. **Scot**=아직도 Norfolk에서 흔히 사용되는 말 이름이다.
617   **surcote**=overcoat. 흔히 상류 계급의 사람들이 입었다. **pers**=blue, bluish gray. **upon he hade**=he had on.
618   **baar**=bore.
619   **Northfolk**=Norfolk.
620   **Biside**=near. **toun**=village. **men clepen**=is called. **Baldeswell**=Norfold 에 있는 지금의 Bawdeswell이라는 작은 마을.
621   **Tukked**=tucked. His coat was tucked up around him with a belt. **frere**=friar.
622   **hyndreste**=hindmost, rearmost. 일행 중 제일 뒤에서 따라온 데 대해서는 몇 가지 해석이 가능하다. 여기서처럼 여러 사람이 집단으로 순례를 떠나는 것은 가는 도중 만나게 될 여러 가지 위험에 공동으로 대처하기 위한 것인데, 그렇다면 그가 가장 뒤에서 좇아왔다는 것은 그가 겁이 많거나, 아니면 약아서 일부러 그리 했다고 볼 수도 있고, 아니면 그와 사이가 나쁜 Miller와 멀리 떨어져 있고 싶어 그리 하였다고 볼 수도 있으며, 또는 그가 사교성이 없어서 그렇다고 볼 수도 있다. 그러나 또 다른 이유는 그가 타고 온 말이 시원치 않았기 때문인지도 모른다. **route**=company, group.

The Summoner

623 **Somonour**=중세의 재판소에는 일반재판소(secular court) 와 교회재판소(ecclesiastical court)의 두 가지가 있었으며, 후자는 주교(bishop)나 부주교(archdeacon)가 재판을 담당했다. 다루는 죄목은 십일조 미납, 간음, 신성모독, 이단, 고리대금업, 위증 등 일반재판소에서 다루지 않는 것들이었다. 극형은 파문(excommunication)

⟨The Summoner⟩

이며, 40일이 지나도 교회재판소의 결정을 따르지 않으면 민간의 대법원(Chancery)에 통보되어 체포, 투옥된다. 그 체포영장은 Significavit nobis venerabilis pater…(=The venerable bishop has certified…)로 시작되기 때문에 Significavit라고 불렀다. Summoner는 본래 종교재판소의 일개 소환관리에 불과하나, 자기 입장을 이용하여 갖가지 비행을 사행하여 비난의 대상이 되었다.

624 **a fyr-reed cherubynnes face**=a red-hot cherub's face. 천사는 통통하고 빨간 얼굴을 가진 것으로 알려져 있다.

625 **saucefleem**=afflicted with red pimples and inflammation of the skin. **eyen narwe**=narrow slit-like eyes. 볼이 통통하기 때문에 상대적으로 눈이 작아 보인다.

626 **hoot**=hot. **sparwe**=sparrow. 제비는 음란(lecherous)하다고 알려져 있었다.

627 **scaled browes**=scabby eyebrows. **piled**=partly hairless, scanty.

628 **visage**=face. **aferd**=afraid.

629 **quyksilver**=mercury. **nas**=was not. **lytarge**=litharge, white lead. **brymstoon**=brimstone, sulphur.

630 **Boras**=borax(분사). **ceruce**=ceruse, a cosmetic made from white lead. **oille of tartre**=cream of tartar. **noon**=not any kind. 이 모두는

탈모증(alopicia)을 위한 약들이나 피부병에도 약효가 있다.

631　**oinement**=ointment; these are all medicines for "sauce-fleem." **byte**= bite, scour, corrode.

632　**helpen of**=rid (him) of. **whelkes**=pimples filled with pus.

633　**knobbes**=lumps.

634　**eek**=also. **lekes**=leeks, a plant something like an onion.

635　**strong wyn, reed as blood**=강한 빨간 포도주는 소화 능력을 저하 시킴으로써 피부병(saucefleem)을 일으키는 것으로 알려져 있었다.

636　**crie**=shout. **as he were wood**=as if he were mad. **wood**=mad.

639　**termes**=stock phrases.

640　**decree**=decree (of canon law), ordinance (of the pope, the bishop, or the church).

641　**no wonder is**=it's no wonder. **herde**=heard.

642　**eek**=moreover. **jay**=a noisy bird, with some of the characteristics of the magpie and parrot. Jays were taught to say "Wat."

643　**clepen**=call. **Watte**=Wat (short for 'Walter').

644　**whoso koude**=if anyone should. **grope**=examine minutely, test, probe.

645　**philosophie**=learning, knowledge.

646　**ay**=ever. **Questio quid iuris**=I ask which law applies to this case. 상투적인 법률 술어이다.

647　**gentil harlot**=easy-going rascal. trifler

648　**felawe**=comrade.

649　**suffre**=allow. **for**=in return for.

650　**a good felawe**=a rascal. **have**=keep, enjoy. **his**=the fellow's (not the summoner's).

651　**atte fulle**=completely, entirely. at the end (of the year)라는 해석도 있다. **excuse hym**=excuse him from the church court. 즉 모른 척 눈감아준다는 뜻.

652　**prively**=secretly. **a fynch…pulle**=to pull finch=pluck the feathers of a finch=seduce a girl=to have sexual relations with a woman.

653　**foond**=found. **owher**=anywhere. **a good felawe**=a good companion.

654   **awe**=fear.

655   **in swich caas**=in such matters. **ercedekenes curs**=archdeacon's curse=excommunication by the archdeacon (the presiding officer of the church court).

656   **But if a mannes soule were in his purs**=unless the sinner thought his soul was in his purse.

658   **Purs is the ercedekenes helle**=the curse could be lifted upon payment of money.

659   **woot**=know. **in dede**=in reality, certainly.

660   **Of cursyng oghte ech gilty man him drede**=every guilty man ought to be afraid of excommunication. **him**은 재귀대명사이다.

661   **slee**=slay (the soul). **right**=just. **assoillyng**=absolution.

662   **And also war hymn of a *Significavit***=and he should also beware of a *Significavit*=let him guard against a *Significavit*=Summoner를 통해 재판소에 손을 쓴다는 뜻. **war**=guard against, be careful, take care. *Significavit*=the opening Latin word of a writ, issued by the Archdeacon to the civil authorities, certifying that an excommunicated man had remained obstinate after forty days; the penalty was imprisonment. 체포영장. **war hym**=aware.

663   **in daunger hadde he**=he dominated (controlled). **daunger**=control. **at his owene gise**=at will, as he pleases, after his own fashion. **gise**=disposal.

664   **girles**=young people of both sexes. 사람에 따라서는 girles를 현대의 girls로 해석하기도 한다. **diocise**=diocese (the area over which a bishop has responsibility).

665   **counseil**=secrets, private matters. **al hir reed**=their only counsellor.

666   **gerland**=a hoop adorned with flowers, garland (of leaves and flowers), wreath.

667   **greet**=large. **ale-stake**=a support for a garland, which was often used as a part of the sign for an alehouse. 광고를 위해 술집 문 위에 길 위에 수평으로 장대를 걸어 놓고 그 끝에 화초를 걸어두는

경우가 있었다. Good wine needs no bush라는 표현은 여기서 나온 것.

668 **bokeler**=shield, buckler. **cake**=a round, flat loaf of bread.

The Pardoner

669 **Pardoner**=a man, sometimes in minor orders, authorized to sell papal indulgences. 소개된 마지막 순례자이며 가장 타락한 사람이다. Pardoner의 기능은 세 가지로 나눌 수 있는데, 첫째는 면죄부를 파는 것, 둘째는 유물을 신도들에게 보여주거나 만지거나 입맞춤하게 해주는 것, 셋째는 설교하는 것이다. 면죄부(papal indulgence)는 작은 쪽지에 법왕의 도장이 찍

〈The Pardoner〉

힌 것으로서 pardon (indulgence)이라고 부르며 개당 1페니 정도를 받고 팔았는데, 이것은 정확히 말해 죄를 경감(remission of penance)해주기는 하나 죄를 완전히 사(remission of sins)해주는 면죄부(absolution)는 아니다. Absolution은 사제들이 발행했다. Pardoner 가운데는 면죄부 판 돈을 전부 교회에 바치지 않고 일부 착복하는 일이 생겼을 뿐만 아니라, 비행을 눈감아 주는 대가로 돈을 받는 일이 생기면서 부정과 부패가 만연하게 되고, 이것이 16세기의 종교개혁을 가져오는 도화선이 된다. 한편 Pardoner의 여성스러움에 주목할 필요가 있는데, 그는 목소리가 높으며, 노란 머리칼은 어깨까지 치렁치렁 내려와 있는가 하면 수염은 전혀 없고, 눈이 둥그런 것이 남자다운 데가 없다. 그가 Summoner와 사랑의 노래를 합창할 정도로 친하다는 것은 다른 뜻을 가질 수 있다.

670 **Rouncivale**=런던의 Charing Cross 근처에 있던 부속수도원(cell)으

로서, 면죄부 판매로 악명이 높았다. **compeer**=comrade, fellow.

671 **was comen from the court of Rome**=the Pardoner claims to come from the Roman Curia, the source of authorized indulgences. 물론 이것은 Pardoner가 하는 말일 뿐 사실 여부는 알 수 없다.

672 **soong**=sang. **Come hider, to me!**=come hither to me. 당시 유행했던 노래의 한 대목이거나 후렴인 듯. Rome과 me가 각운(rhyme)을 맞추고 있다는 것은 어말의 -e가 발음되었다는 것을 뜻한다.

673 **bar to hym a stif burdoun**=bore him a strong bass accompaniment= accompanied him in a strong bass. 이 두 사람이 동성연애 관계에 있다는 것을 암시하고 있다. **burdoun**=the low-pitched undersong accompanying the melody.

674 **trompe**=trumpet.

675 **wex**=wax.

676 **heeng**=hung. **strike**=hank. **flex**=flax.

677 **ounces**=small strands, tiny bunches. **that he hadde**=머리 숱이 많지 않았다는 것을 암시한다.

678 **therwith he his shouldres overspradde**=he spread his hair over his shoulders.

679 **colpons**=shreds. **oon and oon**=one by one, separately.

680 **for jolitee**=for sport. for elegance라는 해석도 가능한데, 그것은 jolitee가 다음에서 보듯 두 가지 뜻을 모두 가지고 있기 때문이다. **jolitee**=fun, levity, attractiveness, beauty, elegance. **wered**=wore.

681 **trussed**=packed. **walet**=a small bag or knapsack.

682 **Hym thoughte**=it seemed to him that. **of the newe jet**=in the latest style, following the latest fashion.

683 **Dischevelee**=loose, unconfined. **save**=except for. **bare**=bareheaded.

684 **glarynge**=staring wildly, shining.

685 **vernycle**=a small copy of St. Veronica's handkerchief, which was said to have miraculously received the imprint of Christ's face when she lent it him on his way to Calvary. The veil was kept at St. Peter's in Rome. Pilgrims to rome often wore copies of it.

686   **biforn**=before.

687   **Bretful**=brimful. **pardoun**=pardons, indulgences. **comen from Rome al hoot**=로마에서 막 돌아온. **hoot**=hot like cakes freshly made (part of the Pardoner's sales-talk).

688   **smal**=thin. **goot**=goat.

690   **as**=as if. **late yshave**=just shaved.

691   **trowe**=believe. **geldyng**=castrated horse, eunuch. Pardoner에게는 여자다운 데가 많다.

692   **craft**=trade, occupation. **fro Berwyk into Ware**=from Berwick-on-Tweed to Ware, Hertfordshire=from the north of England to the south=throughout England. 가능한 여러 지명 가운데서 Ware를 쓴 것은 mare와 각운을 맞추기 위함인 듯.

693   **swich**=such.

694   **male**=bag. **pilwe-beer**=pillowcase.

695   **Lady**=Lady's, i.e., Mary's veil.

696   **gobet**=a small piece, gobbet. **seyl**=sail.

697   **whan that**=when. **wente**=traveled, walked, sailed, etc.

698   **see**=sea. **hente**=seized, in reference either to Jesus's recruitment of Peter, a fisherman (*Matthew* 4:18), or to his rescuing of Peter after his attempt to walk on the water (*Matthew* 14:29).

699   **croys**=cross. **latoun**=a metal made of copper and zinc, cheap, brassy metal. **stones**=precious stones (or imitations).

700   **glas**=a glass container.

701   **reliokes**=relics. **fond**=found.

702   **povre person**=poor parson. **upon lond**=in the country.

703   **gat hym**=got for himself, i.e., by charging parishioners a fee for kissing the relics.

704   **tweye**=two.

705   **feyned**=feigned, false, spurious. **japes**=tricks, deceits.

706   **made the person and the peple his apes**=made monkeys of them=fooled them. **apes**=apes, fools, dupes.

707   **trewely to tellen**=to be serious. **trewely**=truly. **atte laste**=finally, after all, in the end.

708   **a noble ecclesiaste**=a worthy divine. 물론 noble은 풍자적으로 쓰인 것.

709   **rede**=read. **lessoun**=passage from the Bible. 아침 저녁, 혹은 그 밖의 canonical hours에 읽는 성서의 일절. **storie**=series of lessons. 예를 들면 성인전(Saint's Life) 따위. liturgy

710   **alderbest**=best of all. **offertorie**=an anthem sung during the offering. 성찬식에 앞서 부르는 노래로서 이 때 사람들은 봉헌물(offering)을 헌납한다.

711   **wiste**=knew.

712   **moste**=must. **preche**=preach. **affile**=file, make smooth.

713   **murierly**=more merrily. 여기서처럼 비교급에 부사 어미 -ly를 첨가하는 것은 매우 드문 경우이다.

714   **murierly**=more merrily.

715   **in a clause**=in a few words, briefly. **clause**=short sentence.

716   **estaat**=rank, condition. **arrya**=dress, condition.

718   **gentil**=excellent.

719   **highte**=was called. **fast**=close. **Belle**=probably another inn in Southwark.

720   **to yow for to telle**=to tell you.

721   **How that we baren us**=what we did with ourselves. **baren**=bore, conducted ourselves. **ilke**=same.

722   **were⋯alyght**=had alighted (from our horses).

723   **wol**=will. **viage**=trip, journey.

724   **remenaunt**=rest, remainder.

725   **of youre curteisye**=kindly, if you please. 여기서의 Chaucer의 사과는 Decameron에서의 Boccaccio의 사과와 흡사하다.

726   **n'arette it nat**=do not blame it on. **my vileynye**=to my ill-breeding.

728   **hir**=their. **cheere**=behavior, demeanor.

729   **Ne thogh I speke hir wordes proprely**=not even if I speak their words, with accuracy in each case. **proprely**=exactly, literally.

Chaucer · 133

730   **al so wel as**=as well as.
731   **who so**=whosoever. **telle a tale after a man**=repeat a tale after a man.
732   **moot**=must. **reherce**=repeat. **neigh**=nearly, closely.
733   **Everich a**=every. **charge**=power, responsibility.
734   **Al speke he never so rudeliche and large**=however rudely and freely he speaks. **al speke he**=although he should speak. 여기서 he 는 731행에서 언급한 사람. **never so**=however. **large**=freely, broadly.
735   **ellis**=otherwise.
736   **feyne**=invent, feign. **fynde**=invent.
737   **spare**=spare anyone, relent. **he**=731행의 사람.
738   **he moot as wel seye o word as another**=he is as bound to say one word as another. **moot**=may. **o word**=one word.
739   **Crist spak hymself ful brode in hooly writ**=Christ himself spoke very broadly in the Scriptures. **brode**=broadly, indelicately.
740   **woot**=know.
741   **whoso kan hym rede**=if anyone can read him (=Plato). 당시 영국에서 희랍어를 읽을 수 있는 사람은 없었다. **whoso**=whoever. **rede**= read.
742   **moote**=must. **cosyn**=cousin.
744   **Al have I nat**=although I have not. **degree**=order of rank. 당시 선후에 대한 개념은 매우 엄격했다.
746   **My wit is short**=I am not sufficiently clever. **wit**=intelligence, understanding.
747   **Greet chiere made oure Hoost us everichon**=our host entertained us all very well. **chiere**=weldome. **everichon**=everyone.
748   **soper**=supper (a communal meal). **anon**=forthwith, at once.
749   **vitaille**=food. **at the beste**=in the best, way, most excellently.
750   **wel to drynke us leste**=it pleased us well to drink=we were pleased to drink. **us leste**=it pleased us.
751   **semely**=suitable, fitting. **Hoost**=Host, innkeeper. 뒤에 가서 그의 이

름이 Herry Bailly라는 것이 알려지는데 Southwark에는 실제로 Herry Bailly라는 이름을 가진 여관집 주인이 있었다. **withalle**=moreover, too.

752 **For to been a marchal in an halle**=(fit) to have been a marshal in a hall. **marchal**=official in charge of a feast or banquet.

753 **stepe**=prominent.

754 **fairer**=more excellent. **burgeys**=a substantial citizen. burgher. **Chepe**=Cheapside, the market of the City of London. 여관집 주인이 살고 있는 Southwark는 City보다 격이 떨어지므로 이 대목은 여관집 주인에 대해 높이는 말이 된다.

755 **ytaught**=taught (in his trade).

756 **of manhod hym lakkede right naught**=he was in no way lacking in manhoo. **hym lakkede**=there was lacking in him.

758 **playen**=joke, be sociable, play, entertain.

759 **myrthe**=pleasure, amusement.

760 **maad oure rekenynges**=paid our bills.

761 **lordynges**=my masters. 요즘의 Ladies and Gentlemen처럼 쓰였다.

762 **Ye been to my right welcome, hertely**=you are indeed heartily welcome to my house. **hertely**=heartily.

763 **if that I shal nat lye**=if I am to speak truth.

764 **saugh nat**=have not seen.

765 **Atones**=at one time. **herberwe**=inn, harbor.

766 **Fayn**=gladly. **wolde**=would. **doon yow myrthe**=entertain you. **doon**=cause, give. **wiste I how**=if I knew how.

767 **I am right now bythoght**=I have just now thought of, I am struck by a thought.

768 **To doon yow ese**=to please or entertain you.

769 **goon**=are going. **God yow speede**=may God bring you success. spede는 가정법 현재형으로서 기원을 나타낸다.

770 **The blisful martir quite yow yore meede**=May the blessed martyr (=St. thomas) bring you your reward. **quite**=repay, give in return.

	meede=reward.
771	**wel I woot**=as I well know. **by the weye**=on your way, along the road.
772	**Ye shapen yow to talen and to pleye**=You are preparing to tell stories and jest. **shapen yow**=prepare yourselves. **talen**=tell tales, converse. **pleye**=play, amuse oneself.
773	**confort**=comfort, pleasure. **ne**=nor. **myrthe**=pleasure, amusement. **is noon**=there is no.
774	**domb as a stoon**=dumb as a stone.
775	**maken yow disport**=devise entertainment for you. **disport**=diversion. **disport**=pleasure, amusement.
776	**erst**=first, before. **doon yow som confort**=amuse you in some way.
777	**yow liketh alle**=it pleases you all. liketh는 비인칭 동사이다. **by oon assent**=in complete agreement, unanimously.
778	**stonden at my juggement**=accept my decision. **stonden at**=stand by, accept.
779	**werken**=do.
781	**by my fader soule that is deed**=by the soul of my father, who is dead.
782	**But ye be myrie, I wol yeve yow myn heed**=if you do not enjoy it, you can strike off my head. **But**=unless. **yeve**=give. **yeve**=give. **heed**= head.
783	**Hoold up youre hondes**=in sign of agreement.
784	**Oure conseil was nat longe for to seche**=it was not long before we reached our decision. **conseil**=decision, opinion. **seche**=seek.
785	**Us thoughte it was noght worth to make it wys**=it seemed to us not worth deliberating over. **us thoughte**=it seemed to us. **worth to make it wys**=worth while deliberating.
786	**graunted**=agreed with. 주어는 we. **withouten moore avys**=without any more thinking. **avys**=deliberation, consideration.
787	**bad**=asked, ordered. **voirdit as hym leste**=whatever decision it

136 · Middle English

	pleased him. **voirdit**=verdict, decision.
788	**quod**=said. **herkneth for the beste**=listen carefully. **herkneth**=hearken.
789	**But taak it nought, I prey yow, in desdeyn**=but do not treat it with disdain, I beg you.
791	**ech**=each. **to shorte with oure weye**=to shorten our journey with.
792	**viage**=trip. **tweye**=two. 순례자들은 일행 30명(작자 포함)이었으므로 오고 가며 각자 두 개씩 이야기를 하게 되면 도합 120개를 하게 된다. 뒤에 가서 이 계획을 축소 수정하기는 하지만 Chaucer는 본래의 이 계획을 실현시키지 못했다.
793	**To Caunterbyrt-ward, I mene it so**=I mean, on the way to Canterbury. **mene**=mean.
794	**othere**=another.
795	**Of aventures that whilom han bifalle**=of adventures that have happened in the past. **whilom**=once upon a time. **han**=have의 현재, 복수. **bifalle**= happened, befallen.
796	**which**=whichever. **bereth hym**=performs, manages.
797	**in this caas**=on this occasion.
798	**sentence**=moral instruction. **solaas**=solace, comfort, amusement, delight.
799	**soper**=supper. **at oure aller cost**=at the cost of all of us.
801	**agayn**=back.
802	**mury**=merry.
803	**goodly**=gladly.
804	**cost**=expense. **gyde**=guide.
805	**whoso wole my juggement withseye**=whoever shall dispute my judgement. **wole**=will. **withseye**=oppose, contradict.
806	**paye al**=pay for all.
807	**vouche sauf**=vouchsafe, grant.
808	**anon**=at once. **mo**=more.
809	**erly shape me therfore**=get ready for the journey early. **shape me**=prepare myself.

810   **othes swore**=(we) swore our oaths.

811   **preyden**=(we) prayed, asked.

813   **governour**=president.

814   **juge and reportour**=judge and umpire.

815   **sette a soper**=arrange a supper. **at a certeyn pris**=at a set price.

816   **reuled been**=be ruled, be directed. **at his devys**=at his pleasure. **devys**=will, desire, disposal.

817   **In heigh and lowe**=in things both great and small, in all respects. **oon assent**=common assent, unanimously.

818   **acorded**=agreed.

819   **fet**=fetched. **anon**=immediately. 잠자리에 들기 전에 포도주를 조금 마시는 것이 관례였다.

820   **dronken**=drank. **echon**=each one.

822   **A-morwe**=in the morning.

823   **oure aller cok**=the cock who wakened us all.

824   **garded**=gathered. **togidre**=together.

825   **riden a litel moore than paas**=rode at little more than a walking speed. **riden**=rode. **paas**=a foot-pace or walk.

826   **wateryng of seint Thomas**=St. Thomas a Watering, a watering place for horses near the second milestone on the Canterbury road. 런던에서 2마일 쯤 Canterbury쪽으로 가다 있던 개울로서 지금은 없다. Seint Thomas란 물론 Thomas à Becket를 말한다.

827   **bigan his hors areste**=pulled his horse up. **areste**=to stop.

828   **leste**=may please.

829   **woot**=know. **foreward**=agreement, promise. **it yow recorde**=I recall it to you.

830   **If even-song and morwe-song accorde**=if evening-song and morning-song agree=if what you say in the morning agrees with what you said last night.

832   **mote**=may.

832-4   i.e., as surely as I ever hope to drink wine or ale, whoever defies

	my rulings shall pay···
835	**draweth cut**=draw lots. **draweth**=Knyght, Prioresse, Clerk 등에 대한 공손함을 나타내기 위해서 복수형의 명령문이 사용되고 있다. 841행의 ley hont to, every man!에서는 보통의 단수형을 쓰고 있다. 여관 집 주인은 상대에 따라 말을 잘 골라 쓸 줄 아는 사람으로 묘사되어 있다. **cut**=lots. **er**=before. **ferrer twynne**=depart farther.
836	**He which**=the one who.
838	**accord**=decision.
839	**neer**=nearer.
840	**lat be**=leave off. **shamefastnesse**=shyness, bashfulness, modesty.
841	**Ne studieth noght**=nor do not deliberate.
842	**wight**=person.
843	**shortly**=quickly.
844	**Were it**=whether it was. **by aventure, or sort or cas**=either by luck, or fate, or chance. 이들은 모두 같은 뜻의 단어들이다. 동의어를 나열하는 것은 Chaucer가 흔히 사용하는 표현 방법이다.
845	**sothe**=truth, sooth. **fil**=fell.
847	**moste**=must. **as was resoun**=as was reasonable.
848	**foreward**=agreement. **composicioun**=agreement, arrangement. 이 두 단어도 뜻의 별 차이가 없다.
849	**han herd**=have heard. **what**=why. **nedeth**=is the need for. **mo**=more.
850	**saugh**=saw.
851	**As**=since. **he that**=the one who. **wys**=wise.
852	**by his free assent**=voluntarily, willingly.
853	**Syn**=since.
854	**What**=간투사. **a Goddes name**=in God's name. **a**=in.
855	**herkneth**=listen!
857	**murye**=merry. **cheere**=countenance, manner.

Here Begins the Book of the Tales of Canterbury

When April with its gentle showers has pierced the March drought to the root and bathed every plant in the moisture which will hasten the flowering: when Zephyrus with its sweet breath has stirred the new shoots in every wood and field, and the young sun has run its half-course in the Ram, and small birds sing melodiously, so touched in their hearts by Nature that they sleep all night with open eyes—then folks long to go on pilgrimages, and palmers to visit foreign shores and distant shrines, known in various lands; and especially from every shire's end of England they travel to Canterbury, to seek the holy blessed martyr who helped them when they were sick.

One day in that season when I stopped at the Tabard in Southwark, ready to go on my pilgrimage to Canterbury with a truly devout heart, it happened that a group of twenty-nine people came into that inn in the evening. They were people of various ranks who had come together by chance, and they were all pilgrims who planned to ride to Canterbury. The rooms and stables were large enough for each of us to be well lodged, and shortly after the sun had gone down, I had talked with each of these pilgrims and had soon made myself one of their group. We made our plans to get up early in order to start our trip, which I am going to tell you about.

But, nevertheless, while I have time and space, before I go farther in this account, it seems reasonable to tell you all about each of the pilgrims, as they appeared to me; who they were, and of what rank, and also what sort of clothes they wore. And I shall begin with a Knight.

There was among us a brave KNIGHT who had loved

chivalry, truth, and honor, generosity and courtesy, from the time of his first horseback rides. He had performed admirably in his lord's wars, during which he had traveled as widely as any man, in both Christendom and heathen countries, and he had always been cited for his bravery. He had been at Alexandria when it was conquered, and had sat at the head of the table many times in Prussia, above all the foreign knights. He had fought successfully in Lithuania and in Russia more frequently than any other Christian knight of similar rank. Also he had been in Granada at the siege of Algeciras, and had fought in Benmarin. He had been at Ayas and Attalia when they were won, and had taken part in many an armed expedition in the Mediterranean. He had fought in fifteen large battles, in addition to the three times he had defended our faith in lists in Algeria, and each time he had killed his opponent. This same brave Knight had once been with the lord of Palathia to fight against another heathen in Turkey, and he had always been given valuable loot. But though he was brave, he was prudent, and as meek in his conduct as a maid. He had never yet in all his life spoken discourteously to anybody. He was a true and perfect gentle Knight. But let me tell you of his clothing and equipment: his horses were good, but he was not gaily dressed. He wore a thick cotton coat, which was all stained by his breastplates, for he had just returned from his travels and had set out at once on his pilgrimage.

With him there was his son, a young SQUIRE, a lover and a lusty bachelor, with hair as curly as if it had been set. He was about twenty years old, I would say, and he was of average height, remarkably agile, and very strong. He had already been on cavalry raids in Flanders, in Artois, and in Picardy, where he had borne himself well for one so young, in an effort to win favor with his lady. His clothes were as covered as a meadow with white and red flowers. All day he sang or played the flute; in fact, he was joyful as the month of May. His cloak was short, with long, wide sleeves, and he sat his horse well and rode excellently. He could compose the words and music for songs, joust and also dance, and draw and write very well. So ardently did he love that he slept no more at night than a nightingale. He was courteous, humble, and helpful, and carved at the table for his father.

The Knight had brought along only one servant, for he wished to travel that way, and this YEOMAN was dressed in a green coat and hood. He carefully carried a sheaf of bright, keen peacock arrows attached to his belt, and a strong bow in his hand. He knew very well how to care for his equipment, and the feathers on his arrows never drooped. His hair was cut short, and his complexion was brown. he understood all the tricks of woodcraft. He wore a bright leather wristguard, and carried a sword and a small shield on one side, and a fine ornamented dagger, as sharp as the point of a spear, on the other. A Christopher hung on his breast, and he had a hunter's horn with a green cord. In my opinion he was a real forester.

There was also a Nun, a PRIORESS, whose smile was very quiet and simple. Her harshest curse was "by St. Loy," and she was named Madam Eglantine. She sang the divine service very well, with excellent nasal intonation, and spoke French fluently and carefully with the accent of the school at Stratford-Bow, for the French of Paris was unknown to her. Her table manners were admirable: she allowed no crumb to fall from her lips, nor did she wet her fingers deeply in her sauce; she knew exactly how to carry the food to her mouth and made sure that no drops spilled upon her breast. She was very much interested in etiquette. So carefully did she wipe her lips that no trace of grease could be seen in her cup when she had drunk from it. She reached for her food very daintily, and truly she was very merry, with a pleasant disposition and an amiable manner. She took pains to imitate court behavior, to be dignified in bearing, and to be considered worthy of respect. But to tell you of her tender feelings: she was so kind and so full of pity that she would weep if she saw a dead or bleeding mouse caught in a trap. She had several small dogs which she fed with roasted meat or milk and fine bread; if one of her dogs died, or if someone beat it with a stick, she cried bitterly. Indeed, with her everything was tenderness and a soft heart. Her wimple was very neatly pleated, her nose shapely, her eyes blue, and her mouth very small, soft, and red. But, truly, she had a fair forehead; it was almost a hand's-breadth wide, I swear, for, to tell the truth, she was no particularly small. I noticed that her cloak was very well made. On her arm she wore a coral rosary with large green beads for the paternosters, from which hung a brightly shining golden brooch. And on this brooch was first inscribed a capital A, surmounted by a crown, and after that Amor vincit omnia. This Prioress had another NUN, who was her chaplain, and three priests with her.

There was a MONK, an outstanding one, whose job it was to supervise the monastery's estates, and who loved hunting. He was a manly person, quite capable of serving as abbot. He had many excellent horses in his stable, and when he rode you could hear his bridle jingling in the whistling wind as clearly and also as loudly as the chapel bell at the subordinate monastery where this lord was prior. Because the rule of St. Maurus or of St. Benedict was old and somewhat stringent, this monk let old-fashioned things go and followed new-fangled ideas. He didn't give a plucked hen for that text which says that hunters are not holy, and that a monk who is irresponsible is like a fish out of water—that is to say, a monk out of his cell. For he thought that text not worth an oyster; and I said his reasoning was good. Why should he study and drive himself crazy, always poring over a book in his cloister, or work and slave with his hands as St. Augustine orders? How shall that serve the world? Let Augustine have his labor for himself! Therefore this monk was a true hunter: he had greyhounds as swift as birds in flight; his greatest pleasure, for which he would spare no cost, was to ride and hunt the hare. I saw his sleeves edged at the wrist with fur, and that the finest in the land; and he had a very rare pin made of gold, with a love knot in the larger end, to fasten his hood under his chin. His head was bald and shone like glass, as did his face also, as if he had been oiled. He was a fine, fat lord, and in good shape. His protruding eyes rolled in his head and gleamed like coals under a pot. His boots were supple, and his horse richly equipped. Now surely he was a fair prelate; he was not pale as a tormented ghost. Of all roasts he loved a fat swan best. His horse was as brown as a berry.

There was a wanton, merry FRIAR, a licensed beggar and a very gay man. No member of all four orders knew so much of gossip and flattering talk. He had found husbands for many young women at his own expense. A noble representative he was of his order. Among the franklins all over his district, and also among the respectable women in the towns, he was well liked and intimate, for he had, as he said himself, more power of confession than a parish priest, since he was licensed by his order. He heard confession very agreeably, and his absolution was pleasant. When he thought he would get a good present, he was an easy man in giving penance. For to give a present to a poor order is a sign that a man is well shriven. He even boasted that he knew that a man who contributed was repentant, for there are many men with hearts so stern that they cannot weep, even when they are contrite. Therefore, instead of weeping and praying, people could give silver to the poor friars. His cloak was always stuffed full of knives and pins to be given to pretty women. And, certainly, he had a pleasant voice: he could sing and play the fiddle excellently. At ballad-singing he won the prize hands down. His neck was as white as the lily, but he was as strong as a champion wrestler. He knew the taverns well in every town, and cared more for every innkeeper and barmaid than for a leper or a beggar; it was not fitting, as far as he could see, for such an important man to be acquainted with lepers. It is not honest, and it will not advance a man, to deal with such poor folks; rather, he should deal with the rich and with the food-merchants. And, above everything, wherever there was a chance for profit, this Friar was courteous and humbly helpful. There was no man anywhere more capable at this work. He was the best beggar in his order, and paid a certain sum for his grant so that none of his brethren came into his district. And even if a widow did not own a shoe, his greeting was so pleasant that before he left he would have got a coin. The money which he picked up on the sly amounted to more than his regular income. And he could frolic just like a puppy. During court meetings he could be of great help, for then he was not like a cloisterer with a coat as threadbare as a poor scholar's but like a master or a pope. His short coat was of double worsted, as neat as if it were freshly pressed. He intentionally lisped a bit in his joking, in order to make his English roll sweetly from his tongue, and when he played the harp after singing, his eyes twinkled in his head just like the stars on a frosty night. This worthy licensed beggar was named Hubert.

There was a MERCHANT with a forked beard, dressed in clothes of varied colors and sitting proudly on his horse; he wore a beaver hat from Flanders, and his boots were neatly fastened. He spoke his opinions very pompously, talking always about the increase in his profits. He wished the sea were kept open at all cost between Middelburg and Orwell, and was expert in selling money on the exchange. This responsible man kept his wits about him: so closemouthed was he about his dealings in bargaining and in borrowing and lending that no one knew when he was in debt. Nevertheless, he was really a worthy man; but, to tell the truth, I don't know what he was called.

There was also a CLERIC from Oxford, who had long ago applied himself to the study of logic. His horse was as thin as a rake, and he himself, I assure you, was by no means fat, but looked hollow and solemn. His overcoat was threadbare, for as yet he had found no benefice, and he was not worldly enough to hold a secular position. For he would rather have twenty books of Aristotle and his philosophy bound in red or black at the head of his bed than rich clothes, or a fiddle, or a gay psaltery. But though he was a philosopher, he still had but little gold in his chest, for he spent all he could get out of his friends on books and on schooling, and prayed earnestly for the souls of those who gave him money with which to go to school. He was most concerned and occupied with studying. He spoke not one word more than was necessary, and that which he did say was correct and modest, brief and to the point, and filled with worthwhile meaning. His talk centered on moral themes, and gladly would he learn and gladly teach.

A LAWYER, careful and wise, a most excellent man long practiced in legal discourse, was also there. He was discreet and well thought of—at least he seemed so, his words were so wise. Many times he had served as justice at assizes, appointed by letters from the King and also in the regular way. He had earned many large fees and presents of clothes as a result of his skill and his wide reputation. There was nowhere so able a buyer of land: he always sought unentailed ownership, and his papers were never invalidated. No man was so busy as he, and yet he seemed busier than he was. He had all the cases and decisions which had occurred since the time of King William at the tip of his tongue. He could compose and draw up legal paper so that no one could complain bout his phrasing, and he could recite every statute by heart. He rode unostentatiously in a coat of mixed color, with a silk belt on which there were small bars—I shall tell no more about his dress.

    A FRANKLIN was with the Lawyer. His beard was as white as a daisy, and he was sanguine by nature. Dearly did he love his bread dipped in wine in the morning. He had the habit of living for pleasure, for he was a true son of Epicurus, who held that pure pleasure was truly perfect bliss. He was a substantial landowner, St. Julian in his part of the country. Always his bread and ale were of the best, and nobody had a better cellar. His house was never without baked fish and meat in such quantity that it snowed food and drink, the choices that you could imagine. His menus changed in accordance with the various seasons of the year. Many a fat bird was in his coop, and many a bream and pike in his fishpond. Woe to his cook unless the sauce were pungent and sharp and all the equipment in order. All day long his table stood ready laid in the hall. He was lord and sire of the sessions and had frequently served as member of parliament from his shire. A short dagger and a pouch of silk hung from his milk-white belt. He had served as administrator and as auditor for his shire. Nowhere was there such a worthy subvassal.

    A HABERDASHER and a CARPENTER, a WEAVER, a DYER, and a TAPESTRY-MAKER were with us, all clothed in the uniform of a great and important guild. Their equipment was all freshly and newly decorated: their knives were mounted with silver, not with brass; their belts and pouches were in every respect well and cleanly made. Indeed, each of them seemed suited to sit on a dais in the guildhall as burgess. Each, because of his wisdom, was also to serve as alderman. For they owned sufficient goods and money, as even their wives had to agree, or else they certainly would be blameworthy. It is a very fine thing to be called "Madam," to go in first to evening services, and to have a train carried like royalty.

These guildsmen had a COOK with them for the trip to boil chickens with the bones and with the flavoring powder and the spice. He could easily recognize a draught of London ale, and could roast and boil, broil, fry, make stew, and bake good pies. But it was a shame, I thought, that he had a large sore on his shin. For he could make blancmange with the best.

There was a SAILOR who lived far in the west; for all I know he was from Dartmouth. He rode upon a nag as best he could, in a coarse gown which came to his knees. Under his arm he had a dagger which hung down on a cord about his neck. The hot summer sun had tanned him heavily, and certainly he was a good fellow. Often while the wine-merchant slept, he had tapped the wine casks he brought from Bordeaux. He gave no heed to scruples. When he fought and had the upper hand, he made his prisoners walk the plank. But in his business—the correct reckoning of tides and streams; the handling of the ship's controls; the knowledge of the harbors, the moon, and the compass—there was none so good from Hull to Carthage. He was bold and wise in any undertaking. His beard had been shaken by many a tempest. He knew the condition of all the anchorages from Gotland Isle to Cape Finisterre, and every creek in Spain and Brittany. His ship was called the "Magdalen."

With us there was a PHYSICIAN; in all the world there was not another like him for talk of medicines and of surgery, for he was trained in astrology. He skillfully and carefully observed his patient through the astrological hours, and was quite able to place the waxen images of his patient so that a fortunate planet was ascendant. He knew the cause of every disease—whether hot, cold, moist, or dry—and how it developed, and of what humour. Indeed, he was the perfect practitioner: the cause and root of the disease determined, at once he gave the sick man his remedy. He had his apothecaries quite ready to send him drugs and syrups, for each of them worked to the other's profit—their friendship was not newly begun. This Physician knew well ancient Aesculapius and Dioscorides, and also Rufus, Hippocrates, Haly and Galen, Serapion, Rhazes, Avicenna, Averroes, Damascenus and Constantine, Bernard, Gatesden, and Gilbertine. His diet was moderate—not too much, but that little nourishing and digestible. But little time did he devote to the study of the Bible. He was dressed in red and blue cloth lined with taffeta and with silk; and yet he was not quick to spend his money. He held on to that which he gained during a plague. For, in medicine, gold is healthful in drinks; therefore, he especially loved gold.

Thee was a good WIFE from near BATH, but she was somewhat deaf, which was a shame. She had such skill in clothmaking that she surpassed the weavers of Ypres and Ghent. In all her parish there was no woman who could go before her to the offertory; and if someone did, the Wife of Bath was certainly so angry that she lost all charitable feeling. Her kerchiefs were of fine texture; those she wore upon her head on Sunday weighed, I swear, ten pounds. Her fine scarlet hose were carefully tied, and her shoes were uncracked and new. Her face was bold and fair and red. All of her life she had been an estimable woman: she had had five husbands, not to mention other company in her youth—but of that we need not speak now. And three times she had been to Jerusalem; she had crossed many a foreign river; she had been to Rome, to Bologna, to St. James' shrine in Galicia, and to Cologne. About journeying through the country she knew a great deal. To tell the truth she was gap-toothed. She sat her gentle horse easily, and wore a fine headdress with a hat as broad as a buckler or a shield, a riding skirt about her large hips, and a pair of sharp spurs on her heels. She knew how to laugh and joke in company, and all the remedies of love, for her skill was great in that old game.

There was a good man of the church, a poor parish PRIEST, but rich in holy thoughts and works. He was also a learned man, a cleric, who wished to preach Christ's gospel truly and to teach his parishioners devoutly. He was benign, wonderfully diligent, and extremely patient in adversity, as he had proved many times. He did not at all like to have anyone excommunicated for non-payment of tithes; rather, he would give, without doubt, a portion of the offering and also of his salary to his poor parishioners. He needed little to fill his own needs. His parish was wide and the houses far apart, but he never failed, rain or shine, sick or well, to visit the farthest in his parish, be he rich or poor, traveling on foot with a staff in his hand. To his congregation he gave this noble example: first he practiced good deeds, and afterward he preached them. He took this idea from the gospels and added to it another: if gold rust, what shall iron do? For if a priest whom we trust is not worthy, it is no wonder that an ignorant man sins. And it is a shame, if a priest only realized it, to see a wicked priest and a godly congregation. Surely a parson should set an example by his godliness as to how his parishioners should live. This Priest did not hire out his benefice and leave his people in difficulties while he ran off to St. Paul's in London to look for an endowment singing masses for the dead, or to be retained by a guild. He stayed at home and guarded his parish well so that evil did not corrupt it. He was a pastor and not a mercenary. And yet, though he himself was holy and virtuous, he was not contemptuous of sinners, nor overbearing and proud in his talk; rather, he was discreet and kind in his teaching. His business was to draw folk to heaven by fairness and by setting a good example. But if any sinner, whether of high or low birth, was obstinate, this Parson would at once rebuke him for it sharply. I don't believe there is a better priest anywhere. He cared nothing for pomp and reverence, nor did he affect an overly nice conscience; he taught the lore of Christ and His twelve Apostles, but first he followed it himself.

With him there was a PLOWMAN, his brother, who had hauled many a load of manure. He was a good and true laborer, living in peace and perfect charity. With all his heart he loved God best at all times, whether it profited him or not, and next he loved his neighbor as himself. He would thresh and also ditch and dig, free of charge, for the sake of Christ, to help a poor neighbor, if it were at all possible. He paid his tithes promptly and honestly, both by working himself and with his goods. Dressed in a laborer's coat, he rode upon a mare.

There were also a Reeve, a Miller, a Summoner, and a Pardoner, a Manciple, and myself—there were no more.

The MILLER was a very husky fellow, tremendous in bone and in brawn which he used well to get the best of all comers: in wrestling he always won the prize. He was stocky, broad, and thickset. There was no door which he could not pull off its hinges or break by ramming it with his head. His beard was as red as any sow or fox, and as broad as a spade. At the right on top of his nose he had a wart, from which there grew a tuft of hairs red as the bristles of a sow's ears, and his nostrils were wide and black. A sword and a shield hung at his side. His mouth was as huge as a large furnace, and he was a jokester and a ribald clown, most of whose jests were of sin and scurrility. He knew quite well how to steal grain and charge thrice over, but yet he really remained reasonably honest. The coat he wore was white and the hood blue. He could play the bagpipe well and led us out of town to its music.

There was a friendly MANCIPLE of an Inn of Court whom other stewards might well imitate in order to buy provisions wisely. For no matter whether he bought for cash or on credit, he always watched his purchases so closely that he was constantly solvent and even ahead. Now isn't that a fine gift from God, that such an uneducated man can outwit a whole heap of learned men? He had more than thirty masters, who were expert and deep in legal matters; a full dozen of them were capable of serving as steward of the moneys and the lands of any lord in England, and of making that lord live within his own income and honorably out of debt (unless he were crazy), or just as sparingly as he wished. And these lawyers could take care of any emergency that occurred in the administration of a shire; and yet this Manciple made fools of them all.

The REEVE was a slender, choleric man. His beard was shaved as close as possible, and his hair was cut round by his ears and clipped short in front like a priest's. His legs were as long and lean as sticks, completely lacking calves. He knew fully how to keep a granary and a bin; there was no accountant who could get the best of him. From the drought and from the rainfall he could tell the expected yield of his seed and grain. His lord's sheep, cattle, dairy, swine, horses, equipment, and poultry were wholly under this Reeve's care, and his word had been accepted on the accounting ever since his lord was twenty years old. There was no one who could find him in arrears. There was no bailiff, no sheepherder, nor any other laborer, whose petty tricks and stealings were not known to the reeve; they were as afraid of him as of death. His house was well placed upon a heath and shadowed by green trees. He was better able to buy than was his lord. He had privately accumulated considerable money, for he knew very well how to please his lord subtly, to give and lend him money from the lord's own stock and therefore to receive thanks, plus a coat and hood. As a youth he had learned a good trade: he was a very fine woodworker, a carpenter. This Reeve rode upon a large, fine, dappled-gray horse called Scot. He wore a long blue topcoat, and carried a rusty sword by his side. This Reeve that I am telling about was from Norfolk, near a town called Bawdswell. His coat was tucked up like a friar's, and he always rode last in our procession.

There was a SUMMONER with us there who had a fiery-red babyish face, for he was leprous and had close-set eyes. He was as passionate and lecherous as a sparrow, and had black scabby brows and a scraggly beard. Children were frightened by his face. There was no quicksilver, litharge, or brimstone, borax, white lead, or any oil of tartar, or ointment which would rid of him of his white pimples or of the bumps on his face. He really loved garlic, onions, and also leeks, and to drink strong wine, red as blood, after which he would speak and shout like a madman. Then, when he had drunk his fill of the wine, he would speak no word but Latin; he knew a few phrases, two or three, that he had learned out of some church paper—that is not unusual, for he heard Latin all day; and you know very well how a jay bird can say "Wat" as well as the Pope. But if anyone attempted to discuss other learned matter with the Summoner, it was at once evident that he had spent all of his philosophy; he would always cry: "The question is what is the law?" He was a friendly and a kind rascal; you couldn't find a better fellow. For a quart of wine, he would allow a good fellow to have his mistress for a year, and excuse him fully. And he could pull the same trick quite expertly on someone else. If he came across a good companion, he would teach him to have no fear of the archdeacon's excommunication, unless that man's soul was in his purse; for the punishment was sure to be in his purse, since, as the Summoner said, "The purse is the archdeacon's Hell." But I know very well that he certainly lied; every guilty man ought to be afraid of excommunication, which will as surely kill the soul as absolution will save it, and a man should also beware of a Significavit. This Summoner controlled all the young people of the diocese in his own way, and he knew their secrets and was their favorite adviser. He had placed a bouquet on his head, large enough to decorate an alehouse signpost. He had made himself a shield of a cake.

With him there rode an amiable PARDONER from Rouncivalle, his friend and colleague, who had just come from the court at Rome. Loudly he sang, "Come hither, Love, to me!" The Summoner, singing bass, harmonized with him; never was there a trumpet with half so loud a tone. This Pardoner had hair of a waxy yellow, but it hung as smoothly as strands of flax, and he wore what hair he had gathered into small bunches on top but then thinly spread out over his shoulders. But for sport he did not wear his hood, for it was tied up in his bag. He affected to ride all in the new fashion, uncovered except for his little cap. He had eyes which glared like those of a hare. A religious talisman was sewn to his cap. He carried his bag, stuffed full of pardons hot from Rome, before him in his lap. His voice was small and goatlike. He had no beard, and never would have; his face was as smooth as if freshly shaven. I believe he was a eunuch. But in his business, there was not another such pardoner from Berwyck to Ware. For in his bag he had a pillowcase which he said had served as the veil of Our Lady; he claimed to have a piece of the sail with which St. Peter went to sea until Jesus Christ caught him. He had a metal cross embedded with stones, and also he had pig's bones in a jar. And with these same relics, when he found a poor parson living out in the country, he made more money in one day than the parson made in two months. And thus, with feigned flattery and tricks, he made monkeys of the parson and the people. But, finally, to tell the truth, he was in church a noble ecclesiastic. He could read a lesson or a parable very effectively, but best of all he could sing the offertory; for he knew very well that, when that service was over, he must sweeten his tongue and preach to make money as best he could. Therefore, he sang merrily and loud.

Now I have told you very briefly about the rank, the dress and the number of these pilgrims, and also why this group was assembled in Southwark at this good inn called the Tabard, close to the Bell. But the time has come to tell you what we did that same night we arrived at the inn, and afterwards I shall tell you about our trip and all the rest of our pilgrimage. But, first, I beg you in your kindness not to consider me vulgar because I speak plainly in this account and give you the statements and the actions of these pilgrims, or if I repeat their exact words. For you know just as well as I that whosoever repeats a tale must include every word as nearly as he possibly can, if it is in the story, no matter how crude and low; otherwise, he tells an untrue tale, or makes up things, or finds new words. He cannot spare even his brother's feelings; he must say one word just as well as any other. Christ himself spoke quite crudely in Holy Writ, and you know very well that there is no vulgarity in that. Even Plato says, to those who can read him, that the words must be cousin to the deeds. Also I ask you to firgive me for not arranging the people in my tale by their rank as they should be. My wit is short, as you can well imagine.

OUR HOST made each of us very comfortable and soon sat us down to supper. He served us with the best food; the wine was strong, and we were glad to drink. Our Host was a seemly man, fit to serve as major-domo of a banquet hall. He was a large man with protruding eyes—no more impressive burgess is to be found in

Cheapside—frank in his speech, wise, and well schooled, and nothing lacking in manliness. Also, he was a very merry man, and after supper began to play and told many jokes, among other things, after we had paid our bills. Then he said: "Now, ladies and gentlemen, truly you are heartily welcome here, for by my troth, if I do not lie, all this year I haven't seen so gay a group together in this inn as now. I would like to make you happy if I knew the way; in fact, I just now thought of a way to please you, and it shall cost you nothing.

"You are going to Canterbury—God speed you, and may the blessed martyr give you your reward! And I know very well that as you go along the road you plan to tell tales and to play, for truly, there's no fun or pleasure in riding along as dumb as a stone. Therefore, I shall make you a proposition, as I said before, and do you a favor. And if you are unanimously agreed to stand by my judgment and to do as I shall suggest, tomorrow when you ride along the road, by the soul of my dead father, if you don't have fun I'll give you my head! Hold up your hands without more talk."

It didn't take us long to reach a decision. We didn't think the matter worth much careful discussion, and we voted his way without debate. Then we tld him to explain his plan as he wished.

"Ladies and gentlemen," he said, "now listen carefully; but, I beg you, don't be contemptuous. Here is the point, to be brief and plain: that each of you, to make our trip seem short, shall tell two tales of old adventures on the way to Canterbury—I mean it that way—and two more coming home. And the one of you who tells the best tales of all, that is to say, those greatest in moral teaching and in entertainment value, shall have a supper at the expense of all of us here in this inn, right by this column, when we come back from Canterbury. And, to make your trip more enjoyable, I will ride with you myself, at my own expense, and be your guide; and whoever will not accept my judgment along the way will have to bear the full expense of the trip for everybody. Now, if you agree to this plan, say so at once, without any more talk, and I shall immediately get myself ready."

We agreed, and gladly gave our oaths to obey; then we asked him also to agree to serve as our manager, and to judge and report our tales, and to arrange for a supper at a set price. Also, we agreed to be ruled in all things as he saw fit. Thus unanimously we accepted his suggestion, and at once the wine was fetched. We drank, and everyone went to bed without further loitering.

The next morning, when the day began to dawn, our Host got up, roused us, and gathered us all together in a bunch. Then we rode the short distance to the Well of St. Thomas, where the Host halted his horse and said:

"Ladies and gentlemen, listen, if you please; you remember your agreement, and I remind you of it. Now let's see who shall tell the fist story. Just as surely as I hope always to drink wine and ale, whoever rebels against my judgment shall stand the whole expense of this trip. Now draw straws, before we go farther; whoever draws the shortest shall be first. Sir Knight," he said, "my master and my lord, now draw a straw, for that is my wish. Come near, my lady Prioress," he said, "and you, Sir Cleric, don't be bashful or think too hard. Fall to, everyone!"

We all immediately drew straws, and, to make a long story short, either by luck, or chance, or fortune, the truth is that the draw fell to the Knight, for which everyone was content and glad; and in accordance with our promise and agreement, as you have heard, he must tell his tale. What need is there to say more?

When this good man saw the situation, since he was wise and willingly held to his promise, he said: "Well, since I must start the game, I welcome the decision in the name of God! Now, let's ride on, and listen to what I say."

After those words we rode ahead on our way, and he at once very cheerfully began his tale, and spoke in the following manner.

(tr. by R. M. Lumiansky)

II MIDDLE ENGLISH Minor Works

- 12th Century
- 13th Century
- 14th Century
- 15th Century

12th Century

1. Peterborough Chronicle

1   1137. Ðis gære fōr þe Kīng Stēphne ofer sæ tō Normandī and thēr wes underfāngen, forþī ðat hī wēnden ðat hē sculde bēn alsuic alse the ēom wes, and for hē hadde gēt his trēsōr; ac hē tōdēld it and scatered sotlīce. Micel hadde
5   Henrī Kīng gadered gōld and sylver, and nā gōd ne dide me for his sāule thārof.

Þā þe Kīng Stēphne tō Englānde cōm, þā mācod hē his gadering æt Oxenefōrd and þār hē nam þe bischop Rogēr of Sereberī, and Alexander biscop of Lincol and te cancelēr
10   Rogēr, hise nēves, and dide ælle in prisūn til hī iāfen up here castles. Þā the suīkes undergæton ðat hē mīlde man was and softe and gōd, and nā justīse ne dide, þā diden hī alle wunder. Hī hadden him manrēd māked and āthes suōren, ac hī nān treuthe ne hēolden; alle hī wǣron
15   forswōren and here treothes forlōren, for ǣvric rīce man his castles mākede and agǣnes him hēolden, and fylden þe lānd ful of castles. Hī suencten suȳðe þe wrecce men of þe lānd mid castelweorces. Þā þe castles wāren māked, þā fylden hī mid dēovles and yvele men. Þā nāmen hī þā men þe hī
20   wēnden ðat anī gōd hefden, bāthe be nihtes and be dæies, carlmen and wimmen, and diden heom in prisūn efter gōld and sylver, and pīned heom untellendlice pīning. For ne wǣ ren nǣvre nān martyrs swā pīned alse hī wǣron; me hēnged

Minor Works · 161

up bī the fēt and smōked heom mid fūl smōke; me hēnged
bī the þūmbes ōther bī the hēfed, and hēngen brynīges on
her fēt; me dide cnotted strēnges abūton here hǣved and
wrythen tō ðat it gǣde tō þe hǣrnes. Hī diden heom in
quarterne þār nadres and snākes and pades wǣron inne, and
drāpen heom swā. Sume hī diden in crūcet-hūs, ðat is in ān
cǣste þat was scort and nareu and undēp, and dide scǣrpe
stānes þērinne and þrēngde þe man þǣrinne ðat him brǣcon
alle þe limes. In manī of þe castles wǣron lof and grin, ðat
wǣron rachentēges ðat twā ōþer thrē men hadden onōh tō
bǣron ōnne; þat was swā māced, ðat is, fǣstned tō ān
bēom, and diden ān scǣrp īren abūton þe mannes thrōte and
his hals, ðat hē ne myhte nōwiderwardes, ne sitten ne līen
ne slēpen, oc bǣron al ðat īren. Manī þūsen hī drāpen mid
hūngǣr.

Ī ne can ne Ī ne mai tellen alle þē wunder, ne alle þē
pīnes ðat hī diden wrecce men on þis lānd; and ðat lastede
þā nigentēne wintre wīle Stēphne was kīng, and ǣvre it was
werse and werse. Hī lǣiden gǣldes on thē tūnes ǣvre
umwīle and clepeden it tenserīe. Þā þē wreccce men ne
hadden nān mōre tō gyven, þā rǣveden hī and brendon alle
thē tūnes ðat wēl þū myhtes faren all a dǣis fare, sculdest
thū nēvre fīnden man in tūne sittende ne lānd tiled. Þā was
cōrn dǣre and flēsc and cǣse and butere, for nān ne was ō
þē lānd. Wrecce men sturven of hūnger; sume iēden on
ælmes þe wāren sum wīle rīce men; sume flugen ūt of
lānde. Wes nǣvre gǣt māre wrecccehēd on lānd, ne nǣvre
hēthen men werse ne diden þan hī diden; for ōversithon ne

forbāren hī nouther circe ne cyrce-iærd, oc nāmen al þē gōd ðat aarinne was and brenden sythen þē cyrce and al tegædere. Ne hī ne forbāren biscopes lānd, ne abbotes, ne prēostes, ac ræveden munekes and clerekes and ǣvric man ōther þe ōwer myhte. Ġif twā men ōþer ðrē cōman rīdend tō ān tūn, al þē tūnscipe flugæn for heom; wēnden ðat hi wǣron rævēres. Þē biscopes and lēred men heom cursede ǣvre, oc was heom naht þarof for hī wēron al forcursæd and forsuoren and forloren. Warsæ me tilede, þe ērthe ne bar nān cōrn, for þē lānd was al fordōn mid suilce dǣdes and hī sǣden openlīce ðat Crīst slēp and his halechen. Suilc and māre þanne wē cunnen sǣin wē þoleden nigentēne wintre for ūre sinnes.

*Anglo-Saxon Chronicle*는 우리나라의 『삼국사기』에 해당하는 것으로서 Alfred 대왕 때부터 시작되었는바, 몇 가지 판본 가운데서 1080년 이후의 사건까지를 기록하고 있는 것은 여기 인용한 *Peterborough Chronicle*(Oxford대학의 Bodleian Library 소장)이 유일하다.

비록 이 글의 연대는 1137년이나 그 내용으로 보아 Stepehn왕의 치세가 끝난 1154년 이후에 쓰였을 것으로 짐작된다. 여기 실린 사건들의 진위는 역사가들에 의해 입증된 바 있다.

● 방언 : North East Midland
● 철자와 발음 : 여기 인용한 글에는 아직도 고대영어 철자의 잔재가 많이 남아 있다. thorn(þ)[θ/ð]과 ash(æ)[æ]도 그대로 사용되고 있으며, [y]나 [tʃ], [ʃ]를 나타내기 위해 각기 g나 c, sc가 사용되었다는 점(예: gǣre [yɛːre], rice=[ritʃe], biscop=[biʃop])이 그렇다. 그러나 [k]를 나타내기 위해 ch가 사용되었다든지(예: rachentēges [rɑkenteːyes]), 고대영어의 þ대신 th가 사용되었다는 점(예: thēr[θeːr]), cw대신 qu를 사용했다는 점(예: quarterne [kwɑrterne]) 등에서 프랑스어의 영향을 볼 수 있다.
● 문법 : 굴절은 거의 소실되어 강변화와 약변화의 구별이 사라졌으며, 대부분의 경우 명사의 복수형은 -(e)s 하나만으로 나타내었다. 이 글의 성격상 동사의 현재형은 나타나지 않으며 동사의 단수 과거형은 -e로, 그리고 복수형은 -en으로 나타낸다.
● 어휘 : 이미 적지 않은 수의 프랑스어 차용어가 보인다 (예: prisūn, justīse, castle, martyrs)

1   **Đis gǣre**[yɛːre]=this year. *Chronicle*에서 새 항목 앞에서 상투적으로 쓰이는 표현이다. **fōr**=fāren(=to fare, go, travel)의 과거. **þe**=the. **Kīng Stēphne**[kiːŋg stéːvne]=Blois백작으로서 영국으로 건너와 1135년에 스스로가 왕이 되었다. **ofer sǣ**[ɔver sɛː]=over the sea=from the other side of the English Channel. Stephen 왕이 Normandy에 간 것은 3월이고 돌아온 것은(cf, 7행 cōm) 12월이었다.

2　　　　**thēr**=there=in Normany. **wes underfāngen**=was accepted (as leader). **underfōn**=accept, receive. **forþī ðat**[fɔrθi: θat]=because. **hī**=they. **wēnden**=wēnen(=to expect, think)의 복수 과거형.

3　　　　**sculde**[ʃulde]=should. **alsuic alse**[alswitʃ alse]=just the same as. **alsuic**=all such. alse=also. **ēom**=uncle=Henry 1세 (1100~35). **gēt**[ye:t] =약변화 동사 geten(=to get)의 과거분사로 보는 견해와 yet로 보는 두 가지 견해가 있다. 여기서는 후자의 입장을 취하겠다.

4　　　　**trēsōr**[trɛ:zo:r]=treasure. **ac**=but. **tōdēld**=tōdēlen(=to divide, distribute)의 과거. **scatered**[ʃatered]=scattered. **sotlīce**[sɔtli:tʃe]=foolishly. **Micel**[mitʃel]=much. Henri King=King Henry라고 하는 대신 한국어에서처럼 Henry King이라고 하는 것은 고대영어 이래의 관습이다. 이 점에서 새로운 어순을 사용하고 있는 1행의 Kīng Stēphne와 대조를 이룬다. 당시 빠른 속도로 변해가고 있던 중세영어의 한 단면을 보여준다.

5　　　　**gadered**=gaderen(=to gather)의 과거분사.

5-6　　　**nā gōd ne dide me for his sāule thārof**=anyone did no good for his sould with it=no good was done for his soul with it. **nā**=nōn=none, no. **gōd**=good (deed). **dide**=did. 원형은 dōn.

6　　　　**me**=one, they. 부정대명사 men의 약형이다. cf, OE man, mon. G. man. 이와 같은 용법은 25, 26, 27, 63행에서도 다시 보인다. 한편 me는 능동의 동사와 함께 쓰이면 수동의 뜻이 된다. **sāule**=soul. **thārof**=of it, with it.

7　　　　**þā~þā**=when~then. 이것은 고대영어 이래의 용법이다. **cōm**=came. 원형은 comen. **þā**=then. **mācod**=made. 원형은 māken.

8　　　　**gadering æt Oxeneford**[ɔksenefɔ:rd]=the Assembly at Oxford. 1139년 6월에 있었던 모임이다. **gadering**=gathering. **þār**=there (at Oxford). **nam**=nimen(=to take, seize, capture)의 과거.

8-9　　　**Rogēr of Sereberī**[rɔdʒér ɔf séreberi:]=Roger of Salisbury([sólzbèri]).

9　　　　**Lincol**=Lincoln. **te**=þe. þe는 t나 d 뒤에서 te가 된다. **canceler**=chancellor.

Minor Works · 165

10   **hise nēves**[his neːves]=his nephews=Alexander biscop of Lincol and te canceler Rogēr. hise는 his의 복수형. mīn이나 þīn의 변화에 유추해서 변화했던 것 같다. **dide ælle in prisūn**= put them all in prison. til=until. Old Norse의 차용어로서 이 뜻으로 쓰인 최초의 예. 고대 영어에서 이 뜻으로는 oþ-þæt가 쓰였다. **iāfen up**[yɑːven up]=ʒiven up=gave up.

11   **here**=their. **suīkes**=traitors. **undergǣton**[underyɛ́ːtɔn]=perceived, understood. 원형은 undergeten.

11-2   **þā~þā**=when~then.

11   **mīlde**=mild, gentle.

12   **softe**=soft, kind, gracious. **nā justīse**[yustiːse] **ne dide**=did not do justice=inflicted no punishment. justīse dōn(=punish)는 프랑스어의 faire justice를 그대로 영어로 옮긴 번역차용어(calque)이다.

13   **wunder**=atrocities, terrible crimes.

13-4   **Hī hadden**[hɑdden] **him manrēd māked and āthes**[ɑːθes] **suōren** [swoːren]=**Hī hadden māked him manrēd and suōren āthes**=they had made him homage and swore oaths. 이때까지만 해도 완료형의 어순이 현대 독일어처럼 have+목적어(manrēd/āthes)+과거분사(māked/ suōren)의 순서이다. cf. Ich have ein Brief geschrieben(=I have written a letter). **manrēd**=homage. **āthes**=ōþe=oath.

14   **suōren**=sworn. 원형은 swēren. **hī nān**=not one of them. **treuthe**[treuθe] =trewþe=truth, faith, pledge. **hēolden**=kept, held. 원형은 hōlden. **alle hī**=all of them(=the oaths).

15   **forswōren**=prejured, false to the pledge, disloyal, forsworn. 원형은 forswēren. **treothes**=trewþe=faith, truth. **forlōren**=lost. 앞에 wǣron이 생략되었다. 원형은 forlēsen. **ǣvric**[eːvritʃ]=every. **rīce man**=rich man, powerful man, noble man.

16   **agǣnes**[ɑyéːnes] **him**=against him(=King Stephen). **heolden**=hōlden (=to hold)의 과거 복수형. 주어가 ǣvric(=every)이므로 단수형이 사용되어야 하지만 ǣvric의 의미 냉용은 복수이므로 복수의 동

사가 사용되고 있다. **fylden**[filden]=filled. 이것도 복수형이다. 원형은 fillen.

17　**suencten**[swent∫ten]=oppressed. 원형은 swenchen. **suȳðe**[swi:ðe]=swūþe=very greatly, extremely. **wreccce**[wrett∫e]=wretched, poor.

18　**mid**=with. cf. G. mit. **castelweorces**[kɑstelweorkes]=forced labor on the building of castles. castel(=castle)+weorc(=work (=forced labor)). **þā~þā**=when~then. **māked**=made. **fylden hī**=they filled. 목적어는 castle.

19　**mid dēovles and yvele**[ivele] **men**=with devils and evil men. **þā**=then. **nāmen**=seized. 원형은 nimen.

19-20　**þā men þe hī wēndon ðat anī gōd hefden**[hefden]=those people who they thought had any wealth. **þe**=고대영어에서와 마찬가지로 관계대명사. **gōd**=goods, property. **hefden**=had. 원형은 haven.

20　**anī**=any. **bāthe**[bɑ:θe]**~and**=both~and. ON에서 가져다 쓴 최초의 예. 이 뜻에 해당하는 고대영어 표현은 ægþer ge~ge였다. **be nihtes** [nihtes] **and be dæies**[dɛies]=by day and by night. nihtes와 dæies는 각기 niht와 day의 소유격으로서 이른바 부사적 속격(adverbial genitive) 으로 쓰인 것이다. 따라서 be(=by)라는 전치사는 필요 없지만, 여기서는 이들 단어의 어미의 문법적 기능이 약해지면서 nihtes와 dæies가 복수형으로 느껴져 전치사가 쓰였다. 현대영어의 예로는 Working *nights* is different from working *days* (밤에 일하는 것은 낮에 일하는 것과 다르다)가 있다. cf, G. eines Tages.

21　**carlmen and wimmen**[kɑrlmen ɑnd wimmen]=men and women. man은 현대영어에서처럼 '남자'라는 뜻 외에 '인간'이라는 뜻도 있다. **carlmen**=carl(=churl)+men(=men). **immen**=wimman(=woman)의 복수형. 고대영어의 wīfman이 동화작용에 의해 f가 후속하는 m과 같아지면서 wimman이 되었다. **heom**=them. **efter**=after, in qeust of.

21-2　**efter gōld and sylver**=in order to get gold and silver.

22	**pīned heom untellendlice**[untellendlitʃe] **pīning**=inflicted unspeakable tortures on them. **pīned**=tortured, tormented. 원형은 pinen. **pīning**= torture, tormente, suffering. **pīned pīning**=dreamed a dream과 같은 이른바 동족목적어(cognate accusative)의 예. **untellendlice**=inexpressible.
23	**nǣvre**=never. **martyrs**=martyrs. **swā**=so.
23-4	**me hēnged up bī the fēt**=they hanged (them) up by the feet. hēnged 뒤에 목적어 heom(=them)이 생략되었다. **me**=they. cf. G. man. **bī**=by. **fēt**=feet.
24	**fūl**=foul. **me hēnged**=they were hung.
25	**þūmbes**=thumbs. **ōther**=or. cf. G. oder. **hēfed**[hɛːved]=hēved=head. **hēngen**=hang. 원형은 hāngen. **brynīges**[bryniːes]=coats of chain.
26	**her**=their. **cnotted**[knɔtted]=knotted. **strēnges**[streːŋges]=strings, cords. **abūton**=around, about. **here hǣved**=their head.
27	**wrythen tō ðat it gǣde**[yɛːde] **tō þe hǣrnes**=twisted to the point that (the cords) went into the brains (through the skull). **wrythen**= writhed. **tō ðat**=until. **it**=it. 문맥상으로는 strēnges를 지칭하고 있으므로 복수형이 사용되었어야 했다. gǣde=gōn(=to go)의 과거. **hǣrnes**= harn=brains.
28	**quarterne**[kwɑrterne]=prison-cell. **þār**=there, where. 관계부사로 사용되었다. **nadres**=adders. 현대영어의 adder는 a nadder를 an adder로 잘못 분석해서 생긴 모양이다. **pades**=toads.
29	**drāpen**=killed. 원형은 drēpen. **crūcet-hūs**[kruːtʃethuːs]=torture-cage. cf. L. cruciātus=torture. **ān**=one.
30	**cæste**=chest. **scort**[ʃɔrt] **and nareu and undēp**=short and narrow and shallow. **undēp**=not deep=shallow. **scærpe**[ʃærp]=sharp.
31	**þērinne**=therein. **prēngde**[θreːnide]=pressed. 원형은 þrengen.
31-2	**ðat him brǣcon alle þe limes**=until all the limbs broke to them= until all their limbs broke. **brǣcon**=broke. 원형은 brēken. **him**=여격으로서 소유를 나타낸다. **limes**=limbs.
32	**manī**=many. **lof and grin**=정확한 뜻은 알 수 없으나 죄수들의 목

에 감았던 일종의 족쇄로 여겨진다.

33   **rachentēges**[rɑkente:yes]=chains, fetters. 고대영어의 racente(=chain) 과 tēah(=fetter)의 합성에 의해 이루어진 단어이다.

33-4   **twā ōþer thrē men hadden onōh tō bǣron ōnne**=so heavy that two or three men would have difficulty carrying a single one. **onōh**[ɔnɔ́ːx]= inōʒ=enough. **bǣron**=bēren(=to bear, carry). **ōnne**=only, with difficulty.

34   **ðat is**=that is to say.

35   **bēom**=beam. **īren**=iron. **mannes**=man's. **thrōte**=throat.

36   **hals**=neck. **ne~ne**=neither~nor. **myhte**=might. 뒤에 turn himself라는 뜻의 동사가 생략되었다. **nōwiderwardes**=in no direction.

37   **oc**=but. **bǣron**=bear, carry. **þūsen**=thousand.

37-8   **drāpen mid hūngær**=killed with hunger.

39   **ne~ne~ne~ne**=neither~nor. **mai**=may. **wunder**=tortures.

40   **pīnes**=torments, pain, tortures.

40-1   **ðat lastede þā nigentēne wintre wīle Stēphne was kīng**=that lasted nineteen years while Stephen was king. 이로서 이 글이 Stephen의 치세가 끝난 뒤에 쓰였다는 결정적인 증거가 된다. **wīle**=while.

42   **ǣvre**=ever. **werse and werse**=worse and worse. **læiden**=laid. 원형은 leyen. **gældes**=ʒeldes=taxes. **tūnes**=towns.

42-3   **ǣvre umwīle**=at regularly recurring intervals, ever from time to time. **umwīle**=awhile, momently.

43   **clepeden**=called. **tenserīe**= tax exacted by lords from their vassals for protection and defense. cf. Lt. tensare=to protect. **þā~þā**= when~then.

43-4   **ne~nān**=2중부정이 아니고 고대영어에서와 마찬가지로 부정의 강조이다.

44   **rēveden**=robbed. 원형은 rēven.

44-5   **brendon alle thē tūnes**=burned all the towns. 다음과 같은 도시들을 방화했다. Worcester 1139, Nottingham 1140, 1153, Winchester 1141, Oxford 1142, Cambridge 1144. brendon의 원형은 brenne.

faren=fare, go. ðat=so that.

45-6 wēl bū myhtes faren all a dæis fare, sculdest[ʃuldest] thū nēvre finden⋯=in such a fashion that you might well travel a whole day's journey, you wouldn't find⋯. faren=to go. fare=journey. sculdest=should. 강한 추정을 나타낸다. thū=thou.

46 sittende=sitting, living. sitten(=to sit)의 현재분사. tiled=cultivated.

47 cōrn dǣre=expensive corn. flēsc[fleʃ]=meat, flesh. cǣse[tʃɛ:ze] and butere=cheese and butter. for=because. ō=on.

48 sturven of hūnger=starved of hunger. sume= som=some one.

48-9 iēden on ælmes=lived on charity, alms. iēden=ʒēde=went.

49 þe=of those who. sum wīle=at one time. flugen=fled, flied. 원형은 flȳe.

50 gǣt=ʒet=yet. māre wrecccehēd=more misery.

51 hēthen men=the Danes. ōversithon=too frequently. 그러나 everywehre afterwards(ōver(=anywhere)+sithon(=afterwards))의 해석도 가능하다.

52 forbāren=forbore, spared. 원형은 forbēren. nouther circe ne cyrce-iǣrd=neither church nor churchyard. oc=but.

53 sythen=then, after that.

53-4 al tegædere=all together.

54 Ne~ne=neither~nor.

55 prēostes=of priests. munekes=of monks. clerekes=of clerics.

55-6 ǣvric[ɛvritʃ] man ōther þe ōwer myhte=every man (robbed) another anywhere he could. ōwer=anywhere.

56 Ġif twā men ōþer ðrē cōman rīdend=riding. rȳden(=to ride)의 현재분사.

57 tūn=village. tūnscipe= the inhabitants. 문법적으로는 단수형이나 뜻이 복수이므로 동사도 복수형의 동사(flugæn)로 받고 있다. flugæn=fled. flȳe(=to fly)의 과거. for heom=because of them. wēnden=thinking.

58 rǣvēres= robbers. lēred men=learned men. cursede=cursed.

59 was heom naht þarof=they cared nothing for it. forcursæd=cursed.

60　　**forsuoren**=falsely sworn. forswēren(=to forswear, perjure)의 과거분사. **forloren**=damned. **Warsæ me tilede**=wherever men tilled. **Warsæ**=whērsō=everywhere, wher-so. **ērthe**=earth. **ne~nān**=부정의 강조.

61　　**fordōn**=destroyed. 원형도 fordōn. **suilce dǣdes**=such deeds.

61-2　**hī sǣden openlīce**[ɔpenli:tʃe]=they said openly. **Crīst slēp**=cf. Matt. viii, 24.

62　　**halechen**=saints.

62-3　**Suilc**[suiltʃ] **and māre þanne wē cunnen sǣin**=such things and more than we can say.

63　　**þoleden**=suffered. 원형은 þolen.

  1137년. 이 해에 Stephen왕이 바다 건너 Normandy로 가서 그 곳 사람들이 그를 받아들이게 되는데, 그것은 그들이 그가 삼촌과 같으리라는 생각과, 또 그가 아직도 재산을 가지고 있으리라는 생각에서였다. 그러나 그는 돈을 마구 줘버리고, 또 어리석게 써버렸다. Henry 왕이 많은 금은보화를 모아놓았었는데, 그의 영혼을 위한 좋은 일에는 하나도 사용되지 않았다.

  Stephen왕은 영국에 돌아오자 Oxford 회의를 열고 거기서 Salisbury 주교인 Roger와 그의 조카들인 Lincoln 주교 Alexander와 대법원장 Roger를 잡아다 옥에 가둠으로써 이들이 성을 포기하게 만들었다. 배반자들이 왕이 순하고 부드러운데다가 착한 사람으로서 벌줄 줄을 모른다는 것을 알게 되자, 그들은 갖가지 잔악한 행위를 저지르게 된다. 이전에 그들은 왕에게 충성을 맹세하고 서약한 바도 있으나 그것을 지키는 이는 아무도 없었다. 왜냐하면 모든 권세있는 사람들은 성을 짓고 그것을 왕에게 내놓지 않고 가지고 있었으며, 땅을 온통 성곽으로 메웠기 때문이다. 그들은 자기 땅의 불쌍한 사람들을 성곽 공사의 강제노동에 혹독하게 내몰았다. 일이 끝나면 그들은 성곽을 악당들과 고약한 인간들로 채워나갔다. 그리고는 누구든 돈이 있다고 생각되는 사람은 남녀 가릴 것 없이 밤낮으로 붙잡아다 돈을 빼앗기 위해 감옥에 처넣고는 말할 수 없는 고문을 가했다. 어느 순교자인들 그들보다 더한 고초를 당했겠는가. 그들은 잡아온 사람들을 발로 거꾸로 매달고 고약한 연기를 마시게 했다. 또는 엄지손가락이나 머리로 매달고 발에는 무거운 갑옷을 매달았으며, 매듭진 끈을 머리에 감아 끈이 머릿속으로 파고들어갈 때까지 조였다. 그들은 잡아온 사람들을 독사와 뱀과 두꺼비를 넣어둔 골방에 집어넣어 죽게 했다. 또 어떤 사람들은 '고문 상자'라고 부르는 곳에 넣었는데, 그것은 짧고 좁고 얕은 상자로서 그 안에는 날카로운 돌이 들어 있었으며, 그 안에 사람을 넣고는 사지가 찢어질 때까지 내려 눌렀다. 많은 성에는 족쇄가 있었는데, 그것은 하도 무거워서 두세 명의 장정이 가까스로 들 수 있을 정도였다. 그것을 대들보에 매달고 사람들의 목둘레에 날카로운 쇄를 달아 사람들이 꼼짝달싹 하지도, 앉지도, 눕지도 자지도 못한 채 그것을 견디고 있게 했다. 수천 명의 사람들이 굶어 죽었다.

나는 그들이 이 땅의 불쌍한 사람들에 행한 모든 일들을 말할 수도, 말해도 안 된다. 이 같은 일은 Stephen왕이 재위하던 19년 동안 계속되었으며, 사태는 더욱 악화되었다. 그들은 줄곧 마을에 '보호세'라고 부르는 세금을 징수했다. 불쌍한 사람들이 더 이상 내놓을 것이 없어지면 그들을 강탈했으며, 모든 마을들을 다 태워버려 온 종일을 걸어도 마을에 사는 사람 하나, 또 밭갈이 해 놓은 땅을 결코 만날 수 없었다. 곡물과 고기, 치즈, 버터가 없었기 때문에 값이 비쌌다. 불쌍한 사람들은 굶어죽어 갔다. 어떤 사람들은 전에 좀 잘 살던 사람들에 동냥을 해 살아나갔으며, 또 어떤 이들은 국외로 도망갔다. 이 땅에 이처럼 비참한 때는 없었다. 설사 덴마크의 이교도들도 이렇지는 않았다. 번번이 교회나 교회 마당 할 것 없이 쓸 만한 것은 모두 약탈했으며, 그 뒤에는 교회와 그 밖의 모든 것을 태워버렸다. 주교나 수도원장이나 사제의 땅이라고 해서 봐주는 법도 없었고, 수도사와 목사들을 비롯하여 걸려드는 모든 사람들을 강탈했다. 두서너 사람이 말을 타고 동리에 들어오면 마을 사람들은 그들을 강도로 알고 모두 도망을 갔다. 주교와 배운 사람들이 그들을 저주했으나 그것이 그들에게는 아무 소용이 없었던 것이, 그들은 이미 모두 저주 받고 천대받고 내버려진 자들이었기 때문이다. 어디든 땅을 갈아도 곡식이 자라지 않았는데, 그것은 땅이 그런 행위에 의해 파괴되었기 때문이었다. 사람들은 내놓고 예수님도 주무시고, 그 제자들도 자는 모양이라고 말했다. 이런 일들, 그리고 말할 수 없는 더 많은 일들을 우리들은 우리의 죄 때문에 19년 동안이나 감내해야 했다.

2. ANCRENE WISSE (The Love of Christ)

1   A leafdi wes mid hire fān biset al abūten, hire lōnd al
destrūet ant hēo al pōvre, inwið ān eorðene castel. A mihti
kinges luve wes þāh biturnd upon hire, swā unimēte swīðe
þet hē for wōhlech sēnde hire his sōnden, ān efter ōðer,
5   ofte somet monie, sēnde hire bēawbelez bāðe feole ant feire,
sucurs of liveneð, help of his hēhē hīrd tō halden hire
castel. Hēo underfēng al as ōn unrecheles ant swā wes
hēard iheortet þet hire luve ne mahte hē nēaver bēo þe
nēorre. Hwet wult tū māre? Hē cōm himseolf on ēnde,
10   schawde hire his feire neb, as þē þe wes of alle men
feherest tō bihālden, spec se swīðe swōtelīche ant wōrdes se
murie þet hā mahten dēade arēaren tō līve, wrahte feole
wundres ant dude muchele meistrīes bivōren hire ēhsihðe,
schawde hire his mihte, talde hire of his kinedōm, bēad tō
15   makien hire cwēn of al þet hē āhte.

Al þis ne hēold nāwt. Nes þis hoker wunder? For hēo
nes nēaver wurðe for te bēon his þuften. Ah swā, þurh his
deboneirtē, luve hefde ōvercumen him þet hē seide on ēnde:
'Dāme, þū art iweorret, ant þīne vān bēoð se strōnge þet tū
20   ne maht nānesweis, wiðūte mī sucurs edflēon hare hōnden,
þet hā ne dōn þē tō schēome dēað efter al þī wēane. Ich
chulle, for þe luve of þē, neome þet feht upo mē, ant
arudde þē of ham þe þī dēað sēcheð. Ich wāt þāh tō sōðe
þet ich schal bituhen ham neomen dēaðes wunde: ant ich hit
25   wulle heortelīche for te ofgān þīn heorte. Nū þenne, bisēche
ich þē, for þe luve þet ich cūðe þē, þet tū luvie mē lānhūre

efter þe ilke dēað, hwen þū naldest līves! Þes king dude al
þus, arudde hire of alle hire vān, ant wes himseolf tō
wundre itūket, ant islein on ēnde. Þurh mirācle arās þāh
from dēaðe tō līve. Nēre þeos ilke leafdi of uveles cunnes
cunde, ȝef hā ōver alle þīng ne luvede him hērefter?

Þes king is Jēsu, Godes sune, þet al o þisse wīse wohede
ūre sawle þe dēoflen hefden biset. Ant hē, as nōble wohere
efter monie messagērs ant feole gōd dēden, cōm tō prūvien
his luve, and schawde þurh cnihtschipe þet hē wes luvewurðe,
as wēren sumhwīle cnihtes iwunet tō dōnne, dude him i
turneiment ant hefde for his lēoves luve his schēld i feht, as
kēne cniht, on euche half iþurlet. His schēld þe wrēah his
Goddhēad wes his lēove līcome þet wes ispread o rōde,
brād as schēld buven in his istrahte earmes, nearow bineoðen,
as þe ān fōt, efter monies wene, sēt upo þe ōðer. Þet þis
schēld naveð sīden is for bitacnunge þet his decīples, þe
schulden stōnden bī him ant habben ibēon his sīden, fluhen
alle from him ant lēafden him as fremede as þe godspel
seið: *Relicto eo, omnes fugerunt.* Þis schēld is iȝeven us aȝein
alle temptatiūns, as Jeremīe witneð: *Dabis scutum cordis laborem
tuum.* Nawt ane þis schēld ne schilt us from alle uveles ah
dēð ȝet māre, crūneð us in heovene: *Scuto bonae voluntatis.*
'Lāverd,' hē seið, Davīð, 'wið þe schēld of þī gōde wil þū
havest us icrūnet.' Schēld, hē seið, of gōd will; for willes
hē þolede al þet he þolede. Ysaias: *Oblatus est quia voluit.*

'Me, Lāverd,' þū seist, 'hwertō? Ne mahte hē wið lēasse
grēf habben arud us?' Ȝeoi, iwiss, ful lihtlīche; ah hē nalde.
For-hwī? For te bineomen us euch bitellunge aȝein him of

ūre luve, þet hē sē dēore bohte. Me būð lihtlīche þīng þet me luveð lūtel. Hē bohte us wið his heorte blōd, dēorre prīs nes nēaver, for te ofdrāhen of us ūre luve tōward him þet costnede him sē sāre.

I schēld bēoð þrēo þīnges, þe trēo ant te leðer ant te litunge. Alswā wes i þis schēld : þe trēo of þe rōde, þet leðer of Godes līcome, þe litunge of þe reade blōd þet hēowede hire sē feire. Eft, þe þridde reisūn: Efter kēne cnihtes deað, me hōngeð hēhe i chirche his schēld on his mungunge. Alswā is þis schēld, þet is þe crūcifix, i chirche iset i swuch stūde þer me hit sōnest sēo, for te þenchen þērbī o Jēsu Crīstes cnihtschipe þet hē dude o rōde. His lēomon bihālde þron hū hē bohte hire luve, lette þurlin his schēld, openin his sīde, to schawin hire his heorte, tō schawin hire openlīche hū inwardlīche he luvede hire ant tō ofdrāhen hire heorte.

Ancrene Wisse([aŋkrene wisse])(*A Guide to Anchoresses* (=female anchoret(=hermit))=*The Nuns' Guide*)는 본래 *Ancrene Riwle*(*The Anchoresses' Rule=The Nuns' Rule*)을 고쳐 쓴 것이다. 운둔 생활을 시작하려는 세 자매의 부탁을 받고 앞으로의 생활 지침으로 준비한 것이다. 12세기 후반부터 신과 더욱 가까워지려는 노력에서 교회의 부속 건물에서 운둔 생활을 하는 사람들이 많았다.

　　전체는 서문과 8부(books)로 되어 있으며, 여기 인용한 글은 7부의 '사랑'이라는 제목의 글에서 예수의 사랑을 그린 부분만을 발췌한 것이다. 이 작품은 라틴어와 프랑스어로 된 것도 여러 판이 있는데, 영어와 프랑스어, 라틴어판 중 어느 것이 원본인지는 알려져 있지 않으며, 여러 노력에도 불구하고 작자도 아직 미상인 채 남아 있다. 작품에 쓰인 영어는 12세기 후반의 것으로 알려져 있다.

　　산문적 문체로 높은 평가를 받고 있는 *Ancrene Wisse*는 고대영어 시대의 Ælfric과 Wulfstan을 16세기의 위대한 성서 작가들에 연결하는 중요한 작품으로 여겨지고 있다. Sweet는 다음과 같은 열정적인 평을 하고 있다.

　　A.R.(=*Ancrene Riwle*) is one of the most perfect models of simple, natural, eloquent prose in our language; without it indeed, the history of English prose from the close of the Old E. period down to the beginning of the seventeenth century would be little more than a dreary blank. (Sweet 1884, *First Middle English Primer*, vi).

- 방언 : West Midland
- 철자와 발음 : 여전히 고대영어의 þ, ð, hw가 사용되고 있으며, 어두에 오는 f는 항상 [v]를 나타내며, h는 [y]를 나타내기도 한다 (예: fehercest [veyerest]).
- 어휘 : 상당히 많은 프랑스어 차용어가 발견된다 (예: grace, religiun).

1	A leafdi wes····=there was a lady····. leafdi[lɛvdi]=lady. wes=was. mid=by, with. hire=her. fān[vɑːn]=fō(=foe)의 복수형. 여기서는 속세의 인간들을 가리킨다. biset=besitten(=to beset, besiege)의 과거분사. al=all. abūten=about, on all sides. lōnd=land.
2	destrūet=destroien(=to destroy, rave, devastate, ruin)의 과거분사. ant=and. hēo[hœː]=she. pōvre=poor. cf. F. pauvre. inwið=within, in. eorðene castel=earthen castle=세속의 주거. castel=castle.
2-3	A mihti kinges luve=여기 예수는 중세의 기사처럼 묘사되어 있다. kinges=king's.
3	þāh=though, however. biturnd=biturnen(=to turn, set)의 과거분사. upon hire=upon her.
3-4	swā~þet=so~that. unimēte=immeasurably. swīðe=greatly.
4	for wōhlech=in courtship. for[vɔr]=for. wōhlech[woːuxletʃ] =courtship. sōnden=sond(=messenger)의 복수. ān efter ōðer=one after another.
5	ofte=often. somet=together. monie=many. bauble. bēawbelez= splendid gifts. bāðe~ant=both~and. feole[vœle]=many. feire[vɛire]=fair, fine, precious.
6	sucurs=succour, help, support. liveneð= means of living, provision of food, sustenance. hēhē[heːye] hīrd= mighty army. hēhē=high, noble. halden=hold.
7	underfēng=underfōn(=to accept, receive)의 과거. as ōn unrecheles [unretʃeles]=like an indifferent person. ōn=one, person. unrecheles= heedless, indifferent.
7-8	swā~þet=so~that.
8	hēard iheortet=hard-hearted. ne~nēaver=부정을 강조하는 누적부정. mahte[mɑxte]=may, can, be allowed. bēo[bœː]=be.
9	nēorre[nœːre]=neor(=near)의 비교급. wult=will, want, desire. māre= more. on ēnde=in the end, at last.
10	schawde[ʃaude]=showed. 원형은 shewen. neb=face. þē þe=he who.
11	feherest[veyerest]=feier(=fair)의 최상급. bihālden=behold, look upon.

	spec=spoke. 원형은 speken. **se**=so. **swīðe**=greatly. **swōtelīche**[swoːtlitʃe]= sweetly, agreeably.
11-2	**se~se~þet**=so~so~that.
12	**murie**=merry, pleasant, lovely, beautiful. **hā**=they. **mahten**=might. **dēade**=(the) dead. **arēaren tō līve**=raise the dead to life. **arēaren**[ɑːrɛːren]= raise up. **līve**=life. **wrahte**[wrɑxte]=wurchen(=to work, perform, compose)의 과거.
13	**wundres**=marvels. **dude**=did. 원형은 dōn. **muchele**=much, great. **meistrīes**=a great accomplishment, master, great deed, noble deed. **bivōren**=before. **ēhsihðe**[eysiçθe]=eyesight.
14	**mihte**=might, power. **talde**=tellen(=to tell, relate)의 과거. **kinedōm**= kingdom. **bēad**=beden(=to offer)의 과거.
15	**makien hire cwēn of al þet hē āhte**=make her queen of all that he possessed. **makien**=make. **āhte**=owen(=to own, possess)의 과거.
16	**hēold**=availed, avoil, be of use. **nāwt**=naught, nothing. **Nes**=ne+ wes=was not. **hoker**=scorn, disdain, insult. **wunder**=astonishing, wondrous.
17	**nēaver**=never. **wurðe**=worthy. **þuften**=handmaid. **Ah**=but. **swā~þet**= to such a point that, so much~that.
18	**deboneirtē**=gentleness, graciousness. **hefde**=had. **ōvercumen**=overcome. **seide**=said. 원형은 seggen. **on ēnde**=in the end, at last.
19	**iweorret**=werriern(=to atack)의 과거분사. **vān**=fō(=foe)의 복수형. **bēoð**=are. **se strōnge þet**=so strong that.
20	**maht**=be able to, have power, can. 원형은 mouen. **nānesweis**=not at all, in no way. **wiðūte**=without. **mī**=my. **edflēon**=escape. **hare**=their. **hōnden**=hands.
21	**þet**=so that, in order that. **dōn**=put. **tō schēome dēað**=to shameful death. **wēane**=misery, woe.
22	**chulle**=will. 선행하는 Ich에 동화. **neome**=take. **feht**=fight.
23	**arudde**=rescue, save. **of ham þe þī dēað sēcheð**=from those who seek thy death. **sēcheð**=seek. 원형은 sechen. **wāt**=know. 원형은

	wieten. þāh= though, however. to sōðe=in truth, truly, for sure.
24	schal=shall. bituhen=between, among. dēaðes wunde=mortal wound. dēaðes=of death, deadly. wunde=ound.
25	wulle=will, wish, desire. heortelīche=heartily, cordially. for te=for to, in order to. ofgān=obtain, win. heorte=heart. Nū=now. þenne=then. bisēche=eseech.
26	þe luve þet ich cūðe þe=the love that I made known to thee. cūðen=make known, show, tell. þet=so that. luvie=love. 원형은 luvien. lānhūre=at least. cf. OE la= indeed)+and hurn(=at all events).
27	ilke=same. dēað=death. hwen þū naldest līves!=when thou wouldst not (do so) while (I was) alive! naldest=ne+woldest=would not=did not want. Þes=this. dude=did. 원형은 dōn.
28	þus=thus. arudde=rescued, saved. 원형은 aredden.
28-9	tō wundre=outrageously, cruelly.
29	itūket=tukien(=to ill-treat)의 과거분사. 어두의 i-는 과거분사를 나타내던 고대영어 ġe-([ye])의 잔재. islein=slain. 원형은 slen. 어두의 i-는 itūket의 경우와 같다. arās=arisen(=to arise)의 과거.
30	Nēre=ne+were=were not=would not.
30-1	of uveles cunnes cunde=of evil sort's nature=of the nature of an evil sort. uveles=evil. cunnes=kind, sort.
31	cunde=nature. ȝef[yef]=if. ȝ는 고대영어의 ġ의 잔재. hā=they. 여기서는 문맥상 she로 해석한다. hērefter=hereafter.
32	sune=son. wīse=way, manner. cf. ModE likewise. wohede=wohen (=to woo, seek)의 과거.
33	sawle=soul. þe dēoflen hefden biset=that devils had besieged. wohere=wooer, lover.
34	monie messagērs=many messengers. feole[vœle]=many. gōd dēden=good dees, acts of kindness. prūvien=prove.
35	schawde=schawen(=to showed, revealed, manifested)의 과거. cnihtschipe=chivalry, knightly deed, knightship. luvewurðe=worthy of love.
36	sumhwīle=at one time, formerly. iwunet=accustomed. 원형은 wonen.

	tō dōnne=to do.
36-7	**dude him in turneiment**=performed in the tournament. **i turneiment**= in tournament.
37-8	**hefde~his schēld~iþurlet**=had his shield pierced. 수동을 나타낸다. **for his lēoves luve**=for the love of his beloved. **schēld**[ʃɛːld]=shield. **i feht**=in the fight.
38	**kēne**=courageous, bold, keen. **cniht**[kniçt]=knight. **on euche half**=on every side. **iþurlet**=þurian(=to pierce)의 과거분사. **wrēah**=wrīen(=to cover, hide)의 과거.
39	**Goddhēad**=godhead, divinity. **lēove(lēf)**=dear. **līcome**=fleshly body. **ispread**=sprēdan(=to spread)의 과거분사. **o rōde**=on the rood, on the cross.
40	**brād**=broad. **buven**=above. **istrahte**=stretched. **earmes(arm)**=arm. **nearow (narwe)**=arrow. **bineoðen**=beneath.
41	**as þe ān fōt**⋯=12세기 말까지만 해도 십자가의 예수는 지금처럼 두 발을 한데 포개고 있는 대신 두 발에 따로 못이 박힌 상태였다. **monies**=many (a one). **wene**–expect, believe. 원형은 wēnen. **sēt upo þe ōðer**=set upon the other foot.
42	**naveð**=ne+haveð=did not have. **sīden**=sides. **bitacnunge**=betokening. **decīples þe**=disciples who.
43	**schulden stōnden bī him ant habben ibēon his sīden**=should have stood beside him and have been his sides. **bī**=by, beside. **him**= usus. ant habben ibēon his sīden,
43-4	**fluhen alle**=alle fluen=all fled. **fluen**=flȳe(=to fly)의 과거. **lēafden**= left. 원형은 lēven. **as fremede**=as a stranger. **fremede**=foreign, strange.
45	*Relicto eo, omnes fugerunt.*=위의 말을 Latin어로 바꿔 쓴 것으로서 All leaving him, they fled의 뜻. cf. Matthew 26:56. (Then all the disciples deserted him and fled.) **iȝeven**=given. **aȝein**(agayn)=against.
46	**temptatiūns**=temptation. **witneð**=witnien(=to testify, bear witness)의 3인칭 단수.
46-7	*Dabis scutum cordis laborem tuum.*=You will give your labor as a

shield for the heart. cf. Lamentations 3:65. (Give them anguish of heart: your curse be on them!)

47 **Nawt ane~ah**=not only~but also. **schilt**=schilden(=to protect)의 3인칭 단수. **uveles**=evils. **ah(ac)**=but.

48 **dēð**=does. 원형은 dōn. **ʒet māre**=yet more. **crūneð**=crūnen(=to crown)의 3인칭 단수. **heovene**=heaven. *Scuto bonae voluntatis.*= with a shield of good will. cf. Psalm 5:12. (you cover them with favor as with a shield.)

49 **Lāverd**(lōrd)=lord. **hē**=Davīð. **Davīð**=앞의 hē와 동격이다.

50 **havest**=have. **icrūnet**=crowned. **willes**=voluntarily.

51 **þolede**=suffered. **Ysaias**=Isaiah. *Oblatus est quia voluit.*=He was offered because it was his own will. cf. Isaiah 53:7. (He was oppressed, and he was afflicted, yet he did not open his mouth;)

52 **Me**=interjection. why, now. **Lāverd**(lōrd)=lord. **hwertō**(whērtō)=for what, why. **Ne mahte hē**=could he not. **lēasse**(lesse)=less.

53 **grēf**=grief, sorrow. **arud**=arüdden(=to save)의 과거분사. **ʒeoi**=yes, certainly, yea. **iwiss**=for sure, for certain. **ful**=very. **lihtlīche**=lightly, easily. **ah**=but. **hē nalde**=ne+willan(=to desire, want)의 과거.

54 **For-hwī**(forwhȳ)=why, because. **te bineomen**=in order to deprive. **te**(tō)=to. **bineomen** (benime)=deprive, take away. **euch**(ēch)=each. **bitellunge**=excuse. **aʒein**(agayn)=against.

55 **luve, þet**=the love that. **þet**는 관계대명사. **dēore**(dēre)=dear, dearly. **bohte**=bought. 원형은 bȳen. **Me**=one, they. **būð**=buy. 원형은 bȳen. **lihtlīche**=easily, cheaply. **þīng**=thing.

56 **me luveð lūtel**=people care little for. **lūtel**(lītel)=little. **wið his heorte blōd**=with his heart's blood. **dēorre prīs**=dearer price. **dēorre**=dēre (=dear)의 비교급.

57 **nes nēaver**=there never was. **nes**=ne wes. **for te ofdrāhen**=in order to draw. **of us**=from us.

58 **costnede**=costnin(=to cost)의 과거. **sē**=(sō)so, thus. **sāre**(sōre)=so sorely, bitterly.

59 I=in. bēoð=is. 원형은 bēon. þrēo=three. þīnges=things. trēo(trē)= tree. te=the. leðer=leather. te=the.
60 litunge=color, tint. Alswā(alsō)=also, equally, similarly. rōde=cross.
61 līcome(līcam)=fleshly body, corpse. reade(rēde)=red.
62 hēowede=heowin(=to color, hue)의 과거. sē feire=so fair. Eft=again, once more. þe þridde reisūn=the third reason. Efter(after)=after. kēne= sharp, bold, courageous.
63 cnihtes deað=knight's death. hōngeð=hanfen(=to hand)의 과거. hēhe (heigh)=high.
64 mungunge=memory. Alswā(alsō)=also. crūcifix=crucifix.
65 iset=sette(=to set)의 과거분사. swuch(swich)=such. stūde(stēde)=place. þer=where. 관계부사. sōnest=sōn(=soon, right away, immediately)의 최상급. sēo=see. þenchen(thenken)=think.
66 þērbī=thereby. o=of. Jēsu Crīstes cnihtschipe= Jesus Christ's knightship. dude=dōn(=to do, make)의 과거. o=on. His lēomon bihālde=let his dearly beloved behold.
67 lēomon(lēofmon) =lover, mistress. bihālde=behold. 원형은 bihōlden. þron(þēron)= from this, thereon. hū=how. bohte=bought. 원형은 bȳen. hire luve, lette=let. þurlin=pierce.
68 openin=to open. schawin(schewen)=show.
69 openlīche=openly. inwardlīche=completely, perfectly. luvede(lōved)= loved. 원형은 luvien.

한 숙녀가 있었는데, 온통 원수들에게 둘러싸였을 뿐만 아니라 땅은 모두 파괴되었으며, 이 땅의 주거에 불쌍하게 혼자 있었습니다. 그러나 강력한 왕이 그녀를 말할 수 없게 사랑하게 되어 그녀에게 구애하기 위해 전령을 차례로, 때로는 한 번에 여럿을 보냈습니다. 그리고 살림에 도움이 될 값지고 훌륭한 선물과 그녀의 성을 지킬 고매한 군사들을 보냈습니다. 그녀는 이 모든 것을 대수롭지 않게 받았으며, 그녀는 하도 몰인정한 사람이어서 그는 그녀의 마음에 조금도 다가갈 수가 없었습니다. 무얼 더 바라는가? 마침내 그가 직접 와서 그의 잘 생긴 얼굴을 보였는데, 그는 더 할 수 없이 잘 생긴 남자였습니다. 그는 말도 아주 점잖고 즐겁게 했으므로 그의 말을 들으면 죽은 사람도 벌떡 일어날 지경이었습니다. 그는 그녀가 보는 데서 많은 기적과 신기한 일들을 해보임으로써 그의 힘을 보여주었습니다. 그는 그의 왕국에 대해 이야기 했으며, 그녀로 하여금 자기가 가지고 있는 모든 것의 왕비가 되게 해주겠다는 약속도 했습니다.

그러나 이 모든 것은 소용이 없었습니다. 그녀의 경멸이 대단하지 않습니까? 왜냐하면 그녀는 그의 시녀 자격도 없었기 때문입니다. 그러나 그의 점잖은 성품과 사랑 때문에 마침내 그는 이렇게 말했습니다. "숙녀여, 당신은 지금 공격을 받고 있으며, 당신의 적은 하도 강력해서 내 도움 없이 당신이 그들의 손아귀에 잡혀 수치스러운 주검에서 벗어날 길은 없소이다. 당신에 대한 내 사랑으로 하여 내가 이 싸움을 맡아 당신을 죽이려는 자들로부터 당신을 구하겠소이다. 그러나 그들과 싸우느라면 나도 치명적인 상처를 입게 되겠지만, 그래서 당신의 마음을 얻을 수 있다면 기꺼이 그 일을 맡겠소이다. 그러니 당신에게 대한 내 사랑을 고백한 지금 비록 당신은 살아생전엔 나를 사랑하려 하지 않았으나, 당신을 구하려는 싸움에서 내가 죽거든 나를 사랑해 주길 간청하오." 왕은 이 모든 것을 했습니다. 그는 모든 적으로부터 그녀를 구해냈으며, 자신은 마침내 치욕스럽게 학대받고 처형되었습니다. 그러나 기적에 의해 그는 주검에서 다시 살아났습니다. 이러고도 이 숙녀가 그를 사랑하지 않는다면 고약한 성미의 소유자라고 할 수 밖에 없지 않겠습니까?

이 왕은 악마에 둘러싸인 우리의 영혼을 이런 식으로 구애했던 하나님의 아들 예수입니다. 그리고 그는 고상한 구혼자로서 많은 전령을 보냈고, 많은 선행을 통해 그의 사랑을 증명하기에 이르렀으며, 예전의 기사들이 그러했듯이 그의 기사다운 행위에 의해 그가 사랑을 받을 자격이 있음을 보여주었습니다. 그는 용감한 기사답게 시합에 참가하여 사랑하는 사람의 사랑을 쟁취하기 위한 싸움에서 그의 방패의 네 모퉁이는 모두 구멍이 났습니다. 그의 신성을 가렸던 그의 방패는 팔을 벌리고 십자가에 매달린 그의 몸이었습니다. 방패의 위쪽처럼 팔을 벌리고 있는 그의 몸은 위가 넓었고, 밑은 많은 사람이 믿고 있듯이 한 쪽 다리를 다른 다리에 포개고 있어 좁아졌습니다. 이 방패의 옆 부분이 없다는 것은 그의 옆에 서서 그의 옆구리가 돼주어야 했을 그의 제자들이 스승을 모르는 사람처럼 내팽개치고 모두 도망갔던 깃을 상징합니다. 성경에 가로되, "모두 그를 버리고 도망갔느니라"고 했습니다. 이 방패는 모든 유혹에 대항해서 싸우도록 우리에게 주어진 것입니다. 예레미아는 "그들에게 마음의 고통을 주고 당신의 저주가 그들에게 있게 하라"고 증언하고 있습니다. 이 방패는 모든 악령으로부터 우리를 보호해줄 뿐만 아니라 그보다 더한 일도 합니다. 즉 "선한 방패로" 하늘나라에서 우리에게 왕관을 씌워줍니다. "주님,"하고 다윗이 말합니다. "당신의 선한 방패로 우리에게 면류관을 씌워주셨나이다." 그는 그가 겪어야 했던 고통을 기꺼이 감내했으므로 "선의의 방패"라고 말했습니다. 이사야는 "그는 스스로의 뜻에 의해 그 고통을 감내 했느니라"고 말하고 있습니다. 그러면 당신은 "무엇 때문에요?"라고 말합니다. "덜 고통스러운 방법으로 우리를 구할 수는 없었던가요?" 물론 있지요, 아주 쉬운 방법이 있습니다. 그러나 그는 그렇게 하기를 원치 않았습니다. 왜냐고요? 그것은 그가 그처럼 비싼 대가를 치르고 산 우리를 위한 사랑에 대해 우리가 어떤 핑

계도 대지 못하게 하기 위해서입니다. 싸게 산 물건은 하찮게 여기기 마련입니다. 그는 우리의 사랑을 얻기 위해 그의 심장의 피 -이보다 더 비싼 값이 어디에 있겠습니까- 로 그 사랑을 그처럼 큰 고통을 치르며 샀습니다.

 방패는 세 가지로 이루어져있습니다. 그 첫째는 나무이고, 둘째는 가죽이며, 셋째는 그림입니다. 이 방패가 바로 그러합니다. 십자가가 나무이고, 하나님의 몸이 가죽이며, 그 몸을 그처럼 화려하게 물들인 피가 그림입니다. 세 번째 이유가 있습니다. 용감한 기사가 죽은 뒤 그의 방패는 그를 기억하도록 교회에 높이 걸렸습니다. 마찬가지로 이 방패는 십자가 위에서 예수 그리스도가 보여준 기사다운 용기를 사람들이 회상하도록 교회에서 누구나 쉽게 볼 수 있도록 놓여 있는 십자가입니다. 그를 사랑하는 사람들은 거기서 그가 어떻게 사랑을 샀는가를 회상해야 합니다. 그의 방패는 여기저기 구멍이 났으며, 그의 옆구리에는 심장이 들어나 보이도록 구멍이 나서, 그가 얼마나 분명히, 그리고 진지하게 그녀의 마음을 사로잡기 위해 그녀를 사랑했는가를 보여줍니다.

13th Century

1. THE OWL AND THE NIGHTINGALE

1   Ich was in ōne sumere dāle,
In ōne swīþe dīʒele hāle,
Iherede ich hōlde grēte tāle
An ūle and ōne niʒtingāle.
5   Þat plait was stif and starc and strōng,
Sum-wīle softe and lūd amōng;
An aiþer aʒēn ōþer sval,
And lēt þat vuele mōd ūt al.
And eiþer seide of ōþeres cüste
10   Þat alre worste þat hī wüstc;
And hūre and hūre of ōþeres sōnge
Hī hōlde plaiding swīþe strōng.
   Þe niʒtingāle bigon þe spēche,
In ōne hürne of ōne bēche;
15   And sat up ōne vaire bōʒe,
Þār wēre abūte blosme inōʒe,
In ōre wāste þicke hegge,
Imeind mid spīre and grēne segge.
Hŏ was þe gladur vor þe rīse,
20   And sōng a uēle cünne wīse:
Bet þuʒte þe drēm þat hē wēre
Of harpe and pīpe, þan hē nēre;

>
> Bet þu3te þat hē wēre ishōte
> Of harpe and pīpe, þan of þrōte.

25   Þō stōd ōn ōld stoc þār bisīde,
> Þār þō Ule sōng hire tīde,
> And was mid īui al bigrowe,
> Hit was þāre hūle eardingstowe.
>   Þe ni3tingāle hī isē3,

30   And hī bihōld and ōuersē3,
> And þu3te wēl vūle of þāre hūle,
> For me hī halt lōdlich and fūle.
> 'Vnwi3t,' hō sēde, 'awei þū flō!
> Mē is þe wurs þat ich þē sō!

35   Iwis for þīne vule lēte
> Wēl oft ich mīne sōng forlēte;
> Mīn hörte atflīþ, and falt mī tunge,
> Wonne þū art tō mē iþrunge.
> Mē lüste bet spēten þane singe

40   Of þīne fūle 3o3elinge.'
>   Þēos hūle abōd fort hit was ēve,
> Hö ne mi3te nō lēng bilēve,
> Vor hire hörte was sō grēt
> Þat wēlnē3 hire fnast atschēt:

45   And warp a wōrd þārafter lōnge:
> 'Hū þincþē nū bī mīne sōnge?
> Wēnst þū þat ich ne cünne singe,
> Þe3 ich ne cünne of writelinge?
> Ilōme þū dēst mē grāme,

50   And seist mē bōþe tōne and schāme.

　　　　ȝif ich þē hōlde on mīne uōte,
　　　　[Sō hit bitīde þat ich mōte!]
　　　　And þū wēre ūt of þīne rīse,
　　　　þū scholdest singe an ōþer wīse.'
55　　　　　þe niȝtingāle ȝaf ansvāre:
　　　　'Ȝif ich mē lōkī wit þe bāre,
　　　　And mē schīlde wit þe blēte,
　　　　Ne recche ich noȝt of þīne þrēte;
　　　　Ȝif ich mē hōlde in mīne hegge,
60　　　　Ne recche ich nēver what þū segge.
　　　　Ich wōt þat art unmīlde
　　　　Wiþ höm þat ne muȝe from þē schīlde;
　　　　And þū tūkest wrōþe and uvele
　　　　Whār þū miȝt ōver smale fuȝele.
65　　　　Vorþī þū art lōþ al fuel-künne,
　　　　And alle hŏ þē drīveþ hönne,
　　　　And þē bischrīcheþ and bigrēdet,
　　　　And wēl narewe þē bilēdet;
　　　　And ēk forþē þe sülve mōse
70　　　　Hire þonkes wolde þē tōtōse.
　　　　Þū art lōdlich tō bihōlde,
　　　　And þū art lōþ in monie vōlde;
　　　　Þī bodi is short, þī swēore is smal,
　　　　Grettere is þīn hēued þan þū al;
75　　　　Þīn ēȝene bŏþ cōl-blake and brōde,
　　　　Riȝt swō hō wēren ipeint mid wōde;
　　　　Þū stārest sō þū wille abīten
　　　　Al þat þū miȝt mid cliure smīten;

Þī bile is stif and scharp and hōked,
80 Riȝt sō an ōwel þat is crōked,
Þārmid þū clackes oft and lōnge,
And þat is on of þīne sōnge.
Ac þū þrētest tō mīne flēshe
Mid þīne cliures woldest mē mēshe;
85 Þē wēre icündur tō ōne frogge
[Þat sit at mülne vnder cogge]
Snailes, mūs, and fūle wiȝte,
Bōþ þīne cünde and þīne riȝte.

이 시는 당대 프랑스에서 유행하기 시작한 논쟁시(débat(=debate))를 최초로 영시에 도입한 경우이다. 그 밖에도 이 시는 프랑스의 8음절 2행연구(octosyllabic rimed couplet)를 최초로 영시에 소개한 경우로 기록되는데, 이 기법은 뒤에 Chaucer가 대성하게 된다. 8음절로 이루어진 시행들이 aabbcc…의 모양으로 운이 맞는다.

논쟁시에는 이 작품 외에도 육체―영혼, 여름―겨울, 물―바람, 바이올렛―장미, 학자―기사 사이의 논쟁을 다룬 작품들이 있다. 작자는 미상이나 작품 뒤에서 논쟁의 판정관으로 등장하는 Nicholas de Guilford가 아닐까 생각되기도 한다. 그와 같은 추측을 하게 만드는 또 다른 근거는 이 작품이 그의 고향인 남부 방언으로 쓰여져 있다는 사실이다.

작품은 6월의 어느 날 저녁 부엉이와 나이팅게일이 주고받는 논쟁을 엿듣는 것으로 시작되는데, 우화적인 이 작품의 두 주인공이 상징적으로 사용되고 있는 것이 분명하다. 사람에 따라서는 부엉이는 진지하고 장중한 종교적 교훈시(religious didactic poetry)를 상징하며, 한편 나이팅게일은 르네상스 초기의 새로운 서정적이며 다정다감한 시(lyric and amorous poetry)를 상징한다고도 하며, 또 사람들에 따라서는 부엉이는 수도원을, 그리고 나이팅게일은 사바세계를 상징한다고도 하나 해석은 독자들의 몫이다. 어찌되었든 뒤에 가서 판정관은 나이팅게일의 손을 들어준다.

● 방언 : 작자는 분명히 남부방언을 사용하고 있으나 필사생(scribe)은 West Midland 방언의 사용자였을 것으로 짐작된다. 예: hō(=she).
● 철자와 발음 : u와 v가 구별없이 사용되고 있으나, 대개 어두에서는 v가, 그리고 어중에서는 u가 사용되고 있다. 예: vnder=under. vuele=evil, uersēʒ=oversen.
● 문법 : 관사는 þe(주격), þer(소유격), þan(여격)의 모양으로 사용되었으며, 과거분사는 반드시 접두사 i와 함께 사용되었다. i는 고대영어의 과거분사 접두사인 ge-의 잔재이다.

1. **Ich**=I. **ōne**=a. **sumere**=summer. **dāle**=dale, valley.
2. **swīþe dīʒele hāle**=very secluded nook. **swīþe**=very, greatly. **dīʒele**=secret, hidden. **hāle**=nook, remote corner.
3. **Iherede**=heard. 원형은 heren. **hōlde**=hold. 지각동사 iherede 뒤에서 사용된 부정형. **grēte**=great. **tāle**=talk, debate, conversation.
4. **ūle**=owl. **niʒtingāle**=nightingale. 3행의 hōlde의 의미상의 주어.
5. **þat**=that. **plait**=debate, quarrel. **stif**=stiff, violent, hard, fierce. **starc**=stark, violent. **strōng**=strong.
6. **Sum-wīle**=some+while=sometimes. **softe**=soft, mild. **lūd**=loud. **amōng**=at intervals, at times.
7. **An**=and. **aiþer~ōþer**=either~the other. **aiþer**=either. each of two. **aʒēn**=against. **ōþer**=other. **sval**=swellen(=to swell (with anger))의 과거.
8. **lēt~ūt**=let loose. **lēt**=let. **vuele**=evil, offensive, hostile. **mōd**=mood, temper, spirit. **ūt**=out. **al**=all, entirely, utterly, completely.
9. **seide**=said. 원형은 seggen. **ōþeres**=other's. **cüste**=character, quality.
10. **þat**=the. **alre worste**=worst of all. **alre**=of all. **worste**=worst. **þat**=that. 관계대명사. **hī**=she. 이 작품에서는 owl과 nightingale 모두 여성형을 취급하고 있다. **wüste**=witen(=to know)의 과거.
11. **hūre**=particularly, at least. **hūre and hūre**=especially. **sōnge**=song.
12. **Hī**=they. **hōlde plaiding**=held pleas. **plaiding**=law-suit, dispute. **strōng**=strongly, fiercely. plaiding을 수식하는 형용사로 볼 수도 있다.
13. **bigon**=began. 원형은 bigynnen. **spēche**=speech, law-suit, plea.
14. **hürne**=corner. **bēche**=a piece or strip of land plowed for cultivation.
15. **sat**=sat. 원형은 sitten. **up**=upon. **vaire**=fair, beautiful. **bōʒe**=bough, branch, twig.
16. **þār**=there, where. **abūte**=about, round about, all around. **blosme**=blossom. **inōʒe**=enough, many.
17. **ōre**=a, one. **wāste**=fast, firm, secure, impenetrable. **þicke**=thick. **hegge**=hedge.

18	**Imeind**=mengen(=to mix, mingle, intermingle, interwine)의 과거분사. imeind에서 어두의 I는 과거분사를 나타내는 접두사이다. 고대영어의 ge의 잔재이며 현대독일어의 ge-에 해당한다. **mid**=with. **spīre**=reeds. **grēne**=green. **segge**=sedge.
19	**Hð**=she. **gladur**=glad(=happy, joyful)의 비교급. **vor**=for, because of, on account of. **rīse**=twig, bough, branch.
20	**sōng**=sang. 원형은 singen. **uēle cünne wīse**=many kinds of tunes. **a**=in, on. **uēle**=many. **cünne**=cun(=kin, kind, sort)의 복수 속격. **wīse**=ways, tunes.
21-2	**Bet þuȝte be drēm bat hē wēre Of harpe and pīpe, ban hē nēre**=the sound seemed that it were of harp and pipe rather than it were not=the sound seemed rather to come from harp and pipe than otherwise.
21	**Bet**=better, rather. **þuȝte**=seemed. 원형은 þinchen. 비인칭동사이다. **drēm**=(joyful) sound, melody. **hē**=he=drēm. **wēre**=were. **bēn**(=to be)의 가정법 과거.
22	**harpe**=harp. **pīpe**=pipe. **þan**=than. **hē**=he=drēm. **nēre**=ne+wēre.
23	**ishōte**=shot forth. sheten(=to shoot)의 과거분사. i는 접두사.
24	**Of**=out of. **þrōte**=throat.
25	**Þō**=then. **stōd**=stood. 원형은 stonden. **ōn**=a, an. **stoc**=stock, tree-stump. **þār bisīde**=close by.
26	**Þār**=where. 관계부사. **þō**=the. **Ule**=owl. **hire**=her. **tīde**=tides, hours, canonical hours(성무일과).
27	**Īui**=ivy. **bigrowe**=bigrowen(=to grow over)의 과거분사.
28	**Hit**=it. **þāre**=them that. **hūle**=owl's. **eardingstowe**=dwelling-place.
29	**hī**=her. **isēȝ**=saw. 원형은 sē(o)n.
30	**bihōld and ōuersēȝ**=looked down on. **bihōld**=biholden(=to behold, see, look at)의 과거. **ōuersēȝ**=oversen(=to observe, survey)의 과거.
31	**And þuȝte wēl vūle of þāre hūle**=and it seemed to her quite disgusting with regard to the owl=she thought poorly of the owl. **þuȝte**=seemed. 원형은 þinchen. **wēl**=much, quite. **vūle**=foul, disgusting. **þāre**=the,

that. hūle=owl.

32 me hi halt=one considers her=she is considered. me=one, they. me 는 man의 약형이다. hi=her. halt=holden(=to hold, consider)의 현재. lōdlich=loathsome. fūle=foul.

33 Vnwi3t=monster, evil being. cf. un+wi3t(=creature, person). hō=she. sēde=said. 원형은 seggen. awei=away. þū=thou. flō!=fly! 원형은 flēon(=to fly, flee).

34 Mē=me, to me, for me. þe wurs=the worse. þē=thee. sō!=see!. 원형은 sē(o)n.

35 Iwis=certainly, indeed. þīne=thy. vule=foul. lēte=appearance, behavior, expression.

36 Wēl=very, quite. oft=often. mīne=my. forlēte=forlēten(=to leave off, abandon)의 1인칭 단수 현재.

37 Mīn=my. hōrte=hcart. atflīþ=atflēon(=to flee away, go away)의 3인칭 단수 현재. falt=falden(=to fail)의 3인칭 단수 현재. mī=my. 자음 앞에서는 어말의 n이 탈락한다. tunge=speech.

38 Wonne þū art tō mē iþrunge=when you thrust yourself on me. Wonne=when. þū art tō mē iþrunge=you are forced upon me. iþrunge=þringen(=to press)의 과거분사.

39 me lüste bet=it may please me better=I would rather. lüste=listen (=to please)의 가정법 3인칭 단수 현재. spēten=spit. þane=than.

40 Of þīne fūle 3o3elinge=on account of thy foul goggling. Of=because of. fūle=foul. 3o3elinge=yowling, wailing, hooting.

41 þēos=this. abōd=abiden(=to abide, wait, stay, persist)의 3인칭 단수 과거. fort=until. hit=it. ēve=evening. 부엉이는 밤에만 운다.

42 Hō=she=owl. ne~nō=부정의 강조. mi3te=might. 원형은 mai(=be able to, can). nō lēng=no longer. lēng=longer. lange(=long)의 비교급. bilēve=remain (silent), hold back.

43 Vor=for. hōrte=heart. grēt=great, swollen (with anger).

44 wēlnē3=welll-night, almost, nearly. fnast=breath, breathing. atschēt=atsheten(=to pass out, shot out, drive out)의 3인칭 과거.

45 warp=worpen(=to throw out, utter)의 3인칭 단수 과거. wōrd=word, peech. þārafter=afther that, than. lōnge=long, for long time.

46 Hū þincþē þē?=How does it seem to thee=What do you think? Hū=how. þincþē=þincþ+þē=(it) seems to thee. nū=now. bī=of.

47 Wēnst=wēnen(=to think, suppose)의 2인칭 단수 현재. ne=not. cünne=can(=can, to know (how to))의 2인칭 단수 현재.

48 þeȝ=though. wrītelinge=trilling, warbling.

49 Ilōme=often. dēst=dōn(=to do)의 2인칭 단수 현재. grāme=harm, injury, grief.

50 seist mē tōne=speak to insult me. seist=seggen(=to say, tell, speak)의 2인칭 단수 현재. bōþe~and=both~and. tōne=reproach, insult. schāme=shame, disgrace.

51 ȝif=if. hōlde=could hold. hōlden(=to hold)의 가정법 1인칭 단수. on=in, under. uōte=feet.

52 Sō hit betīde þat~=may it so happen. Sō=흔히 기원문과 함께 사용되었다. bitīde=betīden(=to happen)의 가정법 3인칭 단수. mōte=may, might.

53 wēre=would be. ūt=out. rīse=twigs, small branches.

54 scholdest=should. an ōþer wīse=in another way, in a different tune. wīse=manner.

55 ȝaf=gave. 원형은 ȝeve. ansvāre=answer.

56 ȝif ich mē lōkī wit þe bāre=if I protect myself against the open (space)=if I keep myself in my thicket. ȝif=if. lōkī=look, take care, guard. 원형은 lōken. wit(with)=against. bāre=bare, open (space). 여기서는 명사로 사용되었다.

57 schīlde=shield. blēte=exposed, unsheltered (place). 명사로 사용되었다.

58 recche=care, desire. cf. ModE reck. noȝt=not. þrēte=threat.

59 hegge=hedge.

60 segge=may say. seggen(=to say)의 가정법 현재.

61 wōt=witen(=to know)의 단수 현재. þat art=thou art. unmīlde=un+

milde=unmerciful, cruel.

62 Wiþ=against. höm þat ne muʒe=those who cannot. höm=those. ne muʒe=cannot. chīlde=shield.

63 tūkest=tūkien(=to ill-treat, pluck)의 2인칭 단수 현재. wrōþe=angry. cf. ModE *wrath*. uvele(ēvel)=evil.

64 Whār(whēre)=where. 관계부사. miʒt=may. 원형은 mai. smale=small. fuʒele=(fōwle)=birds. cf. G. *Vogel*, ModE *fowl*.

65 Vorþī(forþi)=therefore, because. lōþ al fuel-künne=hateful to all kinds of birds. lōþ=hateful, loathsome. fuel-künne=foul-kind, birds.

66 alle=all. hǒ=they. þē=thee. drīveþ=drive. hönne(heonne)=hence.

67 bischrīcheþ=shriek at, screech around. bigrēdet=scold, cry out at.

68 wēl narewe=very closely. bilēdet=pursue.

69 ēk(eek)=also. forþē=therefore. sülve mōse=the titmouse itself. sülve=self. mōse=titmouse.

70 Hire þonkes=with her will, willingly. Hire=their. þonkes=thought, mind. wolde=would. 원형은 wille. tōtōse=tear in pieces, rip to shreds.

71 lōdlich(lōþlich)=disagreeable, loathly. bihōlde=behold.

72 lōþ=hateful. in monie volde=in many respects. monie=many. vōlde=way.

73 þī=thy. bodi=body. swēore=neck.

74 Grettere is þīn hēued þan þū al=bigger is thy head than thou all=your head is bigger than all of your body. Grettere=bigger, greater. hēued=head.

75 ēʒene(ēʒe, eye)=eye. bǒþ=both. cōl-blake=black as charcoal. brǒde=broad, big.

76 Riʒt swō=just as it. Riʒt=just, rightly, properly. ipeint=painted. 어두의 i는 과거분사를 나타내는 접두사. mid wōde=with woad. woad는 유럽산 대청 및 여기서 추출한 청색 염료.

77 stārest=stare. abīten=bite.

78 mid=with. cliure(cliver)=claw (of a bird). smīten=smite.

79 þī=thy. bile=bill, beak. stif=stiff. scharp=sharp. hōked=hooked.

80 Riȝt sō=just as. ōwel=flesh-hook. crōked=crooked.
81 Þārmid=with which, whith that. clackes=clack. oft and lōnge=often and long.
82 And þat is on of þīne sōnge=and that is all there is in your song.
83 Ac=but. þrētest=threaten. flēshe=flesh.
84 mēshe=crush.
85 Þē wēre icündur tō ōne frogge=it would be more natural to thee in respect of a frog=a frog would suit thee better. Þē=you. icündur=more natural, more akin, more suitable. frogge=frog.
86 mülne=mill. vnder=under. cogge=cog-wheel(바퀴).
87 Snailes=snails. mūs=mouse. fūle=foul. wiȝte=creature, person.
88 cünde(kīnde)=kind, nature. riȝte=just, rightly, properly.

어느 여름날 나는 아주 후미진 골짜기에서 부엉이와 나이팅게일이 대판 논쟁을 벌이는 것을 들었다. 논쟁은 치열하고 격렬하고 맹렬했다. 때로는 점잖고, 사이사이 큰 소리가 나왔다. 서로가 핏대를 세우고 격한 감정을 토로했다. 서로가 상대방이 자기가 알고 있는 최하라고 말했다. 특히 서로의 노래 솜씨에 대해 치열하게 다투었다.

들판 한 모퉁이에서 나이팅게일이 말을 시작했다. 그 새는 갈대와 푸른 사초들이 촘촘히 뒤엉킨 울타리 한 가운데에 많은 꽃으로 둘러 싸인 예쁜 나무 가지 위에 앉아 있었다. 그 새는 나무 가지 때문에 더 즐거워 보였으며, 많은 종류의 노래를 불렀다. 그 노래는 부인할 수 없게 하프와 피리 소리처럼 들렸다. 그것은 목에서 나온 소리라기보다는 하프와 피리에서 나는 소리 같았다.

그 바로 옆에 나무 그루터기 위에서 부엉이가 성무일과를 알리고 있었는데, 부엉이의 숙소인 그 그루터기는 담쟁이덩굴로 뒤덮여 있었다.

나이팅게일이 부엉이를 보았다. 부엉이를 내려다보고 사람들이 부엉이를 싫어하고 더럽다고 생각하기 때문에 나이팅게일도 부엉이가 매우 혐오스럽고 더럽게 생각되었다. 나이팅게일이 말했다. "이 괴물아, 저리 날아가 버려! 보기만 해도 속이 뒤집혀. 네 추한 꼴만 보아도 노래를 못하게 돼. 네 몸을 내게 가까이 대면 내 심장이 뛰쳐나가고 내 혀가 굳어버려. 듣기 싫은 먹마는 소리를 듣고 있노라면 노래를 하느니 차라리 침을 뱉고 싶어져."

부엉이는 저녁이 될 때까지 참고 있었다. 그러나 그는 더 이상 침묵할 수가 없었다. 왜냐하면 그의 심장이 분노에 부풀어 거의 숨이 막힐 지경이었기 때문이다. 그 뒤 한참 만에 한마디 했다. "그래 지금 내 노래 솜씨는 어떠냐? 비록 내가 너처럼 떠는 소리는 못 내지만 그래도 내가 노래할 줄 모른다고는 할 수는 없겠지. 종종 너는 내게 피해를 입혔고, 모욕을 가하고 창피를 줬어. 네가 내 발톱에 붙잡혀 — 제발 그렇게만 되어라 — 가지 위에 있지 못하게 된다면 아마도 네 노래 소리는 달라질 거야."

나이팅게일이 대답했다. "만약 내가 공터로부터 나를 보호하고 노출된 공간으로부터 나를 지킬 수만 있다면 네 협박 따위는 무서워 할 것이 없어. 만약 내가 울타리 안에만 있다면 네가 무슨 말을 하던 나는 상관할 바가 아니야. 나는 네가 스스로를 방어할 수 없는 것들에 대해 잔인하다는 것을 알고 있어. 너는 할 수만 있다면 작은 새들에게 잔인하고 고약하게 고통을 가하지. 그래서 모든 새들이 너를 싫어하고, 그들 모두가 너를 쫓아내고 너에게 소리 지르고 야단치고 또 바싹 추격하는 거야. 그래서 박새마저도 기꺼이 너를 갈기갈기 찢어놓으려고 하는 거야. 너는 보기에도 흉물스럽고, 여러 면에서 징그러워. 네 몸은 작달막하고, 눈은 커다란데다가 마치 물감 칠을 한 듯 숯덩이처럼 까맣지. 네가 누구를 볼 때는 마치 발톱으로 움켜쥘 수 있는 것이면 무엇이든지 물어뜯고 싶어 하는 표정이고, 부리는 딱딱한데다가 날카로워 푸줏간 갈퀴처럼 구부려져 있지. 그 부리로 너는 자주 한참동안이나 울어대지. 네 노래라는 것은 그것 밖에 안돼. 그런데 너는 네 발톱으로 나를 으깨겠다고 내 살에 위협을 가한다. 너에겐 차라리 바퀴 아래 물레방아에 앉아있는 개구리가 더 어울려. 너는 당연히 달팽이, 생쥐, 더러운 짐승들과 한 족속이야."

2. Hauelok The Dane

1   In þat tīme, sō it bifelle,
    Was in þe lōnd of Denemark
    A riche king, and swȳþe stark;
    Þe nāme of him was Birkabeyn.
5   Hē hāvede manī knict and sweyn;
    Hē was fayer man, and wicht,
    Of bodi hē was þe beste knicht
    Þat ēvere micte lēden ūt hēre,
    Or stēde on rīde, or handlen spēre.
10   Þrē children hē hāvede bī his wīf,
    Hē hem lovede sō his līf;
    Hē hāvede a sone and dougtres twō,
    Swīþe fayre, as fēl it sō.
    Hē þat wile nōn forbēre,
15   Riche ne pōvre, king ne kaysēre,
    Dēth him tōk þan hē best wilde
    Liven; but hyse dayes wēre filde,
    Þat hē ne moucte nō mōre live
    For gōld ne silver, ne for nō gyve.
20   Hwan hē þat wiste, rāþe sēnde
    After prēstes fer and hēnde,
    Chanōūnes gōde and monkes bōþe,
    Him for tō wisse and tō rōðe;
    Him for tō hoslen, and for-tō shrīve,
25   Hwīl his bodi wēre on līve.

Hwan hē was hosled and shriven,
His quiste māked and for him gyven,
Hise knictes dēde hē alle site,
For þoru hem hē wolde wite
30 Hwō micte yēme hise children yunge,
Til þat hē kōūþen spēken wiþ tunge;
Spēken and gangen, in horse rīden,
Knictes and sweynes bī here sīden.
Hē spōken þēroffe, and chōsen sōne
35 A riche man þat under mōne,
Was þe trewest þat hē wēnde,
Godard, þe kinges oune frēnde;
And seyden hē mouchte hem best lōke,
Yif þat hē hem undertōke,
40 Til hise sone mouhte bēre
Helm on hēved, and lēden ūt hēre,
In his hand a spēre stark,
And king bēn māked of Denemark.
Hē wēl trowede þat hē seyde,
45 And on Godard handes leyde,
And seyde, 'Hēre bitēche Ī þē
Mīne children alle þrē,
Al Denemark and al mī fē,
Til þat mī sone of ēlde bē.
50 But þat ich wille, þat þōū swēre
On auter and on messegēre,
On þe belles þat men ringes,
On messebōk þe prēst on singes,

þat þōū mīne children shalt wēl yēme,
þat here kin bē ful wēl quēme,
Til mī sone mōwe bēn knicht,
þanne bitēche him þō his richt,
Denemark and þat þērtil lōnges,
Casteles and tūnes, wodes and wōnges.'
Godard stirt up, and swōr al þat
þe king him bad, and siþen sat
Bī the knichtes þat þēr wāre,
þat wēpen alle swīþe sāre
For þe king þat deide sōne.
Jēsu Crīst that mākede mōne
On þe mirke niht tō shīne,
Wite his soule frō hellepīne,
And lēve þat it mōte wone
In hevenerīche with Godes sone.

    Hwan Birkabeyn was leyd in grāve,
þe ērl dēde sōne tāke þe knāve,
Havelok, þat was þe heir,
Swanborow his sister, Helflēd þe tōþer,
And in þe castel dēde hē hem dō,
þēr nōn ne micte hem comen tō
Of here kyn, þēr þei sperd wōre.
þer hē grēten ofte sōre,
Bōþe for hunger and for kōld,
Or hē wēren þrē winter ōld.
Fēblelīke hē gaf hem clōþes, —
Hē ne yaf a note of hise ōþres;

He hem clōþede riht, ne fedde,
Ne hem ne dēde richelīke bedde.
Þanne Godard was sikerlīke
Under God þe mōste swīke
Þat ēvre in ērþe shāped was,
Withūten ōn, þe wike Judas.
Hāve hē þe malisūn tōday
Of alle þat ēvre spēken may!

운문 로망스(poetic romance)의 하나다. 이야기의 무대는 덴마크와 영국이다. 3001행으로 이루어진 시의 줄거리는 덴마크의 왕자 Havelok이 선왕의 당부를 배반한 신하를 피해 영국으로 건너가 역시 간신 때문에 고통을 겪던 Goldgorough와 결혼한 뒤 덴마크로 가서 그곳의 왕이 되고, 다시 영국으로 쳐들어가 그 곳에서도 왕이 된 뒤 60년간이나 잘 다스리고 살았다는 이야기이다. 이 작품 역시 8음절 2행연구(octosyllabic rimed couplet)로 이루어져 시행들이 aabbcc…의 모양으로 운이 맞는다.

● 방언 : North East Midland
● 철자와 발음 : -ch, -cht는 [çt]나 [xt]로 읽어야 한다. 예: knict [kniçt], moucte[muːxtə]. 한편 ōū[uː]는 ou [ou]와 구별해서 발음해야 한다. ch는 [k]나 [tʃ] 어느 하나로 발음되는데, 이 때의 발음은 현대영어의 발음을 참고하면 된다. [g]나 [ʤ] 중 어느 하나로 발음되는 g의 발음도 마찬가지 방법에 의한다. 어두의 ȝ 대신 처음으로 y가 사용되었다.

1   **In þat tīm**=in that time. '그 때'라는 것은 영국의 왕 Athelwold의 딸 Goldborough가 Goldrich의 손에 맡겨진 때를 말한다. **bifelle**= befell, happened.
2   **lōnd**=land.
3   **riche**=powerful, of hihg rank, rich. **swȳþe**=very, greatly. **stark**=stark, strong.
5   **hāvede**=had. **manī**=many. **knict**=knight. **sweyn**=servant.
6   **He was fayer man, and wicht**=He was fayer and wicht man. **fayer**= fair. **wicht**=brave, valiant.
7   **bodi**=body.
8   **micte**=might. **lēden ūt**=lead out. **hēre**=army.
9   **stēde on rīde**=rīde on stēde=ride on steed. **handlen spēre**=handle

	spear.
10	**þrē**=three. **bī his wīf**=by his wife.
11	**hem**=them. **sō his līf**=as his life.
12	**sone**=son. **dougtres twō**=two daughters.
13	**fayre**=fair. **as fēl it sō**=as it happened so. **fēl**=fallen(=to happen)의 과거.
14	**He**=16행의 **Dēth**(=death). **wile nōn**=will not. **forbēre**=forbear(봐주다).
15	**ne~ne**=neither~nor. **Riche ne pōvre**=rich nor poor. **king ne kaysēre**=king nor emperor.
16	**Dēth**=death. **tōk**=took. 원형은 tāken. **þan**=then, when.
16-7	**hē best wilde Liven**=he wished most to live. **hyse**=his의 복수형.
17	**filde**=fulfilled. 원형은 fillen.
18	**þat**=so that. **moucte**=might. 원형은 mai. **nō mōre live**
19	**ne~ne~nō**=neither~nor~nor. **gyve**=gift.
20	**Hwan**=when. **þat**=자기도 죽어야 한다는 사실. **wiste**=knew. 원형은 witen. **rāþe**=quickly. 현대영어의 rather는 이 단어의 비교급.
20-1	**sēnde After**=sent for.
21	**prēstes**=priests. **fer and hēnde**=far and near. **hēnde**=at hand, near.
22	**Chanōūnes**=canons(성당참사회원). **gōde**=good. **monkes**=monks. **bōþe**=both.
23	**wisse**=guide. **rōðe**=counsel, advise.
24	**hoslen**=housel(=to administer, receive the Holy Communion(성체배령)). **shrīve**=shrive(고해를 듣고 면죄를 선언하다).
25-6	**Hwīl his bodi wēre on līve**=while his body was alive. **on līve**=in life, alive.
26	**Hwan hē was hosled and shriven,**
27	**quiste**=bequest(유산), testament(유언). **māked**=made. **gyven**=given.
28	**Hise knictes**=knights. **dēde**=made. 원형은 dōn. **site**=sit.
29	**þoru**(þurȝ)=through. **hem**=them. **wolde wite**=wished to know.
30	**micte**=might. **yēme**=govern, take care of. **hise children yunge**=young.

31 hē(hī)=they. kōūþen=could. 원형은 can. tunge=tongue.
32 gangen=go, walk. in horse rīden,
33 bī=by. here sīden=their sides.
34 Hē=they. þēroffe=thereof. chōsen=chose. 원형은 chēse. sōne=soon, immediately.
35 riche=powerful, or high rank. mōne=moon.
36 trewest=trēwe(=true)의 최상급. þat=앞줄의 þat를 다시 반복한 것. hē wēnde=they thought. wēnde=wēne(=to think)의 과거.
37 oune frēnde=own friend.
38 seyden=said. 원형은 seyen. lōke=look after, take care of.
39 Yif(ȝif)=if. hem=them. undertōke=undertook.
40 bēre=bear, carry.
41 Helm on hēved=helmet on head. lēden ūt hēre=lead out army.
42 spēre stark=strong spear.
43 And king bēn māked of Denemark=and be made king of Denmark.
44 trowede=believed. 원형은 trowen. þat hē seyde=what they said.
45 And on Godard handes leyde=And leyde handes on Godard. leyde=laid. 원형은 leye.
46 Hēre=here. bitēche=deliver, hand over, entrust. þē=to thee.
47 Mīne children alle þrē,
48 al mī fē=all my property, money.
49 Til þat mī sone of ēlde bē=till my son shall be of age. ēlde=age.
50 þat=뒤의 þat와 상관적으로 사용되고 있다. swēre=swear, gear
51 auter=alter. messegēre=mass-gear(미사복).
52 belles=bells. ringes,
53 messebōk=mass-book, missal. þe~on=on which, wherein. prēst=priest.
54 þat=서약의 내용.
55 here kin=their family. quēme=agreeable, pleasing.
56 mōwe bēn knicht=may be a knight. mōwe의 원형은 mai.
57 þanne=then. bitēche=hand over. þō his richt=those rights of his.
58 þērtil=thereto. lōnges=belong.

59	**Casteles**=castles. **tūnes**=towns. **wodes and wōnges**=woods and plains.
60	**stirt up**=started up, jumped up. 원형은 sterte. **and swōr**=swore.
61	**bad**=bade. 원형은 bidden. **siþen**=then, since then.
62	**Bī**=by. **wāre**=were.
63	**Þat**=who. 관계대명사. **wēpen**=wept. **swībe**=very. **sāre**(sōre)=sorely, bitterly.
64	**deide**=died. 원형은 deie. **sōne**=soon.
65	**mākede**=made.
66	**mirke**=dark. **niht**=night. **shīne**=shine.
67	**Wite**=guard. **soule**=soul. **frō**=from. **hellepīne**=the torment of hell.
68	**lēve**=grant, permit. 여기서는 기원을 나타내는 가정법으로 쓰였다. **it**=his soul. **mōte**=might. **wone**=dwell.
69	**heveneriche**=the kingdom of heaven.
70	**was leyd**=was laid. **grāve**=grave.
71	**ērl**=earl=Godard. **dēde⋯tāke**=did seize. **þe knāve**=boy. cf. G. Knabe. 현대영어의 knave는 '악당'의 뜻.
72	**heir**=heir.
73	**þe tōþer**=þet ōþer에서 þet의 말미 t가 뒤의 ōþer에 첨가된 경우.
74	**castel**=castle. **dēde**=put, place. **hē hem dō**,
75	**þēr**=there, where. 여기서는 관계부사.
76	**here**=their. **kyn**=kindred. family. **þēr**=관계부사. **þei**=they. **sperd**=spēren (=to fasten, lock in, imprison)의 과거분사. **wōre**=were.
77	**hē**=they. **sōre**=sorely, bitterly.
78	**for hunger and for kōld**=춥고 배고파서.
79	**Or**=(ēr)=before. **þrē winter**=three years. cf. fortnight, sennight.
80	**Fēblelīke**=feebly, scarcely, wretchedly. **gaf**=gave. **clōþes**=clothes.
81	**yaf a note of**=전혀 개의치 않았다. cf. Chaucer, *Canterbury Tales*, Prologue, 1. 177: "He yaf nat of that text a pulled hen."(=He valued that text not worth a plucked hen.). **ōþres**=oath.
82	**clōþede**=clothed. **riht**=rightly. **fedde**=fed.

83　　**richelīke**=richly. **bedde**=supply with a bed.
84　　**Þanne**=then. **sikerlīke**=surely, certainly.
85　　**swīke**=traitor.
86　　**ēvre**=ever. **in ērþe**=on earth. **shāped**=shaped, created.
87　　**Withūten**=without, except. **ōn,**=one. **wike**=wicked.
88　　**Hāve hē**=let him have. **hāve**는 hāven(=to have)의 가정법으로서 기원을 나타낸다. **hē þe malisūn**=curse, malediction.

이 때 덴마크 땅에는 유력하고 강력한 왕이 있었는데, 그의 이름은 Birkabeyn이었다. 그는 많은 기사와 하인을 데리고 있었다. 그는 잘생기고 용감한 사람이었다. 그의 몸은 지금까지 말을 타고 군대를 이끌고 창을 휘둘렀던 어떤 사람보다도 뛰어났다. 아내에게서 얻은 세 자녀가 있었는데, 그들을 목숨처럼 사랑했다. 그는 한 아들과 두 딸이 있었는데, 애들은 생김새가 뛰어났다. 그런데 부자나 가난한 사람이나, 왕이나 황제를 가리지 않는 주검이 그가 가장 살고 싶어 하는 때에 그를 데리고 갔다. 그의 명이 끝나 금이나 은이나 그 밖에 무슨 선물을 바쳐도 더 이상 살 수가 없었다.

그 같은 사실을 알게 되자 그는 곧 원근 간에 사제들과 착한 참사회원들과 수도사들을 불러 아직도 그의 몸이 살아 있는 동안 그들에게서 자문과 충고를 구하고, 성체를 배령하고 고해를 하고자 하였다. 성체배령과 고해가 끝나고 유산 분배가 끝난 다음, 그는 기사들을 모두 앉히고 기사들 가운데서 애들이 자라나 말을 하게 될 때까지, 말하고 걷고, 기사와 하인들과 함께 말을 타게 될 때까지 돌봐줄 사람을 찾고자 하였다. 그들은 의론한 결과 달 아래 가장 충성스럽다고 생각한 고위직의 신하이며 왕 자신의 친구이기도 한 Godard를 지체 없이 지목하고, 그가 애들을 돌보기만 한다면 아들이 머리에 투구를 쓰고 손에는 강한 창을 들고 군대를 이끌고 덴마크의 왕이 될 때까지 가장 잘 보살필 사람이라고 말했다. 그들의 말을 확실히 믿은 왕은 Godard에게 손을 올려놓고 말했다. "그대에게 세 자녀와 덴마크 전부와 내 모든 재산을 내 아들이 장성할 때까지 맡기네. 그러나 나는 그대가 제단 위에서 미사복에 대고, 사람들이 울리는 종에 대고, 사제가 노래를 부를 때 쓰는 미사 책에 대고, 내 아들이 기사가 되어 그대로부터 자기의 모든 권리와 덴마크와 거기에 속하는 성과 도시와 숲과 평야를 돌려받을 때까지 내 아들을 잘 돌보며, 또 그의 가족이 잘 지낼 수 있게 보살피겠다는 맹서를 해주기

바라네." Godard는 벌떡 일어나 왕이 명한 모든 것을 서약하고, 거기 있던 기사들 옆에 앉았는데, 기사들은 곧 숨을 걷은 왕을 위해 비통하게 울었다. 어두운 밤에 달이 빛나게 하신 예스 그리스도가 그의 영혼을 지켜 지옥의 고통을 받지 않게 하시며, 하늘나라에서 하나님의 아들과 함께 지낼 수 있기를!

Birkabeyn이 무덤에 묻히자 백작은 당장 후계자인 아들 Havelok과 누이동생 Swanborow와 또 다른 누이동생 Helfled를 잡아다 성에 가두고, 그곳에 그의 가족 중 누구도 갈 수 없게 하였다. 애들은 세살이 되기까지 허기와 추위에 심하게 울었다. 백작은 옷도 잘 주지 않았다. 그는 맹서 따위 알기를 우습게 알았다. 그는 애들에게 옷도 잘 주지 않았고, 제대로 먹이지도 않았고, 좋은 침대를 주지도 않았다. 이때의 Godard는 사악한 유다를 제외하고는 이 세상에 태어난 가장 사악한 배반자였다. 그가 오늘날 말할 수 있는 모든 사람의 저주를 받기를!

14th Century

1. The Bruce (The King And The Three Traitors)

1   Swā hapnyt it that, on a day,
    Hē vent till hwnt, for till assay
    Quhat gammyn wes in that cuntrē;
    And sā hapnyt that day that hē
5   Bȳ a vōdē-sȳde tō sette is gāne,
    Vith his twā hūndis hym allāne;
      Bōt he his swērd ay vith hym bēre.
    Hē had bōt schort quhīll syttyn thāre,
    Quhen hē saw frā the vōde cumand
10 Thrē men vith bowis in thār hand,
    That tōward hym cōm spēdelȳ,
    And hē persāvit that in hȳ,
    Be thair effeir and thair hāvyng,
    That thai lufit hym nā kyn thyng.
15 Hē raiss and his leysche till him drew hē,
    And leit his hōūndis gang all frē.
    God help the kyng nōw for his mycht!
    For, bōt hē nōw bē vīss and vicht,
    He sall bē set in mekill press.
20 For thai thrē men, vithōūten less,
    Wār his fayis all ūtrelȳ,
    And had vachit sō besalȳ,

Tō sēn quhen thai vengeans mycht tāk
Of the kyng for Johne Cwmyns sāk,
That thai thoucht than thai lasēr had;
And sen he hym allāne wes stad,
In hȳ thai thoucht thai sulde him slā,
And gif that thai mycht chēviss swā,
Frā that thai the kyng had slayn,
That thai mycht vyn the vōde agayn,
His men, thai thoucht, thai suld nocht dreid.
In hȳ tōwart the kyng thai ȝeid,
And bēnd thair bowis quhen thai vār neir;
And hē, that drēd in grēt maneir
Thair arowis, for hē nākit was,
In hȳ āne spēkyng tō thāme mais,
And said: 'hē aucht tō shāme, perdē,
Syn Ī am āne and ȝhē ār thrē,
For tō schūt at mē on fēr!
Bōt haf ȝhē hardyment, cum nēr
Vith ȝōur swērdis, mē till assay;
Wyn mē on sic vīss, gif ȝhē may;
ȝhē sall weill mair all prīst bē.'
'Perfay,' quod āne than of the thrē,
'Sall nō man say wē drēde thē swā,
That wē vith arrowis sall thē slā.'
With that thair bowis avay thai kest,
And cōm on frast but langar frest.
The kyng thāme met full hardelȳ,
And smāt the first sō rigorōuslȳ,

That hē fell dēd dōun on the greyn.
And quhen the kyngis hōunde has seyn
Thai men assāle his master swā,
Hē lap till āne and can hym tā
55 Richt bā the nek full felonlȳ,
Till top our taill he gert hym lȳ.
And the kyng, that his swērd up had,
Saw hē sō fair succōur hym maid,
Ōr hē that fallyn wes mycht rȳss,
60 Had hym assālȝeit on sic wīss
That hē the bak strāk ēvyn in twā.
The thrid that saw his fallowis swā
Forōuten recoveryng bē slayne.
Tūk till the vōde his vay agāne.
65 Bōt the kyng followit spēdelȳ;
And als the hōund that wes hym bȳ
Quhen hē the man saw gang hym frā,
Schōt till hym soyn, and can hym tā
Richt bē the nek, and till hym dreuch;
70 And the kyng that ves neir eneuch,
In his rīsyng sic rōwt hym gāf,
That stāne-dēd till the ērd hē drāf.
The kyngis menȝe that wār neir,
Quhen at thai saw on sic maneir
75 The kyng assālit sā suddanlȳ,
Thai sped thāme tōward hym in hȳ,
And askit hōw that cass befell.
And hē all hālȳ can thaim tell,

How thai assālȝeit all thrē,
80 'Perfay,' quod thai, 'wē may weill sē
That it is hard till undirtāk
Sic mellyng vith ȝōw for tō māk,
That sō smertlȳ has slayn thir thrē
Forōūten hurt: — 'Perfay,' said hē,
85 'I slew bōt āne forōūten mā,
God and my hōūnd has slāne the twā.
Thair tresōūne cumrit thāme perfay
For richt vicht men alle thrē vār thai.'

북부 방언으로 쓰여진 historical romance이다. 작자는 John Barbour(1320-1395)로서 Aberdeen에서 부주교(archdeacon)를 지낸 사람이다. 1375년에 쓰여졌고 총 20권 13,549행으로 이루어진 이 작품은 Bannockburn의 영웅 Robert Bruce(1274-1329)의 일대기를 다룬 것으로서 스코틀랜드 문학의 효시이다. 이 시 또한 8음절 2행연구(octosyllabic rimed couplet)의 모양을 갖추고 있다.

- 방언 : Northern
- 철자 : 모음 뒤의 i나 y는 해당 모음이 장모음임을 나타내기 위한 것이다. 예: maid[mɑːd], weill[weːl], soyn[soːn].
  v와 w는 구별없이 사용되었다. 예: vent=went, vith=with.
  ch는 다른 방언에서의 ȝ나 gh를 나타낸다.
  예: mycht=might, nocht=noght.
  한편 quh-는 wh- 대신으로 사용되었다. 예: quhen=when.
  중복자음은 무성음임을 나타낸다. 예: effer[efər]
- 문법 : -is, -ys는 복수, 소유격, 3인칭 단수 현재를 나타낸다. 한편 -it와 -yt는 과거와 과거분사를 나타낸다.
  3인칭의 대명사는 다음과 같다. 예: thai=they. thār/thair=their. thāme/thaim=them(여격).
- 어휘 : 북부와 스코틀랜드의 방언의 어휘가 보인다.
  예: till(=to), sic(=such), but(=but), forouten(=without), gang(=go).

1   **Swā hapnyt it that**=so it happened that.
2   **Hē**=Bruce. 이야기의 무대는 1307년이다. **vent**=went. **till**=to. **hwnt**=hunt. **for till assay**=in order to try.
3   **Quhat**=what. **gammyn**=game. **cuntrē**=country.
4   **sā**(sō)=so.
5   **vōdē-sȳde**(wōde-sīde)=woodside. **sette**=set, be seated. **gāne**=gone. 원형은 gān.

6	**Vith**=with. **twā hūndis**=two hounds. **hym allāne**=alone by himself.
7	**Bōt**=but. **swērd**=sword. **ay**=always. **vith**=with. **bēre**=bear, carry.
8-9	**Hē had bōt schort quhīll syttyn thāre Quhen~**=he had only a short while sat there, when~. **schort**=short. **quhīll**=while. **syttyn**=sat.
9	**Quhen**=when. **frā the vōde**=from the wood. **cumand**=coming. -and는 현재분사 어미. 현대영어의 -ing과 같다. 원형은 comen.
10	**bowis**=bows. **in thār hand**=in their hands.
11	**spēdelȳ**=speedily.
12	**persāvit**=perceived. 원형은 persāve. **in hȳ**=in haste, soon. 북부 방언에서 흔히 쓰이는 용법으로서 별 뜻 없이 쓰이는 경우가 많다.
13	**Be(bī)**=by. **thai**=their. **effeir**=demeanor, attitude. **and thair hāvyng**=behavior, demeanor.
14	**That thai**=they. **lufit**=loved. **nā kyn thyng**=in no way whatsoever.
15	**raiss**=rose. 원형은 rīse. **leysche**=leash. **drew**=drew. 원형은 drawe.
16	**leit**=let. **hōūndis**=hounds. **gang**=go. **all frē**=free.
17	**God help**=may God help. **the kyng nōw for his mycht**=might.
18	**bōt**=unless. **vīss**(wīse)=wise. **vicht**(wicht)=brave, valiant.
19	**in mekill press**=the condition of being hard pressed. **mekill**(mikel)=big, great, much. **press**=condition of being hard pressed, danger.
20	**vithōūten less**=without lie, truly. 별 깊은 뜻 없이 사용되는 구이다.
21	**fayis**(fō)=foes. **ūtrelȳ**=utterly.
22	**vachit**(wachit)=watched. 원형은 wacche. **besalȳ**=busily.
23	**Tō sēn**=to see. **quhen**(whan)=when. **vengeans**=vengeance. **mycht tāk**=might take.
24	**for Johne Cwmyns sāk**=for John Comyn's sake=Bokk II에 의하면 1306년에 Bruce가 왕위에 오르기 얼마 전에 Dumfries의 Franciscan 파의 교회 제단 앞에서 John Comyn을 찔러 죽인 일이 있었다. **sāk**=sake.
25	**thoucht**=thought. **than**=then. **lasēr**=leisure, opportunity.
26	**sen**=since. **allāne**=alone. **stad**=placed (in peril).

27	**In hȳ**=in haste. 12생의 주 참조. **sulde him slā**=should slay him.
28	**And gif**=if. **mycht chēviss swā**=could so succeed.
29	**Frā that**=from the time that.
30	**vyn**=(wyn)=win, gain. **vōde**=wood. **agayn**=again.
31	**thai thoucht**=they thought. 삽입절, **suld nocht dreid**=should not dread. 목적어는 문두의 his men.
32	**In hȳ**=in haste. **tōwart**=toward. **the kyng thai ʒeid**=went. gōn(=to go)의 과거.
33	**bēnd**=bend. **thair bowis**=their bows. **quhen thai vār neir**=when they were near.
34	**that drēd in grēt maneir**=who dreaded greatly.
35	**Thair arowis**=their arrows. **nākit**=naked=unarmed.
36	**āne spēkyng tō thāme mais**=makes a discourse to them. **spēkyng**=speaking, discourse. **mais**=māke(=to make)의 3인칭 단수 현재.
37	**ʒhē aucht tō shāme**=you ought to be ashamed. **perdē**–by God, indeed. cf. OF. par(=by)+dē(=God).
38	**Syn**=since.
39	**tō schūt at mē on fēr**=to shoot at me afar. **fēr**=far, afar.
40	**Bōt**=but. **haf ʒhē**=if you have. **hardyment**=courage, boldness. **cum nēr**=come near.
41	**Vith ʒōūr swērdis**=with your swords. **mē till assay**=to attack me. **till**=to.
42	**Wyn**=win. **on sic vīss**=in such wise. **gif ʒhē may**=if you can.
43	**ʒhē sall weill mair all prīst bē**=you shall be well all the more prised. **weill**=well. **mair**(mōre)=more. **prīst**=prīse(=to praise)의 과거분사.
44	**Perfay**=by faith. **quod**=quēthen(=to sasy, speak)의 과거. **āne than of the thrē**=one of the three.
45	**Sall nō man say**=no man sahll say. **wē drēde thē swā**=we so dread thee.
45-6	**swā~That**=such~that.

46 slā=slay.
47 thair bowis avay thai kest=they cast their bows away.
48 but langar frest=without more delay.
49 thāme=them. met full hardelȳ=met them full boldly, firmly.
50 smāt=smote. rigorōuslȳ=rigorously.
51 dēd=dead. dōūn=down. on the greyn=on the green.
52 seyn=seen.
53 Thai men assāle his master swā=those men assail his master.
54 lap=lēpen(=to leap)의 과거. till āne=to one.
can hym tā=did take him. can(gan)=ginne(=begin)의 단수 과거형이지만 여기서처럼 조동사로 쓰이는 경우가 많다. tā(tāken)=take.
55 Richt bā the nek=right by the neck. full felonlȳ=full cruelly.
56 Till=till. top our taill=head over tail=head over heels, upside down. our=over. he gert hym lȳ=he made him lie. gert=gēr(=to make)의 과거.
57 that his swērd up had=who held up his sword.
58 hē sō fair succōūr hym maid=God made him so fair succour.
59 Ōr(ēr)=before. hē that fallyn wes mycht rȳss=he who was fallen could rise.
60 assālȝeit=assailed. on sic wīss=in such wise.
61 hē the bak strāk ēvyn in twā=that he struck the back just in two. ēvyn=even.
62 thrid=third. fallowis=fellows.
63 Forōūten recoveryng=without recovering. bē slayne=be slain.
64 Tūk=took. till the vōde=to the wood. vay=way. agāne=again.
65 Bōt=but.
66 als(alsō)=also. the hōūnd that wes hym bȳ=the hound that was by him.
67 Quhen hē the man saw gang hym frā=Quhen hē saw the man gang frā hym=when he saw the man go away from him.
68 Schōt=rushed. till hym=to him. soyn(sōne)=soon, immediately. can

	hym tā=did take him.
69	**Richt bē the nek**=right by the neck. **till hym dreuch**=drew to him.
70	**that ves neir eneuch**=who was near enough.
71	**In his rīsyng**=in his rising. **sic rōwt hym gāf**=gave such a stroke. **rōwte**=heavy blow or stroke.
71-2	**sic~That**=such~that.
72	**stāne-dēd till the ērd**=stone-dead to the earth. **ērd**=earth, ground. **hē drāf**=he fell.
73	**menʒe**=men, company of followers, army, host. **that wār neir**=who were near.
74	**Quhen at**=when that, when. **on sic maneir**=in such a manner.
74-5	**saw~The kyng assālit**=saw the king assailed.
75	**sā suddanlȳ**=so suddenly.
76	**sped thāme**=sped themselves. **in hȳ**=in haste.
77	**askit**=asked. **hōw that cass befell**=how that case befell.
78	**hālȳ**=wholly. **can thaim tell**=did tell them.
79	**Hōw thai assālʒeit all thrē**=how they assailed him, all three.
80	**Perfay**=by faith. **weill**=well. **sē**=see.
81	**till undirtāk**=to undertake.
82	**Sic mellyng**=such meeting, fight. **vith ʒōw**=with you. **for tō māk**=make.
83	**smertlȳ**=quickly, suddenly. **thir**=these.
84	**Forōūten hurt**=without hurt.
85	**I slew bōt āne**=I slew but one. **forōūten mā**=without more.
87	**tresōūne**=treason. **cumrit thāme perfay**=annoyed them, indeed. cumrit =cummrt(=to bother, annoy)의 과거.
88	**For richt vicht men alle thrē vār thai**=For thai alle thrē men vār richt vicht=because they were just valiant men, all three. **vicht** (wicht)=brave, valiant.

어느 날 그는 그 고장에 어떤 사냥감이 있는지 알아볼 겸 사냥을 하기위해 갔다. 그날은 두 마리의 사냥개를 데리고 숲가에 혼자 앉아있게 되었다. 그러나 칼은 늘 갖고 있었다.

앉아 있은 지 얼마 안 돼 세 남자가 손에 활을 들고 숲으로부터 그에게로 잰 걸음으로 다가오고 있는 것을 보았다. 그는 그들의 태도나 행동으로 보아 절대로 그를 좋아하는 사람들이 아니라는 것을 알았다. 그는 일어나서 끈을 당겨 사냥개들을 모두 풀어놓았다. 신이여 온 힘을 다해 그를 도우소서! 왜냐면 그가 현명하고 용감하지 못하다면 그는 엄청난 위험에 처할 것이기 때문이다. 그것도 그럴 것이 이들 세 사람은 어김없는 그의 원수들이었고, John Comyn을 위해 복수할 날을 손꼽아 기다려 왔던 참이었고, 지금 그 기회가 왔다고 생각하고 있던 참이었다. 그리고 그가 지금 혼자만 있으므로 지체 없이 그를 죽여야 하고, 성공하는 날에는 숲 전체를 다시 손에 넣을 수 있다고 생각하고 있었다. 그들이 서둘러 왕에게로 달려가 가까이에 이르자 시위를 당겼다. 무장을 하고 있지 않아 그들이 몹시 두려웠던 왕은 그들에게 말을 건넸다. '맙소사, 자네들은 셋씩이나 되면서 혼자 있는 나를 멀리서 쏘겠다니 부끄러운 줄도 모르는가. 만약 자네들에게 용기가 있다면 칼을 들고 내 가까이에 와 나를 치게나. 할 수 있다면 그렇게 한번 해봐. 그러면 훨씬 더 칭송을 받을 거야.' 셋 중 하나가 말했다. '누가 있어 두려움에 우리가 그대를 활로 죽인다고 하겠는가.' 그 말과 더불어 그들은 활을 내려놓고 지체 없이 재빨리 달려 왔다. 왕은 용감하게 그들과 맞서 첫 번째 녀석을 아주 세차게 내려쳐서 풀 위에 쓰러져 죽게 했다. 그리고 왕의 사냥개가 이들이 자기 주인을 공격하는 것을 보았을 때 한 녀석에게로 달려가 잔인하게 그의 목덜미를 한 입 물어 꼬꾸라지게 했다. 왕은 넘어졌던 녀석이 일어나기 전에 그의 등을 쳐 두 쪽을 내고는 신이 그를 공정하게 도와주고 있다는 것을 알았다. 자기 동료들이 회복할 수 없게 살육당하는 것을 본

마지막 녀석은 숲으로 도망갔다. 그러나 왕은 재빨리 그를 뒤쫓아 갔으며, 마찬가지로 옆에 있던 사냥개도 그 사내가 도망가는 것을 보자 급히 그에게 달려가서 바로 목덜미를 물어 자기에게로 끌어 당겼다. 그러자 바로 옆에 있던 왕이 일어나면서 그에게 하도 강력한 일격을 가한 나머지 그는 땅 위에 돌처럼 쓰러져 죽었다. 그처럼 갑작스럽게 자기들 임금님이 공격당하는 것을 본 근처에 있던 왕의 부하들은 그에게로 달려와 사건의 전말을 물었다. 왕은 셋이 자기를 공격하게 된 자초지종을 말해 주었다. 그들이 말했다. '사실 세 사람을 스스로는 상처 하나 없이 도륙한 임금님에게 감히 맞선다는 것은 무모한 짓이라는 것을 알겠습니다.' 그러나 왕이 말했다. '사실은 내가 죽인 것은 더도 말고 한 녀석뿐이네. 신과 내 사냥개가 나머지 둘을 죽였다네. 그들 셋은 단지 용감한 사람들이었으므로 사실 그들의 반역은 그들을 괴롭혔던 거네.'

2. John of Treuisa's Translation of Ranulf Hidgen's Polychronicon

As hyt ys yknowe hōū3 menȳ manēr pēople būþ in þis ȳlōnd, þēr būþ also of sō menȳ pēople lōngāges and tonges; nōþelēs Walschmen and Scottes, þat būþ no3t ymelled wiþ ōþer nāciōns, hōldeþ wēl ny3 here fūrste lōngāge and spēche, bote 3ef Scottes þat wēre som tȳme confederat and wonede wiþ þē Pictes drawe somwhat after here spēche. Bote þē Flemmynges, þat woneþ in þē west sȳde of Wāles, habbeþ yleft here strānge spēche and spēkeþ Saxonlȳch ynow. Alsō Englysch men, þey3 hȳ hadde fram þē bygynnyng þrē manēr spēche, sōūþeron, norþeron, and myddel spēche, in þē myddel of þē lōnd, as hȳ cōme of þrē manēr pēople of Germānia, nōþelēs, bȳ commyxstiōn and mellyng fūrst wiþ Dānes and afterward wiþ Normans, in menȳe þē contray lōngāge ys apeyred, and som useþ strānge wlaffyng, chyteryng, harryng and garryng, gristittyng. Þis apeyryng of þē būrþtonge ys bycause of twey þinges. Ōn ys, for chyldern in scole, a3ēnes þē usāge and manēre of al ōþer nāciōns, būþ compelled for tō lēve here oune lōngāge and for tō construe here lessōns and here þinges ā Freynsch, and habbeþ sūþthe þē Normans cōme fūrst intō Engelōnd. Alsō gentilmen children būþ ytau3t for tō spēke Freynsch fram tȳme þat ā būþ yrokked in here crādel, and conneþ spēke and playe wiþ a cīld hys brouch; and uplōndysch men wol lȳkne hamsylf tō gentilmen, and fōndeþ wiþ grēt bysȳnes for tō Freynsch for tō bē mōre ytōld of.

þys manēre was moche yused tōfōre þe fŭrste moreyn, and ys seþthe somdēl ychaunged. For Jōhan Cornwal, a mayster of gramēre, chayngede þē lōre in gramērscōle and construcciōn of Freynsch intō Englysch; and Richard Pencrych lurnede þat manēre tēchyng of hym, and ōþer men of Pencrych, sō þat nōw̄, þē ȝēr of ōūre Lōrd a þōūsond þrē hondred foure scōre and fȳfe, of þē secunde Kyng Richard after þē conquest nȳne, in al þe gramērscōles of Engelōnd childern lēveþ Frensch and construeþ and lurneþ an Englysch, and habbeþ þērbȳ avauntāge in ōn sȳde and desavauntēge yn anōþer. Here avauntāge ys, þat ā lurneþ here gramēr yn lasse tȳme þan childern wēr ywoned tō dō; disavauntāge ys, þat nōw̄ childern of gramērscōle conneþ nō mōre Frensch þan can here lift heele, and þat ys harm for ham and ā scholle passe þē sē and travayle in strānge lōndes, and in menȳ caas alsō. Alsō gentilmen habbeþ nōw̄ moche yleft for tō tēche here childern Frensch.

Hyt sēmeþ a grēt wondur hōū Englysch, þat ys þē bŭrþtonge of Englysch men and here oune lōngāge and tonge, ys sō dȳvers of sōūn in þis ȳlōnd; and þē lōngāge of Normandȳ ys comlying of anōþer lōnd, and haþ ōn manēr sōūn among al men þat spēkeþ hyt aryȝt in Engelōnd. Nōþelēs, þēr ys as menȳ dȳvers manēr French yn þē rēm of Fraunce as ys dȳvers manēre Englysch in þē rēm of Engelōnd.

Alsō, of þē forseyde Saxon tonge, þat ys dēled ā þrē and ys abyde scarslȳsch wiþ fēaw uplōndysch men, and ys grēt wondur; for men of þē ēst wiþ men of þē west, as hyt wēre undur þē sāme partȳ of hevene, acordeþ mōre in

sōūnyng of spēche þan men of þē norþ wiþ men of þē
⁵⁵ sōūþ. Þērfōre hyt ys þat Mercii, þat būþ men of myddel
Engelōnd, as hyt wēre partenērs of þē ēndes, understōndeþ
betre þē sȳde lōngāges, norþeron and sōūþeron, þan norþeron
and sōūþeron understōndeþ eyþer ōþer.

Al þē lōngāge of þē Norþhümbres, and specialȳch at
⁶⁰ Ʒork, ys sō scharp, slyttying and frōtyng and unschāpe, þat
wē sōūþeron men may þat lōngāge unnēþe understōnde. Ȳ
trowe þat þat ys bycause þat ā būþ nūʒ tō strānge men and
āliens þat spēkeþ strāngelȳch, and alsō bycause þat þē
kynges of Engelōnd woneþ alwey fer fram þat contray; for
⁶⁵ ā būþ mōre yturnd tō þē sōūþ contray, and ʒef ā gōþ tō þē
norþ contray ā gōþ wiþ grēt help and strengthe. Þē cause
whȳ ā būþ mōre in þē sōūp contray þan in þē norþ may bē
betre cōrnlōnd, mōre pēople, mōre nōble cytēs, and mōre
profytāble hāvenes.

이 작품은 본래 Chester의 수도승이었던 Ranulf Higden이 라틴 어로 썼던 *Polychronicon*(=the chronicle of many ages(『만국사』))를 John Trevisa가 번역한 것이다. Higden(1364 사망)은 Chester의 한 사원의 베네딕트 수도승으로서, 창세기부터 1327년까지의 역사를 라틴어로 썼는데, 이것이 대 성공을 거두어 두 번씩이나 영어로 번역되었다. 그 중 하나가 여기 인용한 Trevisa의 번역으로서 1387년의 번역으로 알려져 있다. 번역자인 Trevisa는 Cornwall 출신으로서 Oxford 대학의 Exeter College의 fellow를 거쳐 Berkeley의 교구목사(vicar)를 지냈던 사람이다.

● 방언 : 남서지방의 Gloucestershire([glɔ́stəʃə]) 방언.
● 문법 : hī(=they) 대신 흔히 사용되던 hā외에 ā가 사용되었다. 여기서도 과거분사는 항산 접두사 y-와 함께 쓰이고 있다.

1 **hyt**=it. **ys**=is. **yknowe**=known. 원형은 knowen. **hōū3**=how. **manēr**= manner, kind. **būþ**=are. **bēn**(=to be)의 3인칭 복수 현재. **þis**=this.

2 **ȳlōnd**=island. cf. OE. īġland[i:yland]. **þēr būþ**=there are. **lōngāges**= languages. **tonges**=tongues.

3 **nōþelēs**=nevertheless. **Walschmen**=the Welsh. **Scottes**=the Scotch. **þat**=that, who. 관계대명사. **no3t**=not. **ymelled**=mellen(=to mix, mingle)의 과거분사. 어두의 y은 고대영어 ġe-의 잔재로서 과거분사를 나타내는 접두사. **wiþ**=with.

4 **ōþer**=other. **nāciōns**=nations. **hōldeþ**=holden(=to hold)의 3인칭 복수. **wēl ny3**= well-nigh, almost. **wel**=well. **ny3**=nigh. **here**=their. **hī**(=they)의 속격. **fürste**=first. **spēche**=speech.

5 **bote 3ef**=except that. **bote**=but. **3ef**=if. **þat**=that, who. **wēre**=were. **som**=some. **tȳme**=time. **confederat**=confererated, allied. **wonede**=wonen (=to live, inhabit)의 과거분사.

6 **þē**=the. **Pictes**=Picts. **drawe after**=imitate. **drawe**=drawen (to draw)

의 3인칭 과거 복수.

7　**Flemmynges**=Flemings. **woneþ**=live, inhabit. **sȳde**=side. **Wāles**=Wales. **habbeþ**=have.

8　**yleft**=leven(=to lease)의 과거분사. **spēkeþ**=speak. **Saxonlȳch**=in the Saxon fashion. **ynow**=enough. **Alsō**=also, equally, similarly.

9　**þeyȝ**=though, just because. **hȳ**=they. **hadde**=had. **fram**=from. **þrē**=three.

10　**sōūþeron**=southern. **norþeron**=northern. **myddel**=middle.

11　**lōnd**=land. **cōme of**=derive from, originate in. **cōme**=came. **of Germānia**=from Germany.

12　**commyxstiōn**=intermingling. **mellyng**=mellen(=to mix, mingle)의 현재분사. **Dānes**=the Danes. 9세기에 영국을 침략한 Vikings를 지칭한다.

13　**afterward**=afterwards, after that. **Normans**=the Normans. **in menȳe**=in general. **contray**=country.

14　**apeyred**=apeiren(=to deteriorate)의 과거분사. **som**=some people. **useþ**=use. **wlaffyng**=stammering, indistinc speech. **chyteryng**=chattering. **harryng**=snarling.

15　**garryng**=grating. **gristittyng**=grinding of teeth. **apeyryng**=deterioration, impairment. **būrþtonge**=birth-tongue, native speech.

16　**bycause of**=becasue of. **twey**=two. **Ōn**=one. **for**=for, because. **chyldern**=children. **scole**=school. **aȝēnes**=against.

17-8　**for tō lēve**=to leave.

18　**oune**=own. **construe**=construe, interpret. **here lessōns**=their lessons.

19　**ā**=in. **Freynsch**=French. **habbeþ**=have. **süþthe**=since.

20　**cōme**=came. **gentilmen children**=gentlemen's children.

21　**ytauȝt**=taught. **for tō spēke**=to speak. **fram tȳme þat**=from the time when. **ā**=they. **hȳ**(=they)의 약형. **yrokked**=rocked.

22　**crādel**=cradle.

22-3　**conneþ**=know. **playe**=play. **cīld hys brouch**=child's brooch=child's toy. 이른바 his-속격의 예. 명사 뒤에 속격의 대명사를 사용하여

해당 명사를 속격으로 만드는 이와 같은 용법은 고대영어와 중세영어에서 뿐만 아니라 초기 현대영어에서도 흔히 볼 수 있는 용법이다.

23　**uplōndysch**=countrified, rustic. **wol**=will. **lȳkne**=liken, make~like. **hamsylf**=themselves.

24　**fōndeþ**=try, test, examine. **wiþ grēt bysȳness**=very diligently. **bysȳnes**=business, industry.

24-5　**for tō bē mōre ytōld of**=in order to be thought of, to be taken account of.

25　**ytōld**=tellen(=to consider, regard, account)의 과거분사.

26　**þys manēre**=this fashion. 여기서부터는 Higden의 기술에 대한 Trevisa의 논평이다. **moche**=much. **yused**=used. **tōfōre**=before. **fürste moreyn**=the first plague. 1348-49 사이에 유행했던 페스트를 말한다. 제2차 전염병은 1361-2, 제3차는 1369, 제4차는 1375-6년에 있었다. **fürste**=first. **moreyn**=plague.

27　**seþthe**=since then. **somdēl**=somewhat. **ychaunged**=chaungen(=to 과거분사. **Jōhan Cornwal**-그 이름으로 보아 작자인 Trevisa나 32행의 Richard Pencrych와 마찬가지로 Cornwall 사람이다. **mayster**=master, teacher.

28　**gramēre**=grammar. **chayngede**=changed. **þē**=the. **lōre**=(method of) teaching. **gramērscōle**=grammar school. **construcciōn**=construction, interpretation.

29　**Freynsch**=French. **lurnede**=learned.

30　**manēre**=of manner, of kind. **tēchyng**=teaching. **of**=from.

31　**ʒēr**=year. **a**=one. **þōūsond**=thousand. **þrē**=three. **hondred**=hundred. **foure scōre**=eighty. **scōre**=score.

32　**secunde**=second. **Kyng Richard**=Richard the Second(1377-99). **conquest**=conquest. 여기서는 Richard II세가 즉위한 것을 가리킨다. **nȳne**=nine.

33　**lēveþ**=leave, cease.

34　**construeþ**=construe, interpret. **an**=in. **þērbȳ**=thereby, by that, on that account. **avauntāge**=advantage.

35   **in ōn sȳde**=on one side. **desavauntēge**=disadvantage. **yn anōþer**=on another (side). **Here**=their.

36   **þat**=that. **ā**=they. **lasse**=less. **þan**=than. **wēr**=were.

37   **ywoned**=wont, accustomed.

38   **conneþ**=know. **nō mōre~þan**=no more~than. **can**=knows. 주어는 lift heele(=their left heel). **lift**=left. **heele**=heel.

39   **harm**=harm, damage, bad fortune. **ham**=them. **and**=if, in case. **ā scholle passe þē sē**=in case they should cross the Channel. **scholle**=should. **þē sē**=the sea=the English Channel.

40   **travayle**=travel. **strānge**=strange. foreign. **lōndes**=lands. **caas**=cases, circumstances.

41   **moche**=much. **yleft**=leven(=to leave)의 과거분사. **childern**=to teach their children.

43   **sēmeþ**=seems. **grēt**=great. **wondur**=wonder. **hōū**=how. **bürþtonge**=birth-tongue.

44   **oune**=own.

45   **dȳvers**=diverse, different. **of**=in. **sōūn**=sound. **ȳlōnd**=island.

46   **comlying**=foreigner, intruder, stranger. **of**=from. **haþ**=has. **ōn manēr**=of one manner. **manēr**=of manner.

47   **spēkeþ**=speak. **arȝʒt**=aright, rightly. **Nōþelēs**=nevertheless. **þēr ys**=there is.

48   **menȳ dȳvers manēr**=many diverse kinds of. **rēm**=realm. **of**=of, as to, with regard to.

50   **forseyde**=aforesaid. **dēled**=delen(=to divide)의 과거분사. **ā þrē**=into three.

51   **ys abyde**=has survived. **abyde**=abiden(=to abide)의 과거분사. **scarslȳsch**=scarcely. **wiþ**=with. **fēaw**=few. **uplōndysch**=countrified, rustic.

52   **ēst**=east.

52-3 **as hyt wēre**=as it were.

53   **partȳ**=part. **hevene**=heaven. **acordeþ**=be in accord, fall into an agreement.

54 sōūnyng=pronunciation. spēche=speech. þan=than. norþ=north. sōūþ=south.
55 þērfōre=therefore. Mercii=Mercians. myddel=middle.
56 partenērs=partners, partakers, one who shares certain qualities or traits. ēndes=ends. understōndeþ=understand.
57 betre=better. sȳde lōngāges=a side language spoken in an adjacent area.
58 eyþer ōþer=each other.
59 Norþhümbres=the people of Northumbria. specialȳch=specially.
60 ʒork=York. scharp=sharp, harsh. slyttying=slitting, piercing. frōtyng=grating, grinding. unschāpe=unformed, unpleasant. sōūþeron men=Southern men. we와 동격. unnēþe=hardly, with difficulty.
62 trowe=believe. bycause þat=becasue. 이때의 þat는 별 뜻이 없다. ā=they. nūʒ= nigh, near. strănge=strange, foreign.
63 āliens=aliens, strangers. spēkeþ=speak. străngelȳch=strangley.
64 woneþ=live. alwey=always. fer=far. contray=country.
65 ā=they. yturnd–inclined to, fond of. ʒef=if. gōþ=go.
66 help=help. 여기서는 military aid, military force, reinforcements의 뜻. strengthe=strength. cause=cause.
68 cōrnlōnd=corn-land, wheat-land. nōble=noble, great, splendid. cytēs=cities.
69 profytāble=profitable. hāvenes=havens, harbors, ports.

이 땅에 많은 민족들이 살고 있듯이 말과 언어도 많다는 것은 잘 알려져 있다. 다른 민족과 섞이지 않았던 웨일즈인과 스코트 사람들은 거의 자신들의 처음 말과 언어를 간직하고 있으나, 한동안 픽트족과 어울려 살았던 스코틀랜드인들은 어느 정도 그들의 말을 본받게 되었다. 그러나 웨일즈 서쪽에 사는 플랑드르 사람들은 그들 본래의 낯선 말을 버리고 이제는 제법 색슨 어를 잘 한다. 또한 영국 사람들은 본래 독일에서 따로 살던 세 민족으로서 이들도 처음에는 남부 어와 북부 어, 그리고 땅 한 가운데에선 중부 어를 사용하였다. 그러나 처음에는 덴마크인들과, 그리고 나중에는 노르웨이인들과 혼합하고 융합함으로서, 이 땅의 언어는 전반적으로 망가지게 되고, 어떤 사람들은 이상한 말을 더듬고, 씨부렁거리거나, 재잘거리거나, 으르렁거리거나, 거슬리는 소리를 내거나, 이가는 소리를 낸다. 이렇게 언어가 타락하는데 에는 두 가지 원인이 있다. 그 하나는 학교에 다니는 어린애들이 노르만인들이 영국 땅에 온 이래로 그들 본래의 말을 버리고, 지금 배우는 내용과 사물들을 프랑스어로 번역하는 것을 강요받고 있기 때문이다. 동시에 양반가의 자식들은 요람 속에서 말을 시작하고 애들 장난감을 가지고 놀 때부터 프랑스어를 말하도록 교육을 받는다. 그리고 시골 사람들은 양반 흉내를 내서 남에게 대접받을 수 있도록 프랑스어를 하기 위해 매우 열심히 노력한다.

　　1차 흑사병이 돌 때까지는 대개 이런 식이었으나 그 뒤로는 사정이 좀 달라졌다. 왜냐하면 문법 선생님이신 John Cornwall이 초등학교에서 문법을 가르치는 방법과 프랑스어를 영어로 번역하는 법을 바꿨기 때문이다. Richard Pencrych가 그에게서 가리킴을 받았고, 그 뒤에 다른 사람들이 Pencrych에게서 배웠기 때문이다. 그리하여 2세께서 즉위하신지 9년째 되는 오늘날 1385년에는 초등학교의 모든 학생들이 프랑스어를 그만두고 영어로 배우고 영어로 번역한다. 그런데 이것은 이점과 단점을 가지고 있다. 이점이란 애들이 보통 배우는 것보다 더 빨리 문법을 배운다는 사실이고, 단점은 애들이 자기들이 신고 다니는 신발 왼짝보다도 더 프랑스어를 모른다는 사실이다. 이것은 그들이 해협을 건너 외국 땅으로 여행을 가거나 그 밖의 많은 경우에 손해가 된다. 지금은 많은 양반들마저도 애들이 프랑스어 배우는 것을 그만두게 했다.

영국 사람들의 모국어이고 그들 자신의 말이고 언어인 이 땅의 영어가 그처럼 발음이 다양하다는 것은 놀랍게 보인다. 노르망디의 언어는 다른 땅에서 수입해 온 말인데도 영국에서 이 말을 바르게 사용하는 사람들은 한 가지 발음으로 말한다. 그러나 프랑스 땅에서는 영국에서와 마찬가지로 다양한 프랑스어를 들을 수 있다.

또한 세 가지 방언을 가지고 있는 앞서 말한 색슨 어에 대해 말하자면, 몇몇 시골 사람들을 제외하고는 거의 남아나지 않다는 것은 참으로 놀랄 일이다. 왜냐하면 이른바 같은 하늘 아래 있는 동쪽에 사는 사람들과 서쪽에 사는 사람들의 발음이 북쪽에 사는 사람의 발음과 남쪽에 사는 사람들의 발음보다 더 가깝기 때문이다. 그리하여 영국 한 가운데서 양쪽의 파트너처럼 존재하는 머시아어가 북쪽 사람과 남쪽 사람들이 직접 상대를 이해하는 것보다 더 잘 그들을 이해할 수 있다.

노덤브리언인들이 쓰는 모든 말, 특히 그 가운데서도 요크 어는 너무 날카롭고 째는 듯하고 귀에 거슬리며 불쾌하게 들린다. 그리하여 우리 남쪽 사람들은 그들의 말을 거의 알아듣지 못한다. 그 까닭은 그들이 알지 못할 말을 사용하는 외국 사람이나 이방인과 거의 한가지이며, 영국의 왕들이 항상 그 고장으로부터 먼 곳에 살았기 때문이라고 생각한다. 그리하여 왕들은 보다 남쪽 말에 익숙해졌기 때문이다. 그들이 북쪽에 갈 때에는 많은 대군을 몰고 간다. 왕들이 북쪽보다 남쪽에 더 많이 있는 것은 남쪽에 곡식이 더 많고, 사람과 멋진 도시, 그리고 보다 수익이 많이 나는 항구가 많기 때문이다.

3. Wicliff's Bible

The Lord's Prayer (MATTHEW vi. 9-13)

1   Oure fadir that art in heuenes, halewid be thi name; thi kyngdoom come to; be thi wille don in erthe as in heuene; ȝyue to vs this dai oure breed ouer othir substaunce; and forȝyue to vs oure dettis, as we forȝyuen to oure dettouris;
5   and lede vs not in to temptacioun, but delyuere vs fro yuel. Amen.

Ten Young Women (MATTHEW xxv. 1-13)

1   Thanne the kyngdoom of heuenes schal be liik to ten virgyns, whiche token her laumpis, and wenten out aȝens the hosebonde and the wiif; and fyue of hem weren foolis, and fyue prudent. But the fyue foolis token her laumpis,
5   and token not oile with hem; but the prudent token oile in her vessels with the laumpis. And whilis the hosebonde tariede, alle thei nappiden and slepten. But at mydnyȝt a cryȝ was maad, Lo! the spouse cometh, go ȝe oute to mete with him. Thanne alle tho virgyns risen vp, and araieden
10 her laumpis. And the foolis seiden to the wise, Ȝyue ȝe to vs of ȝoure oile, for oure laumpis ben quenchid. The prudent answeriden, and seiden, Lest perauenture it suffice not to vs and to ȝou, go ȝe rather to men that sellen, and bie to ȝou. And while thei wenten for to bie, the spouse
15 cam; and tho that weren redi, entreden with him to the weddyngis; and the ȝate was schit. And at the last the

othere virgyns camen, and seiden, Lord, lord, opene to vs. And he answeride, and seide, Treuli Y seie to ȝou. Y knowe ȝou not. Therfor wake ȝe, for ȝe witen not the dai ne the our.

The Prodigal Son (LUKE xv. 11-32)

A man hadde two sones; and þe ȝonger of hem seide unto his fadir; 'Fadir, ȝyve me a porcioun of þe substance þat falliþ me.' And þe fadir departide him his goodis. And soone aftir, þis ȝonge sone gederide al þat fel to him, and wente forþ in pilgrimage in to a fer contré; and þer he wastide his goodis, lyvynge in lecherie. And after þat he hadde endid alle his goodis, þer fel a gret hungre in þat lond, and he bigan to be nedy. And he wente oute, and clevede to oon of þe citizeins of þat contré, and þis citisein sente him into his toun, to kepe swyn. And þis sone coveitide to fille his beli wiþ þese-holes þat þe hogges eten, and no man ȝaf him. And he, turninge aȝen, seide: 'How many hynen in my fadirs hous ben ful of loves, and y perishe here for hungre. Y shal rise, and go to my fadir, and seie to him: "Fadir, I have synned in heven, and bifore þee; now y am not worþi to be clepid þi sone, make me as oon of þin hynen."'

And he roos, and cam to his fadir. And ȝit whanne he was fer, his fadir sawe him, and was moved bi mercy, and renning aȝens his sone, fel on his nekke, and kiste him. And þe sone seide to him: 'Fadir, y have synned in hevene, and bifore þee; now I am not worþi to be clepid þi sone.' And þe fadir seide to his servauntis anoon: 'Bringe ȝe forþ þe firste stoole, and cloþe ȝe him, and ȝyve ȝe a ryng in his hond, and shoon upon his feet. And bringe ȝe a fat calf, and sle him, and ete we, and fede us; for þis sone of myn was deed, and is quykened aȝen, and he was parishid, and is foundun.' And þei bigunne to feede hem.

And his eldere sone was in þe feeld; and whanne he cam, and was nyȝ þe hous, he herde a symphonie and oþer noise of mynystralcye. And þis eldere sone clepide oon of þe sevauntis, and axide what weren þes þingis. And he seide to him: 'þi broþir is comen, and þi fadir haþ slayn a fat calf, for he haþ resceyved him saaf.' But þis eldere sone hadde dedeyn, and wolde not come in; þerfore his fadir wente out, and bigan to preie him. And he answeride, and seide to his fair: 'Lo, so many ȝeeris y serve to þee, y passide nevere þi mandement; and þou ȝavest me nevere a kide, for to fede me wiþ my frendis. But after þat he, þis sone, þat murþeride his goodis wiþ hooris, is come, þou hast killid to him a fat calf.' And þe fadir seide to him: 'Sone, þou art ever more wiþ me, and alle my goodis ben þine. But it was nede to ete and to make mery, for he, þis þi broþir, was deed, and lyvede aȝen; he was perishid, and is founden.'

종교개혁가이며 종교혁명의 선구자인 Wycliff(1328?-1384)는 Oxford에서 공부하고 Oxford에서 가르쳤다. 다른 사람들과 마찬가지로 그도 초기에는 주로 라틴어로 글을 썼으나 보다 많은 사람들이 읽을 수 있도록 뒤에는 영어로 글을 썼고, 제자와 함께 라틴어 성경(Vulgate)을 번역했다.
● 방언 : Southeast Midland
● 철자와 발음 : v와 u는 구별 없이 사용되고 있으며, 어두에서는 v가, 어중에서는 u가 사용되었다.

The Lord's Prayer

1. **Oure**=our. **fadir**=father. **that**=that, who. 관계대명사. **art**=are. **in heuenes**=in heavens. **halewid**=hallowed. **be**=may be. 기원을 나타내는 가정법 현재. **thi name**=thy name.
2. **kyngdoom**=kingdom. **come to**=achieve. 여기서의 come도 기원을 나타내는 가정법 현재. **be~don**=may be done. **wille**=will. **in erthe**=on earth.
3. **ȝyue**=give. **vs**=us. **this dai**=this day, today. **breed**=bread. **othir**=other. **substaunce**=substance.
4. **forȝyue**=forgive. **dettis**=debts. **dettouris**=debtors.
5. **lede**=lead. **in to**=into. **temptacioun**=temptation. **delyuere**=deliver. **fro**=from. **yuel**= evil.

Ten Young Women

1. **Thanne**=then. **schal**=shall. 예언을 나타낸다. **liik**=like.
2. **virgyns**=virgins. **whiche**=which, who. **token**=took. **her**=their. **wenten**=went. **aȝens**=to, towards. 여기서는 to meet의 뜻.
3. **hosebonde**=bridegroom. **wiif**=wife. **fyue**=five. **hem**=them. **weren**=were. **foolis**=foolish.

4   **prudent**=prudent, wise. **her**=their. **oile**=oil.
5   **hem**=them.
6   **her**=their. **whilis**=while.
7   **tariede**=tarried, delayed (in arrival). **thei**=they. **nappiden**=napped, slumbered. **slepten**=slept. **mydnyȝt**=midnight.
8   **cryȝ**=cry. **maad**=made. **spouse**=bridegroom. **cometh**=comes. **ȝe**=ye. **oute**=out. **to mete**=to meet.
9   **tho**=those. **risen**=rose. **vp**=up. **araieden**=arisen(=to prepare)의 3인칭 복수 과거.
10   **her**=their. **seiden**=said. **the wise**=the wise virgins. **ȝyue**=give. **ȝe**=ye.
11   **of**=(some) of. 부분을 나타내는 of. **ȝoure**=your. **for**=for, because. **ben quenchid**=became extinguished, ceased to burn.
12   **answeriden**=answered. **seiden**=said. **perauenture**=perhaps, possibly. **suffice**=be sufficient.
13   **sellen**=sell.
14   **bie**=buy. **to**=for. **ȝou**=yourselves.
15   **cam**=came. **tho that**=those who. **redi**=ready. **entreden**=entered.
16   **weddyngis**=weddings, wedding banquets. **ȝate**=gate. **schit**=shut. **at the last**=at last.
17   **camen**=came.
18   **Treuli**=truly. **Y**=I.
19   **Therfor**=therefore. **for**=for, because. **witen**=know.
20   **our**=hour.

The Prodigal Son

1   **ȝonger**=younger. **hem**=them. **seide**=said.
2   **ȝyve**=give. **porcioun**=portion. **substance**=substance.
3   **fallip**=fall, happen etc. as an inheritance. **departide**=divided, shared. **goodis**=goods, wealth.
4   **soone aftir**=soon after. **gederide**=gathered. **al þat fel to him**=all that

	which fell to him.
5	**wente forþ**=went forth. **pilgrimage**=pilgrimage(먼 여행). **in to**=into. **fer**=far. **contré**=country. **þer**=there.
6	**wastide**=wsted. **lyvynge**=living. **lecherie**= lechery.
6-7	**after þat he hadde endid alle his goodis**=after he had squandered all of his wealth. 대과거를 사용함으로써 다음 줄의 fel(=happened) 이전에 일어난 일임을 나타낸다.
7	**þer fel**=there happened. **hungre**=hunger, famine.
8	**lond**=land. **bigan**= began. **nedy**=needy.
9	**clevede to**=clung to, cleaved. **oon of þe**=one of the.
10	**sente**=sent. **toun**=enclosure, enclosed field. **swyn**=swine.
11	**coveitide**=desired, wanted. **beli**=belly. **pese-holes**=pease-hull, pea-pod. **hogges**=hoggs. **eten**=eat.
12	**ʒaf**=gave. **turninge aʒen**=turning back. **hynen**=servants, slaves, hinds.
13	**hous**=house. **loves**=loaves. **y**=I.
14	**perishe**=perish. **hungre**=hunger, starvation.
15	**synned**=sinned. **bifore þee**=before thee.
16	**worþi**=worthy. **to be clepid**= to be called. **oon**=one.
18	**ʒit**=yet. **whanne**=when.
19	**fer**=far. **sawe**=saw. **bi**=by.
20	**renning**=running. **aʒens**=to meet. **nekke**=neck. **kiste**=kissed.
23	**servauntis**=servants. **anoon**=at once. **Bringe**=bring. **ʒe**=ye. 명령문에 사용된 주어.
24	**þe firste stoole**=the best garment. **cloþe**=clothe. 명령문.
25	**hond**=hand. **sle**=slay. 명령문.
26	**him**=the calf. **ete we**=let us eat. **fede us**=feast ourselves.
26-7	**þis sone of myn**=this son of mine.
27	**deed**=dead. **is quykened aʒen**=is brought to life again. **parishid**=perished.
28	**foundun**=found. **feede hem**=feed themselves.
29	**feeld**=field. **whanne**=when.

30	**ny3**=nigh, near. **symphonie**=music.
31	**mynystralcye**=merry-making, minstrelsy. **clepide**=called.
31-2	**oon of þe**=one of the.
32	**sevauntis**=servants. **axide**=asked. **þingis**=affairs, business.
33	**haþ**=has.
34	**resceyved**=received. **saaf**=safe.
35	**dedeyn**=disdain. **wolde not**=would not. **þerfore**=therefore.
36	**preie**=pray, supplicate, ask.
37	**3eeris**=years.
38	**passide**=passed, surpassed, transgressed, disobeyed. **nevere**=never. **þi**=thy. **mandemenet**=commandment, order. **3avest**=gave.
39	**kide**=kid, young goat. **fede**=feed. **frendis**=friends.
39-40	**he, þis sone**=he와 þis sone는 동격이다.
40	**þat**=that, who. 관계대명사. **murþeride**=murdered. **goodis**=wealth. **hooris**=whores.
41	**killid**=killed.
42	**ever more**=evermore, now and always. **alle my goodis**=all of my wealth.
43	**þine**=thine. **it was nede**=it was necessary. **nede**=need.
44	**broþir**=brother. **lyvede**=lived. **a3en**=again.

주기도문

하늘에 계신 우리 아버지여, 이름이 거룩히 여김을 받으시오며, 나라가 임하시오며, 뜻이 하늘에서 이루어진 것 같이 땅에서도 이루어지이다. 오늘 우리에게 일용할 양식을 주시옵고, 우리가 우리에게 죄지은 자를 사하여 준 것 같이 우리 죄를 사하여 주시옵고, 우리를 시험에 들게 하지 마시옵고, 다만 악에서 구하시옵소서.

열 명의 처녀들

그 때에 천국은 마치 등을 들고 신랑을 맞으러 나간 열 처녀와 같다 하리니, 그 중의 다섯은 미련하고 다섯은 슬기 있는지라, 미련한 자들은 등을 가지되 기름을 가지지 아니하고, 슬기 있는 자들은 그릇에 기름을 담아 등과 함께 가져갔더니, 신랑이 더디 오므로 다 졸며 잘 새 밤중에 소리가 나되 보라 신랑이로다, 맞으러 나오라 하매, 이에 그 처녀들이 다 일어나 등을 준비할 새, 미련한 자들이 슬기 있는 자들에게 이르되, 우리 등불이 꺼져가니 너희 기름을 좀 나눠 달라 하거늘 슬기 있는 자들이 대답하여 이르되, 우리와 너희가 쓰기에 다 부족할까 하노니 차라리 파는 자들에게 가서 너희 쓸 것을 사라 하니, 그들이 사러 간 사이에 신랑이 오므로 준비하였던 자들은 함께 혼인 잔치에 들어가고 문은 닫힌지라, 그 후에 남은 처녀들이 와서 이르되 주여, 주여 우리에게 열어 주소서, 대답하여 이르되, 진실로 너희에게 이르노니 내가 너희를 알지 못하노라 하였느니라. 그러니 깨어 있으라. 너희는 그날과 그 때를 알지 못하느니라.

돌아온 탕자

어떤 사람에게 두 아들이 있었는데, 그 둘째가 아버지에게 말하되, 아버지여, 재산 중에서 내게 돌아올 분깃을 내게 주소서 하는 지라, 아버지가 그 살림을 각각 나눠 주었더니, 그 후 며칠

이 안 되어 둘째 아들이 재물을 다 모아 가지고 먼 나라에 가 거기서 허랑방탕하여 그 재산을 낭비하더니, 다 없앤 후 그 나라에 크게 흉년이 들어 그가 비로소 궁핍한지라, 가서 그 나라 백성 중 한 사람에게 붙여 사니 그가 그를 들로 보내어 돼지를 치게 하였는데, 그가 돼지 먹는 쥐엄 열매로 배를 채우고자 하되 주는 자가 없는지라, 이에 스스로 돌이켜 이르되 내 아버지에게는 양식이 풍족한 품꾼이 얼마나 많은가, 나는 여기서 주려 죽는구나. 내가 일어나 아버지께 가서 이르기를, 아버지 내가 하늘과 아버지께 죄를 지었사오니, 지금부터는 아버지의 아들이라 일컬음을 감당하지 못하겠나이다. 나를 품꾼의 하나로 보소서 하리라 하고,

　　이에 일어나서 아버지께로 돌아가니라. 아직도 거리가 먼데 아버지가 그를 보고 측은히 여겨 달려가 목을 안고 입을 맞추니, 아들이 이르되, 아버지 내가 하늘과 아버지께 죄를 지었사오니 지금부터는 아버지의 아들이라 일컬음을 감당하지 못하겠나이다 하니 아버지는 종들에게 이르되, 제일 좋은 옷을 내어다가 입히고, 손에 가락지를 끼우고 발에 신을 신기라. 그리고 살찐 송아지를 끌어다가 잡으라. 우리가 먹고 즐기자. 이 내 아들은 죽었다가 다시 살아났으며 내가 잃었다가 다시 얻었노라 하니 그들이 즐거워하더라.

　　맏아들은 밭에 있다가 돌아와 집에 가까이 왔을 때에 풍악과 춤추는 소리를 듣고 한 종을 불러 이 무슨 일인가 물은 대 대답하되, 당신의 동생이 돌아왔으매 당신의 아버지가 건강한 그를 다시 맞아들이게 됨으로 인하여 살찐 송아지를 잡았나이다 하니 그가 노하여 들어가고자 하지 아니하거늘, 아버지가 나와서 권한 대 아버지께 대답하여 이르되, 내가 여러 해 아버지를 섬겨 명을 어김이 없거늘 내게는 염소 새끼라도 주어 나와 내 벗으로 즐기게 하신 일이 없더니, 아버지의 살림을 창녀들과 함께 삼켜 버린 이 아들이 돌아오매 이를 위하여 살찐 송아지를 잡으셨나이다. 아버지가 이르되, 얘 너는 항상 나와 함께 있으니 내 것이 다 네 것이로되, 이 네 동생은 죽었다가 살아났으며, 내가 잃었다가 얻었기로 우리가 즐거워하고 기뻐하는 것이 마땅하다 하니라.

15th Century

Caxton's Prologue to Eneydos

1   And certaynly our langage now vsed varyeth ferre from that whiche was vsed and spoken whan I was borne. For we englysshe men ben borne vnder the domynacyon of the mone, whiche is neuer stedfaste but euer wauerynge,
5   wexynge one season and waneth and dyscreaseth another season. And that comyn englysshe that is spoken in one shyre varyeth from another, in so moche that in my dayes happened that certayn marchauntes were in a shippe in tamyse for to haue sayled ouer the see into zelande, and for
10   lacke of wynde thei taryed atte forlond, and wente to lande for to refreshe them. And one of theym named sheffelde, a mercer, cam in to an hows and axed for mete, and specyally he axyd after eggys. And the good wyf answerde that she coude speke no frenshe. And the marchaunt was
15   angry, for he also coude speke no frenshe, but wold haue hadde egges and she vnderstode hym not. And thenne at laste another sayd that he wolde haue eyren; then the good wyf sayd that she vnderstod hym wel. Loo, what sholde a man in thyse dayes now wryte, egges or eyren. Certaynly it is harde to playse euery man
20   by cause of dyuerisite and chaunge of langage. For in these dayes euery man that is in ony reputacyon in his countre wyll vtter his commynycacyon and maters in such maners and termes that fewe men shall vnderstonde theym.

Caxton은 Virgil의 *Æneid*의 프랑스어 판을 영어로 번역하여 Henry 7세의 장남인 Prince Arthur에게 헌정했다. 1490년에 번역이 끝난 것으로 기록이 되어 있다. 이미 16세기에 들어서는 당시의 글은 보다시피 읽기 어렵지 않다. 이 글에서 우리는 당시 영어의 실상을 구체적으로 보여주는 한 단면에 접할 수 있다.

1   **certaynly**=certainly. **vsed**=used. **varyeth**=varies, differes. **ferre**=far.
2   **whan**=when.
3   **englysshe men**=Englishmen. **ben**=are. **vnder**=under. **domynacyon**= domination, power to rule or control.
4   **mone**=moon. **neuer**=never. **stedfaste**=steadfast, unchinging, stable in form. **euer**=ever. **wauerynge**=wavering.
5   **wexynge**=waxing, growing. **waneth**=wanes. **dyscreaseth**=decreases.
6   **that**=the. **comyn**=common, vernacular. **englysshe**= English language.
7   **shyre**=shire. **in so moche that~**=so much that~.
8   **marchauntes**=merchants. **shippe**=shipe.
9   **tamyse**=the River Thames. **sayled**=sailed. **ouer**=over. **zelande**=Zealand.
10 **lacke**=lack. **wynde**=wind. **thei**=they. **taryed**=tarreid. **atte**=at the. **forlond**= foreland, headland, promontory. **wente**=went.
11 **refreshe**=refresh. **them**=themselves. **theym**=them. **sheffelde**=Sheffield.
12 **mercer**=mercer(포목상). **hows**=house, shop. **axed**=asked. **mete**=meat, food, meal.
13 **specyally**=specially. **axyd after**=asked for. **eggys**=eggs. **wyf**=wife.
14 **frenshe**=French.
15 **wold**=would, wanted, desired.
16 **vnderstode**=understood. **thenne**=then.
17 **eyren**=eggs. egg의 g를 [y]로 발음하고, 복수 어미로 -en(cf. children)을 사용하고 있다.
18 **vnderstod hym wel**=well. **Loo**=lo, behold. **sholde**=should. **in thyse**

dayes=these days.
19   **wryte**=write. **playse**=please, satisfy.
20   **by cause of**=because of. **dyuerisite**=diversity. **chaunge**=change.
21   **that**=thatm who. **ony**=any. **reputacyon**=reputation.

분명히 지금 우리가 사용하고 있는 언어는 내가 태어났을 때 말하고 사용되던 것과는 몹시 다르다. 왜냐하면 우리 영국 사람들은 달의 영향 아래서 태어났는데, 달은 잠시도 가만있지 않고 한 동안 흔들리며 자라나는가 하면 금방 기울면서 줄어든다. 어떤 고장에서 사용되는 영어가 다른 고장에서 사용되는 것과 너무나 달라서, 내가 어렸을 때 템스 강에 Zealand로 가려다가 바람이 없어서 지체되고 있는 배에 몇몇 상인들이 있었는데, 그들이 쉴 겸해서 육지로 올라왔던 일이 있었다. Sheffield라는 이름의 한 사람이 가게에 가서 식사를 주문했고, 특히 '계란(eggs)'을 달라고 했다. 그런데 착한 아주머니가 자기는 프랑스 말을 할 줄 모른다고 대답했다. 그 상인은 화가 나서 자기도 프랑스어는 모른다고 하면서 굳이 계란을 먹고 싶노라고 말했다. 그때 또 다른 상인이 와서 '계란(eyren)'을 달라고 했더니 아주머니는 그의 말을 문제없이 알아들었다. 그러니 이런 상황에서 우리는 eggs라고 써야 하나, 아니면 eyren이라고 써야하나? 언어의 다양성과 변화 때문에 모든 사람을 만족시킨다는 것은 어려운 일이다. 왜냐하면 요즈음 지체 높은 사람들은 모두 자기들이 하는 말을 거의 남들이 알아듣지 못하는 식으로 하기 때문이다.

참고문헌

金鎭萬. 1965. 『캔터베리 이야기』, 서울 : 正音社.
市河三喜/松浪 有. 1986. 『古英語・中英語初步』, 東京 : 硏究社.
水鳥喜喬/米倉 綽. 1997. 『中英語の初步』, 東京 : 英潮社.

Baugh, A. C. ed. 1963. *Chaucer's Major Poetry*. New York : Appleton-Century-Crofts.
Coghill, N. 1951. *The Canterbury Tales*. Penguin Books.
Cook, D. 1961. *The Canterbury Tales of Geoffrey Chaucer*. New York : Anchor Books.
Curry, W. C. 1960. *Chaucer and the Mediaeval Sciences*. New York : Barnes and Noble Inc.
Emerson, A., M. 1915. *A Middle English Reader*. New York : The Macmillan Co.
Fisher, J. H ed. 1977. *The Complete Poetry and Prose of Geoffrey Chaucer*. New York : Holt, Rinehart and Winston.
Ichikawa, S. and R. Matsunami. 1987. *Chaucer's Canterbury Tales : General Prologue*. Tokyo : Kenkyusha.
Kökeritz, H. A. 1961. *Guide to Chaucer's Pronunciation*. New York : Holt, Rinehart and Winston.
Kurath, H., S. Kuhn, J. Reidy & E. R. Lewis. eds. 1954-. *Middle English*

Dictionary. Ann Arbor: The University of Michigan Press.

Lumiansky, R. M. 1948. *The Canterbury Tales of Geoffrey Chaucer*. New York : Washington Square Press.

Manly, J. M. 1959. *Some New Lights on Chaucer*. Gloucester, Mass. : The Macmillan Co.

Mossé, F. 1952. *A Handbook of Middle English*. Baltimore : The Johns Hopkins Press.

Pollard, A. W. 1955. *Chaucer's Canterbury Tales : The Prologue*. New York : Macmillan Co.

Robinson, F. N. ed. 1957. *The Works of Geoffrey Chaucer*. Boston : Houghton Mifflin.

Sweet, H. 1884. *First Middle English Primer*. Oxford : Clarendon Press.

Treharne, E. ed. 2004. *Old and Middle English : c.890-1400*. Blackwell Publishing Co..

MIDDLE ENGLISH 어휘사전

일러두기

중세영어는 모두 굵은 활자체로 표시하였다.

ʒ는 g 다음에 제시하였다.

æ는 a e와, þ는 th와, ü는 u와, 그리고 어중의 y와 i는 동일하게 취급하였다.

학습의 편의를 위하여 표제어로는 단어의 원형뿐만 아니라 흔히 쓰이는 굴절형도 제시하였다.

앞으로의 학습 편의를 위하여 본문의 단어 외에도 흔히 사용되는 단어도 망라하였다.

약자

acc	대격 (accusative)
adj	형용사 (adjective)
adv	부사 (adverb)
art	관사 (article)
collect	집합명사 (collective)
comp	(형용사나 부사의) 비교급 (comparative (adjective or adverb))
conj	접속사 (conjunction)
dat	여격 (dative)
dem	지시사 (demonstrative)
fem	여성 (feminine)
fig	비유적 (figurative)
gen	속격 (genitive)
imper	비인칭 (동사) (impersonal (verb))
ind	직설법 (indicative)
indef art	부정관사 (indefinite article)
indef pron	부정대명사 (indefinite pronoun)
inf	부정사 (infinitive)
interj	감탄사 (interjection)
interr	의문사 (interrogative)
interr pron	의문대명사 (interrogative pronoun)
masc	남성 (masculine)
neut	중성 (neutral)
num	수사 (numeral)
num adj	수 형용사 (numerical adjective)
pers pron	인칭대명사 (personal pronoun)
poss pron	소유대명사 (possessive pronoun)
poss	소유격 (possessive)
pp	과거분사 (past participle)
prep	전치사 (preposition)
pron	대명사 (pronoun)
prop n	고유명사 (proper noun)
prs p	현재분사 (present participle)
prs	현재시제 (present)
pp	과거분사 (past participle)
pt	과거시제 (preterite)
refl	재귀(동사/대명사) (reflexive (verb or pronoun))
sbj	가정법 (subjunctive)
sup	(형용사나 부사의) 최상급 (superlative (adjective or adverb))
v	동사 (verb)

A

a→ān
ā→ōn(e)
abīde(n) *v* wait, stay. *pt sg* abōd
abīte(n) *v* bite
able *a* capable, fit, apt, competent, qualified
abōūte(n), abūte(n), abūton *adv* about, on all sides, *prep* about, around
above(n) *adv, prep* above, higher at the table than
absolucioun *n* forgiveness of a sin as pronounced by a priest or by authority of the Church, remission
ac, acc, oc, ah, auh *conj* but
accord *n* agreement
accordandly *adv* accordingly
ac(c)ordaunt *adj* in accordance with, agreeable to, **accordaunt to resoun**=reasonable, proper
ac(c)orden *v* agree, impers be fitting, correspond, fall into an agreement
achaat *n* act of buying, purchase
achatour *n* a buyer of provisions, purveyor, caterers
adrad *adj* greatly afraid
adrēde(n) *v* be frightened, dread, fear, *pp* adrad
ælle→al(1)
ǣvre, ǣvric→ēvre, everich
aferd *adj* frightened, afraid
affīlen *v* sharpen, polish (one's tongue)
afforce(n) v force, try
after, affterr, efter *prep* according to
affeccyōn→affection
afforce(n) *v* force, try
after, affterr, efter *prep* after, for, according to (the practices of), *adv* afterward, after that, **after the sesoun**=appropriate to the season, **rechen after**=reach for (something), **waiten after**=expect, anticipate

agayn(es), agǣnes, agānē, aʒē(n) *adv* back, again *prep* against, towards
aʒain→agayn
aʒēn→agayn
aʒʒ→ay
ah→ac, owen
ay, aʒʒ *adv* aye, ever, always
ayere *n* air
āhte→owen
aiþer→eiþer
al *adv* although
al(1) *adj* all, *pl* alle, ælle, *pl gen* aller, alre, *adv* entirely, very, quite, **over al**=everywhere, **al bifore**=at the head of the procession
alderbest *adv* best of all
alderman *n* a leading member of the council of the city or borough, alderman, chief of a guild
alestake *n* a stake or post set up before an alehouse, to bear a garland, bush, or other sign, or as a sign itself
algate *adv* every way, always
Algezir *prop n* Algeciras, in Spain
alyght *pp* alit, alighted
alyghten *v* arrive, stop, *pp* alyght
Alisaundre *prop n* Alexandria
aller→al(1)
allāne *adv* alone. **hym allāne** alone by himself
allas *interj* alas
aloft *adv* loft, on high in rank, power, estimation, **lordes aloft** powerful lords
alre-worste worst of all, *adv* entirely, quite
als→alsō
alse, alsuic *pron* (all) such
alsō, alswō, alsuō, alswā, alse, als *adv* also, as, just as, equally, similarly
alsuō, alswā, alswō→alsō
alwey, alway *adv* always, all the while
amblere *n* saddle horse, easy paced horse

among *adv* at intervals, *prep* among
amorwe *adv* in the morning, next morning
an *prep* in
an→**an(n)d**
ān, *indef art* a, an
an(n)d, **an** *conj* and
andswarede→**ondswerien**
āne→**ōn**
angwys *n* anguish
anī, **anȳ** *indef pron* any
anla(a)s *n* dagger, a short two-edged knife worn at the girdle
anōn, **anoon**, **anān** *adv* at once, soon, anon
anōther, **anōthire** *pron v* another
ansuereþ→**ondswerien**
answāre *n* answer
ape(s) *n* dupe
apiked *pp* trimmed, adorned
apiken *v* adorn, array, *pp* **apikend, apiked**
apothecarie *n* pharmacist or druggist who stores, compounds, and sells medicaments of all sorts
aqueyntaunce *n* acquaintance
ār, āre(n)→**bē(n)**
araye *n* array, condition
āre→**ēr**
aredde(n), **arüdde(n)** *v* rescue, deliver *pt sg* arüdde
arēre(n), **areare(n)** *v* raise
aresten *v* stop
aretten *v* reckon, attribute, account
ariȝt, **aryȝt**, **aryht** *adv* aright, exactly, rightly, straight, all right, as it should be
arīse(n) *v* arise, *pt sg* **arās**
arive, aryve *n* arrival, disembarkation
arm, ærm, earm *n* arm
armee *n* military expedition by sea or land
array *n* clothing, dress, attire, gear, equipment

arrerage *n* the condition of being behind in payments or short in one's accounts, **bringen in arrerage**=find (somebody) short in his accounts
ar(r)ow, arwes n arrow, *pl* **ar(r)owis**
art→**bē(n)**
arüdden *v* save, *pt* **arüdde,** *pp* **arüd**
as, ase *conj* as
ascendent *n* that degree of the zodiac which arises above the horizon at a given moment, **fortunen the ascendent** →**fortunen**
aske(n) *v* ask, *pt* **askit**
assay *v* try, attack
assāle(n) *v* assail, attack, *pt* **assālȝeit**, *pp* **assālȝeit**
assent *n* **by oon assent**=in complete agreement, unanimously, **by (one's) free assent**=voluntarily, willingly
assente(n) *v* assent, agree to
assise *n* the session held periodically in each county of England, for the purpose of administering civil and criminal justice, by judges acting under certain special commission
assoil(l)yng *n* removal of excommunication or other ecclesiastical sentence, absolution
astored *pp* stored, provided
astoren *v* provide (oneself) with supplies, *pp* **astorend**
astronomye *n* the science of astronomy, together with the pseudo-science of astrology, as developed by the Greeks and the Arabs
atflīþ *v prs 3sg* flies away
āthe→**ōþe**
atones *adv* at one and the same time
atschēt *v pt* vanished
atte *prep demon pron* at the
atwīte(n) *v* blame
aucht→**owen**

auditour *n* an official who examines and verifies accounts, an auditor or examiner

aught *pron* anything, **for aught I woot**=for all I know

auh→**ac**

Austin *prop n* Agustine

auter *n* alter

avaunce *n* profit

avauncen *adj* be profitable

avaunt *v* boast, **maken avaunt**=boast, declare in a boastful manner

aventure *n* fate, fortune, chance, adventure, **by aventure**=by chance

avȳs, avȳse *n* advice, consultation, discussion, deliberation

awei, awaye, avay *adv* away

B

bā *pron* both

bacheler *n* a young man, probationer for knighthood

bad(d)→**bidde(n)**

bǣron→**bēre(n)**

baillif *n* an agent of a lord or his seneschal for the management of the manor

bak *n* back

bake *pp* baken, baked

bake mete *n* any dish baked in a shell of pastry, such as a meat pie, a tart, a custard

bale *n* sorrow, grief

balled *adj* bald

bar *adj* bare-headed

bar, bare, bāren→**bēre(n)**

bāre *adj* bare, open

bāre→**bēre(n)**

bargayn *n* business transaction or agreement

barge *n* sea-sailing vessel of moderate size

bar(re) *n* ornamental (gold or silver) strip or bar, as on a girdle, a piece of armor, a saddle

barres *n pl* cross-stipes

batailles *n pl* battles

bāthe(n) *v* bathe, soak, suffuse, *pp* **bathend**

bāþe, bāthe→**bōthe**

bawdryk *n* baldric, belt

be→**bī**

bead→**bēoden**

bēam *n* beam

beawbelez *pl n* baublets, trinklets

bēche *n* valley

bedde *v* supply with a bed

bēde *n* bead of rosary, **peir of bēdes**=a rosary

bēden→**bidde**

befell→**bifalle**

beggestere *n* beggar (originally a female beggar)

beiȝ *n* collar, *pl* **bīȝes**

belle *n* chapel bell, a kind of cloak or tunic

Belmarye *prop n* Moorish kingdom in Africa

bē(n), bēo(n) *v* be, *imper* **bē**, *ind prs lsg* **am**, *2sg* **art**, *3sg* **is, iss, es**, *pl* **sinnedenn, āre, ār, āren, bēoþ**, *pt sg* **was, watȝ, wes**, *ves*, **nes**(=ne wes), *pt pl* **wǣron, wǣren, wāren, wēre, wēren, wāre, wōre, wār, vār, nēre**(=ne were), *sbj prs* **bē**, *sbj pt* **wēre, wēren, nēre** (=ne wēre)

bēnde *v* bend *pt* **bēnd**

benefice *n* a ecclesiastical living, an office or position in the church

Benelt *prop n* Benedict

benygne *adj* benign

benime, bineomen, beneme *v* deprive, take away, *pp* **binome, binume**
bēoden *v* offer *pt sg* **bead**
berd *n* beard
bēre(n), bǣron *v* bear, carry, *pt* **bāre, bāren,** *pp* **ybōre, ibōren, bōre, bōren, born, the pris bēren**=take the prize, be the best of
besaly *adv* busily
besynes *n* trouble, care
best(e) *adv sup* best, most, **at the (atte) beste**=in the best way, most excellently, **for the beste**=conductive to the best results, in the best interests of a person or a group, **with the beste**=as well as any one
bet *adv comp* better, more
bēver *n* beaver fur
bī, bē *prep* by, concerning, according to
bidde *v* bid, order, pray, *pt sg* **badd, bad,** *pt pl* **bēden**
bidden *v* bid, *prs 2sg* **bit**
bȳe(n), bügge *v* buy, *pt* **boghte, boghten, bohte, bouhe,** *pp* **ybouʒt, ibouʒt**
bifalle(n) *v* befall, happen, occur, come to pass, *pt* **bifil, bifelle, bifell**
bifil→**befalle**
biforn, bivōren *prep* before
bigynne *v* begin, *pt* **bigon,** *pp* **bygonne**
bigonne→**bigynne**
bigrēden *v* scold, *prs pl* **bigrēdet**
bigrowe *pp a* overgrown
bīʒes→**beiʒ**
bihalde(n)→**bihōlde(n)**
bihōlde(n) *v* behold, see, contemplate, *pt* **bihēold, beohēold, bihēōld**
biknowen *v* own, acknowledge
bile *n* bill
bilēdet *v prs pl* pursue
bilēve *v* remain

bīnde *v* bind, *pp* **ybōūnden**
bineomen→**benime**
binēþ(e), binēōþ, binēōðe(n) *adv* beneath
byn(ne) *n* chest or bin (as for grain, flour, bread)
bire(n) *v impers* be fitting, *pres 3sg* birrb
bischop *n* bishop
bischrīcheþ *v prs pl* shriek at**bisēche** *v* beseech
bisetten *v* beset, beseige, employ, *pp* **biset, bisetten wit**=shape (one's) thoughts, use (one's) head
bisīde *adv* beside, near to
bisīdes *prep* near
bisily *adv* earnestly, assiduously
bisinesse *n* endeavor, effort
bismortered *pp* bespattered, soiled
bit→**bidden**
bitācnunge *n* betokening
bitēche *v* deliver, hand over, entrust
bitellunge *n* excuse
bȳte(n) *v* corrode, bite, *pt sg* **bōt(e)**
biboʒt *pp* thoughtful, discreet
bitīde *v* happen, betide, sbj prs
bitürnen *v* turn
bitwēonen *prep* between, among
bitwixe *prep* between
blayke *adj* pale, white
blake *adj* black
blamen *v* blame, **ben to blame**=be to blame, wrong
blankmanger *n* a dish of chopped chicken or fish boiled with rice
blawene→**blowe**
blēte *adj* exposed
blisful *adj* blissful, blessed
blōd *n* blood, **ran blōde** shed blood, bled
blōme *n* bloom, *pl* **blōneʒ**
blosme *pl n* flowers

blowe *v* blow, *pp* **blawene**
blwe *adj* blue
bōc *n* book
bodi *n* body
bōȝe *n* bough
bohte→**bȳe(n)**
bokeler *n* bucklerm small round shield
bōld *adj* bold
Boloigne *prop n* Boulogne
boold *adj* bold
bo(o)te *n* medical cure or remedy
boote *n* boot
boras *n* borax
bord *n* table, board, **biginnen the bord**= sit at head of the table
bōt→**but**
bōthe, bōþe, bāthe *pron, adv* both
bow *n* bow, *pl* **bowis**
bracer *n* an arm guard or wrist guard used by an archer
brǣcon→**brēke**
brǣsse *n* brass
brawn *n* muscle
bream *n* a freshwater fish, the bream
breathe *n* breath
breed *n* bread
breem *n* bream, a variety of carp
breeth *n* breath
brēke *v* break, *pt pl* **brǣcon**
brenne, bren *v* burn, *pt pl* **brenden, brendon**, *pp* **brent**
breste *n* breast
bretful *adj* filled to the brim, brimful
bretherhed *n* guild, brotherhood
briȝt, bryght *adj* bright
brymstoon *n* brimstone, sulphur
bringe *v* bring, *prs 1sg* **bringe**, *3sg* **brynges**, *pt* **brohht**
brynige *n* coat of mail, *pl* **bryniges**
brōd, brood *adj* broad
brode *adv* broadly, frankly, unreservedly

brustle *n* bristle
bügge→**bȳe**
Burdeux-ward *n* the direction of Bordeaux
burdoun *n* the low-pitched undersong accompanying the melody, burden
būre *n* bower
burgeys *n* burgess, a citizen with full rights and privileges
but, bōt *conj* but, unless, *adv* just, only, *prep* except, without
buterflīȝe *n* butterfly
but if *conj* unless

C

ca(a)s *n* suit, cause, case, chance
cacche *v* catch, *prs 3sg* **caccheth**
cæste *n* chest
cake *n* a flat cake or loaf
calle *v* call
cam→**come**
can *v* know (how), be able, *ind prs* **cünne, kunne, kan, kane**, *pl* **cōūthe**, *pl pt* **kōūþen**, *pp adj* **kōw̄the**
can→**ginne(n)**
cancelēr *n* chancellor
cappe *n* a headdress, a hat, etc., especially a small head covering worn under the hood, **setten cappe**= make a fool of
carf→**kerven**
carl *n* fellow, churl
carlman *n* man, *pl* **carlmen**
caroyne *n* carrion
carpen *v* chatter
carpyng *n* talking, babbling
cas(s) *n* case, chance
caste *v* cast, throw, *prs 3sg* **castys**, *pt* **kest**
castel *n* castle, *pl* **castles, casteles**
castelweorc *n* forced labor on castles

cat *n* cat, *gen* **cattes, cattis**
catel *n* money, property
ceint *n* girdle
cell *n* a subordinate monastic establishment
certeyn *adv* certainly
ceruce *n* ceruse, white lead
chambre *n* private room
champioun *n* an athlete, such as a boxer or a wrestler
chanōūn n canon
chaped *adj* mounted, trimmed
chapeleyne *n* a nun who serves as a private secretary or assistant to the abbess or prioress of a covenant, chaplain
chapman *n* merchant, trader
charge n trust, charge, weight, **ben in charge**=be in (one's) power
charge *v* charge, load, weigh down, *pp* **chargede**
charytē, charitee *n* charity, **ben out of charitee**=lack charity
chaumbre *n* chamber
chaunge *v* change
chaunterie *n* chantry, an endowment for the maintenance of one or several priests to sing a daily mass for the soul of the founder; also such a position held by a priest
cheere *n* behavior, manner, **maken greet cheere**=treat (somebody) hospitably
Chepe *n* Cheapside
cherubyn(nes) *n* an angel of the second order
chēse *v* choose, pt pl **chōsen**
chevysa(a)unce *n* the borrowing of money, especially on security or/and at interest
chēviss *v* succeed
chiere *n* cheer, entertainment
chīld *n* child, *pl* **chidren**

chirche *n* church
chyvachie *n* cavalry expedition, expedition on horseback
chivalrie *n* the ethical code of chivalry; feasts of knightly valor
chōsen→**chēse**
Christofer *n* a small image of St. Christopher
citē *n* city, town
clacke *v* clack, *prs 2sg* **clackest**
clad *pp adj* clothed, bound. →**clōthe**
claspen *v* furnish with buckles
clause *n* clause, sentence, **in a clause**= briefly
cleanly *adv* purely, chastely
clēn *adj* clean
clēne *adv* excellently, cleanly
clēpen *v* call, name, *pt* **clepte**
clēr(e) *n* claw (of a bird), *pl* **clivres**
clerk *n* a (university) student, scholar
clēthe *v* **clōthe**, *pt* **clōþede**, *pp* **clad**
clēve *n* room, dwelling, cottage
cloysterer *n* monk
cloysterles *adj* out of the cloister
clot *n* clay, earth
clōthes *pl n* clothes, garment
clowe *v* claw
cnihtshcipe *n* knightship
cnotted *pp* knotted
cofre *n* money box, coffer
cogge *n* cog
coy *adj* quiet, modest
cōl-blake *adj* black as charcoal
colēr *n* collar
colerik *adj* (of persons or temperament) dominated by the humor choler, choleric
Coloigne *prop n* Cologne
color *n* color
colpon *n* bunch
come(n), cumen *v* come, *imper* **cum**, *pt*

sg **cōm, cam**, *pt pl* **cōmen, cōm**, *prs p* **cumand**
commāndement *n* commandment
commissioun *n* **pleyn commissioun**=full authority invested
compaignye *n* company, a group of persons, sexual union, intercourse
compeer *n* comrade, companion
complexioun n one of the four temperaments or dispositions attributed to the predominance of one of the four humors
composicio(u)n *n* an agreement between two parties
comūne *n* commons, people
comūne *adj* common
con→**can**
concyens *n* conscience
condicioun *n* circumstances of life
confort *n* comfort
conyng *n* cony, rabbit
conscience *n* sensibility, tenderness, scruples, **spiced conscience**=fastidiousness
conseil *n* secret, private matters, decision, counsel
conseille *n* counsel, council
conseille *v* counsel
contemplācyōne *n* contemplation
contrē, cuntrē *n* country
cop *n* the tip (of a nose), top
cōpe *n* cope, the cowl or hood of a friar, etc.
coppe *n* cup
corāge *n* heart, disposition
cordial *n* restorative, stimulant, medicine which invigorates the heart
cosyn *n* cousin, **bēn cosyn to**=be akin to
coste *v* cost, *pt* **coste**, *pp* **costed**
costin *v* cost
counterfeten *v* imitate

countour *n* auditor
countrefete *v* imitate
coupled *pp* coupled, fastened
cōūrs *n* course
cōūrte *n* court
courtepy *n* a short woolen coat or jacket, cape
cōūthe→**can**
coveite(n), coveyte *v* covet, desire, *prs 3sg* **coveiteth**
covenant *n* a formal contract
coverchiefs *n pl* hairdress, kerchiefs, headcovers
covyne *n* fraud, deceit, deceit, agreement
coy *adj* shy
cracche, crachy *v* scratch
crafty *adj* crafty, skilful
crēatūr *n* creature
crēpe *v* creep, *sbj pt* **crōpe**
crīe *v* cry
cryke *n* creek
Cristen *adj* Christian
Cristendom *n* Christendom
Cristophere *n* image of St. Christopher worn as an amulet
croys *n* cross
crōked *pp adj* crooked
crop *n* shoot
crōpe→**crēpe**
crop(pes) n a bud or shoot, tree-top
crōūne, crūne *n* crown, top of head
crūcethūs *n* torture-box
crull *adj* curly
crūnen *v* crow, pp **icrūnet**
cülled→**kille**
cum, cumand→**come**
cummer *v* bother, annoy, *pt* **cumrit**
cumrit→**cummer**
cūnde→**kīnde**
cūnne→**can, kin**
cuntrē→**contrē**

cūpe *n* basket
curat *n* a parish priest
cure *n* attention, heed, care, **taken cure (of)**=pay attention to
curious *adj* exquisite, learned, skilled
curs *n* excommunication
curse *v* curse
cursen *v* excommunicate
curteis *adj* courteous
cüste *n* **character, way**
cut *n* lot or chance as determined by the drawing of straw or sticks of different length, **drauen cut**=draw lots
cūðe→kīþen
cwēne *n* queen

D

day *n* day, *adverbial genitive* **dæies**, *pl* **dayes**
dayerye *n* dairy
dayesye *n* daisy
dāle *n* valley, dale
daliaunce *n* small talk, gossip, conversation
dāme *n* dame, my lady
dar *v* dare, *pt* **dorst**
daunce *n* dance, **the olde daunce**=the whole business, all the tricks
daunger *n* *d*ominion, power to injure
daungerous *adj* difficult, domineering, overbearing
dead→dēd
deaþ(es)→dēþ
deboneirtē *n* gentleness
decīple *n* disciple
dēd, **dead** *adj* dead, the dead
dēde *n* deed
dēde→dō(n)
dedeyn *n* disdain
deed *adj* dead

deef *adj* deaf
deelen *v* have dealings with
defāme *v* defame
degree *n* social class, rank
deie *v* die, *pt* **deide**
deyerye *n* dairy
deel *n* part
deelen *v* deal, have to do with
deyntee *adj* rare, precious
deys *n* a raised platform, dais
deyntee *n* delicious food, dainty, *adj* excellent, fine
delīte *n* delight, pleasure
delȳte *v* delight
delyvere *adj* agile, active
delven *v* dig, cultivate, **dyken and delven**= do the farm work
Denemark *prop n* Denmark
deōr→dēr(e)
dēōre, deorre→dēre
departe(n) *v* divide, share
dēpe *adv* deeply
dēr(e), **deere, dǣre, dēōre** *adj* dear, *comp* **deorre**, *adv* dear
Dertemouthe *n* Dartmouth
desdeyn *n* disdain
despitous *adj* merciless, cruel, scornful
desport *n* bearing, manner, **of great desport**= dignified in manner, diversion, mirth
dēst→dō(n)
destruye, destrüien *v* destroy, *pp* **destrüiet**
dēþ, **dēth, deaþ** *n* death, *gen* **deaðes**
dettelees *adj* debtless, out of debt
deuoyde *v* cast away
dēvel(l) *n* devil, *pl* **dēovles**
devys *n* request, direction, command, appointment
devysen *v* describe, devise, set forth
digne *adj* worthy (of), haughty, overbearing
diʒele *adj* secret, hidden **dyke** *v* dig a ditch

diocise *n* diocese
dischevelee *adj* with the hair hanging loose
dispence *n* spending, expenditure, **esy of dispence**=parsimonious
disport, desport *n* conduct, manner, entertainment, **maken disport**=entertain
dȳvers *adj* divers, different
doked *pp* docked, cropped
dō(n), doo *v* do, place, put, make, *prs 2sg* **dēst**, *3sg* **dōþ, dotʒ**, *pl* **dōn, doo**, *pt sg* **dide, dēde, düde**, *pt pl* **diden**, *prs p* **dōande**, *pp* **dōn**
dong *n* dung
dormant *adj* sleeping, (of a table) fixed, **table dormant**=permanent table
dorst→**dar**
dorste→**durren**
double *adj* double, **double worsted**=heavy worsted
douhter *n* daughter
doumb *adj* dumb
dōūn *adv* down
dōūte *n* fear
drǣf→**drīve**
drāpen→**drēpe**
draughte *n* draft, **drinken draught**=drink something in one pull
drawe *v* draw, *pt* **drew**, **dreuch**
drēde *n* dread, danger
drēde, dreid *v* dread, *pt* **drēd**
drēmē *n* dream
drēpe(n) *v* kill, *pt* **drāpen**
dressen *v* arrange, make ready
drīve *v* drive, fall, sink, *prs pl* **drīveþ**, *pt* **drǣf, drōf**
drōf→**drīve**
drogge *n* drug
droghte *n* drought, dryness of the weather, lack of rain
düde→**dō(n)**

dunne *n* darkness
durren *v* have the courage to do something in one pull
duszeyne *n* dozen

E

earding-stowe *n* dwelling-place
earm→**arm**
ēch, ǣch, ūch(e), euch *pron, adj* each, every
echon *pron* everyone, each one
edflēon *v* escape
eek *adv* also, moreover
effect *n* fact, **in effect**=in deed, in fact
effeir *n* demeanor, attitude
eft, æft *adv* again, once more, **now and eft**=now and again
efter→**after**
eye, ēʒe, īʒe, ȳe *n* eye, *pl* **ēʒen, eyen**
ehsihþe *n* eyesights
eiþer, aiþer *pron, adj* either
ēk(e), eek *adv* also
ēlde *n* age
ēlyng *adj* miserable, wretched
elleʒ, ellis *adv* else, otherwise
elles-whēre *adv* elsewhere
embrouden *v* embroider
encombre *v* get stuck to
encombred *pp* encumbered
ēnde, ǣnde *n* end, **on ēnde**=at last, in the end
enditen *v* compose (a song), draft or write (a document)
eneuch→**inōʒ(e)**
engendre(n) *v* beget, produce, originate
Englaland *prop n* England
enoynt *pp* anointed
enoynten *v* anoint, smear with oil, *pp* **enoynt**

ensample *n* example
enspīre(n)→inspīren
entuned *pp* attuned
entunen *v* chant or recite (a Mass)
envyned *pp* stored with wine, supplied with wine
ēom *n* uncle
eorþen *adj* earthen
ēr, āre, ōr *conj* before
erþēre *n* arbor, garden
ercedeken *n* archdeacon
ērd *n* earth, ground
ēre *n* ear, *pl* erys
ēre→bē(n)
ēre *n* ear, *pl* ēren, ērys
ērl *n* earl
erly *adv* early
erst *adv* earlier, before
ērt→bē(n)
ērthe, ērþe *n* earth
ērtheley *adj* earthly
es→bē(n)
eschaunge *n* exchange
ēse *n* ease
ēsed *pp* entertained
ēsen *v* treat hospitably
ēsy *adj* easy
(e)sta(a)t *n* state, array, rank, condition, in good estat=in good condition
estatlich *adj* dignified, majestic, stately
euchan, euch(e)→ēch
ēve *n* eve, evening
ēvel, ūvel, ȳvel *n adj, adv,* evil
ēven, ēvyn *adv* even, just, average
even-song *n* vesper
ēver(ē), ēvre, ǣvre *adv* ever
everemoore *adv* at all times, always
everich, ǣvric *pron, adj* each
everychon *pron* each one
everydeel *adv* in every part, wholly
evermoore, eavermāre→evermōre

evermōre, evermoore, evermāre *adv* never again, now and always

F

facultee *n* faculty, profession
fæstnen *v* fasten, *pp* fæstned
fayly *v* fail
fayn *adv* gladly, willingly
fair, a fair *n* a good one
fair, fayre, fayer, feire, vaire *adj* fair, beautiful, excellent, *sup* feherest
faire *adv* fairly, well, faire and fetisly= elegantly, faire and wel=completely
fairnesse *n* kindness, gentleness
fays→fō
faith *n* faith, belief
falde(n) *v* fail, falter, *prs 3sg* falt
faldying *n* a kind of woolen coarse cloth
falle(n), valle *v* fall, happen, *pt* fēl, fell, fīl, fēōl *pp* falle, fallyn, ifalle
fallow *n* fellow, *pl* fallowis
falt→falde(n)
famulier *adj* familiar
fān→fō
fāre *v* fare, go, *pt* fōr
farsed *pp* stuffed
farsen *n* stuff, cram
fast *adv* fast, quickly
faste *v* fast, abstain from food
faste *adj* close, very near
fē, fee *n* property, money, payment, a wage
fēble *adj* feeble
fēblelīke *adv* feebly, scarcely, wretchedly
fēde, feede *v* feed, *prs 3sg* fēt, *pt* fedde, *pp* fedde
fēde *pp adj* faded, withered
fee symple *n* property held absolutely,

as contrasted with feetail, used of entailed property
feghtande→**fyghte(n)**
feht→**fiht**
feynen *v* feign, invent (a story), *pp* **feyned** false
feire→**fair**
felawe *n* fellow, **good felawe**=drinking companion, boon, companion, regular guy
felaweship *n* fellowship
fēle *v* feel
fēle, vēle, veole *n, adj* many, much
felony *adv* cruelly
fēr, ferre *adv* far, afar, *adj* distant, remote, *pl* **ferre**, *comp* **ferre**, *sup* **ferreste**
fērlīch *n* terror, fear
fern *adj* distant, remote, ancient
ferre(r) *adv comp* farther
ferreste *adj sup* farthest
ferther *adv* further
ferthyng *n* a small bit, a particle, ferthing, morsel
festen *v* fasten
festne *v* fasten
fet *pp* fetched
fēt(e)→**fōt(e)**
fetys *adj* neat, elegant, featous
fetisly *adv* skilfully, neatly
fetten *v* bring, *pp* **fet**
fiftēne *num* fifteen
fyghte(n) *v* fight, *prs p* **feghtande**
figure *n* a parable or metaphor
fiht, feht *n* fight
fil→**fallen**
fille(n) *v* fill, fulfil, *pt pl* **fylden**, *pp* **filde**
fylthe *n* filth
fīn *n* end
fynch *n* dupe, **pullen a fynch**=do something with cunning, seduce a girl

fīnde(n), fȳnden, fīndenn *v* find, *pt* **fōnd(e), font, fōunde,** *pl* **fōundun, fōnden,** *pp* **fōunden, yfōunde**
fyr-reed *adj* as red as fire
fithele *n* fiddle
Flaundryssh *adj* made in Flanders or by Flemings
flēshe *n* flesh *gen* **flǣshess**
flēte(n) *v* flow, float, *pt* **fleten**
flex *n* flax
flȳe *v* fly, *imper* **flēo**, *pl* **flȳes**, *pt* **fliȝte**
flyghyng(e) *n* flying, flight
floytynge *pres p* fluting
flōr, flōūr, flūr *n* flower
flugen, flugæ, fluhen→**flȳe**
fnast *n* breath
fō, vō, fay *n* foe, *pl* **fān, vān, fayis**
folc, follc *n* folk
fold *n* pen, enclosure, *fig* a parish
folwe(n), follȝhten *v* follow, *pt* **followit**
for, fore, forr, vor *prep* for, because of, concerning, as for, **for tō, for till**=in order to *conj* for, because, since, **for any thyng**=despite everything, at any cost, **for sothe**=truly, **for aught I woot**=for all I know, **for the nones**=at the time, for this occasion, for then once
fōr→**fāre**
forbēre *v* forbear, *pt* **forbāren**
for-bȳ *adv* by, past
forcursæd *pp adj*, cursed
fordō(n) *v* destroy, spoil
fordolked *pp a* stupefied
for(e)ward *n* agreement
forgaa *v* forgo
forȝete *v* forget
forheed *n* forehead
forhwī→**forwhȳ**
forlēse *v* lose, *pp* **forlōren**
forlēte *v* leave off, abandon

forneys, fornys *n* furnace, *fig* something exceedingly bright
forōūten *prep* without
forpyned *n* suffering from torment, greatly pained, tormented, wasted away
forsōþe *adv* forsooth
forster *n* forester
forswēre(n) *v* forswear, perjure, *pp* **forswōren**
forswōren, forsuōren *pp adj*, falsely sworn
fort *conj* until
fōrþen *v* accomplish, carry out, *pt* **fōrbedd**, *pp* **fōrbedd**
forþī, forrþī, forþȳ, vorþi *adv* therefore, *conj* becausez
fortune *n* fortune
fortunen *v* presage
forward *n* agreement
forwhȳ, forhwī *conj* why, because
fōt(e), uōt(e) *n* foot, *pl* **fēt, fēte**
fother *n* cart-load
foughten *pp* fought
foūnde, foūnun→**fȳnde(n)**
fōwle, fuȝele *n* bird, *pl* **foweles, fōwheles**
frā→**frō**
fram, from, vrom *prep* from
frame *n* profit
frankeleyn *n* a landowner and member of the gentry ranking immediately below the nobility, franklin
fraternitee *n* a guild, brotherhood
frē *adj* free
fredom *n* generosity, freedom, liberality
fremede *adj* foreign
frenchype *n* friendship
frēnd *n* friend, *pl* **frēndys**
frendshipe *n* (commercial) alliance
frere *n* friar
frest *n* delay, **but langar frest** without longer delay
frȳte *n* fruit
frō, frā, *prep* from, **frā that** from the time that
frogge *n* frog
fuȝele→**fōwle**
fuȝel-künne *n* race of birds
fūl, vūl *adj* foul, poorly
ful(l) *adj* full, *adv* full, very
fulluhht *n* baptism
fustian *n* a kind of cloth apparently made of cotton, flax, or wool; not necessarily coarse or of poor quality

G

gaa→**gō(n)**
gadere(n), gadre, gedere *v* gather, come together, assemble *pp* **gadered**
gadering *n* gathering, council, assembly
gǣde→**gō(n)**
gǣld→**ȝēld**
gǣre→**ȝēr**
gǣt→**ȝɛt(e)**
gaf→**ȝive(n)**
gay *adj* radiant, bright
Galice *prop n* Galicia in Spain
galyngale *n* an aromatic root, in English, sweet cyperus root, used for spice
gamen *impers* rejoice
gan→**ginne(n)**
gāne→**gō(n)**
gang, gangen *v* go
gat-toothed *adj* having teeth set wide apart
gauded *pp adj* (of a rosary) adorned with large, ornamental beads
gedere→**gadere(n)**
geere *n* equipment, clothing, tools, instruments
gegge *n* maid
geldhalle *n* guildhall
geldyng *n* a gelded horse, gelding
gemme *n* gem, *pl* **gemmeȝ**

gentil *adj* noble, excellent
gēr *v* do, make, *pt* **gert**
gerland *n* garland
Gernade *prop n* Gernada
gernera *n* granary, storehouse for grain
gessen *v* guess, **as I gess**=according to my etimate
gete(n) *v* get
gēt→ȝēt
gif→ȝif
gynglen *v* jingle
ginne(n) *v* begin, *pt* **gan, can**
gipo(u)n *n* a tight tunic often worn under armor, short vest
gipser *n* a pouch hanging from a girdle or sash
girl *n* a child of either sex
girles *n pl* youths
gise *n* manner, way, fashion, **at his owene gise**=after his own fashion, as he pleases
gyve *n* gift
gyven→ȝive(n)
glad *adj* glad, happy, *comp* **gladur**
glarynge *adj* glaring wildly
glē, glēo *n* glee, joy
glīde *v* glide
gobet *n* a fragment, shred
God *n* God
gōd, good, gōūd, gud(e) *n* good, benefit, property, **dide gōd** did good, *adj* good, *comp* **better**, *sup* **best**
goddhead *n* godhead
goddspell *n* gospel *gen* **goddesplelles**
gōlde *n* gold
goliardeys *n* a buffoon, ribald
gō(n), gan *v* go, *inf* **goon**, *pt* **gāede**, *pp* **gāne**
good→gōd
goodly *adv* gladly
goost *n* ghost

goot *n* goat
Gootlond *prop n* the isle of Gottland
governaunce *n* conduct, behavior
governour *n* a leader
grāce *n* grace, favor
grayne *n* grain, *pl* **grayneȝ**
grāme *n* harm
grāve *n* grave
greet *adj* great
grēf(e) *n* grief, sorrow
grehound *n* greyhound
grey *adj* (of eyes) bright, glaring
grēne, greyn *n, adj* green
gresse *n* grass
grēt *adj* great, swollen with anger, *comp* **grettre**
Grete See *prop n* the Mediterranean
grēten *v* weep, *pt pl* **grēten**
gretteste *adj sup* greatest
grēve *v* injure, torture, vex, *pp* **grēved**
grew→growe(n)
grin *n* some instrument of torture
grys *n* a gray fur
grōpe *v* probe, try
gropen *v* examine
grōūnde, grūnde *n* ground, foundation
grounded *adj* learned (in a branch of knowledge)
growe(n) *v* grow
grucche *v* grudge, complain
gud(e)→gōd

ȝ

ȝæf→ȝeve
ȝē, ȝhē *pron 2pl* ye *dat/acc* **ȝōw**, *poss* **ȝōūr, ȝōw̄re**
ȝēde, yēde *pt* went
ȝēld, gǣld *n* taxes
ȝeoi *interj* yes, certainly

ȝēr, gær *n* year
ȝērne *adv* eagerly
ȝērne *v* desire, yearn for, *pt 2sg* ȝerrndesst
ȝēt, ȝūt, gēt *conj, adv* yet, still
ȝeve, yeve, ȝyve *v* give, *pt* yaf, ȝef, *pp* yeven, iȝeven
ȝhē→ȝē
ȝif, ȝiff, gif, yf *conj* if
ȝive(n) *v* give, *pt* ȝaf, gāf, yaf, *pt pl* iāfen, *pp* gyven
ȝoȝeling *n* goggling
ȝōw̄, ȝōūr, ȝōw̄r→ȝē
ȝōw̄reselve *intens pron* yourself, yourselves

H

hā→hēo
habbe→hāve(n)
haberdasshere *n* a dealer in small articles, especially hats and caps
habergeon(s) *n* a coat or jacket of mail or scale armor, often worn under plate armor
hād *n* rank
had, hadden→hāve(n)
hærne *n* brain
hǣved→hēved
haf, hāfe→hāve(n)
hālde→hōlde
hāle *n* recess, nook
halechen, halȝen *n pl* saints
half *adj* half
hāly, hōli, hallȝhe *adj* holy
hāly *adv* wholly
hals *n* neck
halt→hōlde(n)
halve cours *n* half courses
halwe *n* hallow, saint, shrine
ham→hī
han→hāve(n)

hand(es)→hōnd
handle(n) *v* handle
hānge(n) *v* hang, cause to hang, suspend *pt* hēng, hēnged, hēngen, *pp* hanged
happe *v impers* happen, *pt* hapnyt
hard *adj* hard, difficult, heard iheortet hard-hearted
hardely, hardily, hardyly *adv* boldly, firmly, assuredly, certainly
hardyment *n* courage, boldness
harlot *n* a trifler
harlotrie(s) n base, crude, or obscene behavior
harn, hærne *n* brain
harneisen *v* adorn (a weapon, a girdle, etc.)
harpe *n* harp
harre *n* the hinge of a door or lock
has→hāve(n)
hatte→hōte
haunt *n* the place frequented
hāve(n), hāve(n), habbe(n) *v* have, *ind 1sg* hafe, haf, hāve, *3sg* hafeþþ, haþ, hath, has, *pl* hafenn, hāfe, *pt* had, hadde, hāvede, hefde, *pt pl* hadden, hefden, *sbj prs* hāve, haf, *pt* had
hāvyng *n* behavior, demeanor
hē *pron 3sg masc* he *dat/acc* him, hym, *poss* his, hys(e), hys(e), *dat* him
hē→hī
heed *n* head
heer *n* hair
heeth, heeþ *n* heath
hēfed→hēved
hegge *n* hedge
heh(e), heighe→heigh
heigh, hēi *adj* high, in heigh and lough= in all respects, absolutely, hyer hond= victory
heir *n* heir
hēlden→hōlde
hele *n* welfare

hellepīne *n* the torments of hell
helm *n* helmet
helpe *v* help, cure *pp* **holpen**
hem→**hī**
hēnde *adj* gracious
hēnde *adv* near
henten *v* obtain, get
hēo, hī *pron 3sg fem* she, *nom* **hā**, scheo, *dat/acc* **hir(e), hyr, hī,** *poss* **hir(e), hyr,** her
hēo→**hī**
hēolde(n)→**hōlde**
heom→**hē, hī**
heonne *adv* hence
heorte→**hert(e)**
heortelīche *adv* heartily
heoven(e)→**heven**
heowin *v* hue, color
her→**hēo, hī**
herberwe *n* harbor, inn
hērde→**hēre(n)**
her(e)→**hēo, hī**
hēre *adv* here
hēre *n* army
hēr-efter *adv* hereafter
hēre(n) *v* hear, *pt* **herde, iherde,** *pp* **iherd**
hermīte *n* hermit
hert(e), heorte *n* heart
hethen *n* heathen
hethenesse *n* heathen lands
heu, hew(e) *n* hue
heue(n) *v* raise
hēve(n) *v* lift, heave, *pt* **hōf**
hēved, hēfed, hǣved *n* head
heven(e), heoven(e), hewen *n* heaven
hevenerīche *adj* heavenly
hēvie, hēvy *adj* heavy
hēvynes *n* heaviness
hēwe *n* complexion
hī, hē, hēo *pron 3pl* they, *nom* **hā,** *dat/acc* **hem, heom, ham, ham be** those who, *poss* **her(e), hare, hir**
hī→**hēo**
hȳ *n* haste, **in hȳ** in haste, soon
hīde *v* hide
hider *adv* hither
hierde *n* a herdsman
highte was called cf. OE hāten=to call
him→**hē**
hymself, himselve, himsülf *intens pron* himself
hyndreste *sup* of **hinder**(*adj*) lying or situated in the rear, hindermost
hȳne, hīne *n* slave, servant, hind, a farm laborer, *pl* **hīne, hȳnen**
hir(e), hyr→**hēo**
hīrd *n* army, retinue, court
hyre *n* payment, **setten to hyre**=farm out (one's benefice) in return for fixed payment
his(e), hys(e)→**hē**
hit, it, itt *pron 3sg neut* it, *poss* **his**
hō→**whō**
hōked *pp adj* hooked
hoker *n* contempt, disdain
hōlde(n), hālde(n), hēālden *v* hold, keep, **holden after the newe world**= follow the new customs, *prs 3sg,* halt, *pt* **hēold, hēolde,** *pt pl* **hēolden, hēlden,** *sbj pt* **hēolde,** *pp* **hōlden, hālden, ihālden**
hōli→**hāli**
hōliwrite *n* Holy Writ, Bible
holpen→**helpe(n)**
hōlt *n* holt, wood
holwe *adj* hollow
hōnde(e), hand *n* hand, *pl* **hōnden, handes**
honest *adj* befitting one's social status
hōnge, hōngi→**hange(n)**
hōny *n* honey
hooly *adj* holy
hooly *adv* wholly

hoom *n* home
hoomly *adv* in a homely manner
hoore, hooris→**hōre**
ho(o)st *n* the landlord of an inn
hoot *adj* hot
hoot(e) *adv* ardently, passionately
hōre→**hēo**
hōre, hoore *n* whore
hors(e) *n* horse
hosle(n) *v* housel
hostelrye *n* hosterly, inn
hostiller *n* innkeeper
hōte, hātten *v* be called, *pt* **hatte**
hoūnde, hūnd *n* dog, hound, *pl* **hoūndis, hūndis**
hous *n* a religious order or its establishment
housebande *n* husband
hōw̄, hū *adv* how
humour *n* one of the four cardinal fluids, blood, phlegm, choler, and melancholy or black choler
hunger, hūnger *n* hunger
hūre *adv* certainly, especially
hūrne *n* corner
hurt *n* hurt, wound
hūs *n* house
hwan, hwon→**whan**
hwat→**what**
hwērtō→**whērtō**
hwīle→**whīl(e)**
hwnt *n* hunt
hwō→**whō**

I

Ī→**ich**
ī→**in**
iāfen→**ʒive(n)**
ich, icc, ic, ihc, Ī *pron 1sg, dat/acc* **mē**, *poss* **mī(n)**, my

icūndur *adj comp* more akin, more suitable
iēden→**ʒēde**
if→**ʒif**
ifēre *n* companion
īʒe→**eye**
iheortet *pp adj* hearted, **heard iheorted** hard-hearted
iherd(e)→**hēre(n)**
ilke *adj* same, very
ilōme *adv* often, frequently
imeind *pp* mixed, mingled
in, inn, ī *adv, prep* in
infecten *v* invalidate
inne *adv* inside, within
inōʒ(e), inōh, onōh, eneuch *adv* enough
inpassed→**passe(n)**
ipeint *pp* painted
inspīred *v* inspire, breathe life into, *pp* **inspīred**
intill *prep* into
inwardlīce *adv* completely, perfectly, profoundly
inwið *prep* within
īren *n* iron
is, iss→**bē(n)**
isēʒ→**sē(n)**
ishōte→**shōte**
islein→**slē(n)**
isōld→**selle(n)**
istraht *pp adj*, stretched
it→**hit**
itūked→**tūkien**
ibrunge *pp adj*, close
iburlet→**burlin**
īvi *n* ivy
iweorret→**werrie(n)**
iwis, iwys *adv* certainly, for sure, for certain

J

janglere *n* a raconteur
jape *n* trick
Jēsu Crīst Jesus Christ
jet *n* fashion, **of the newe jet**=in the newfangled way, in the latest fashion
joye *n* joy
jolitee *n* beauty, elegance, jolliness
juēle *n* jewel
jugge *v* appraise, estimate
juste *v* joust, tourney
justīse *n* justice, **justīse dōn** inflict punishment

K

kaysēre *n* emperor
kan *v* know, be able
kannunk *n* canon
keep *n* attention, heed, **taken heep (of)**– take heed (of)
ke(e)pen *v* take care, guard, observe, keep
ke(e)pere(e) *n* prior, keeper
kēne *adj* pointed, sharp, keen, hardy, bold
kēpe *v* keep
kerven *v* cut up meat at table, *pt* **carf**
kest→**caste**
kide *n* kid, young goat
kille *v* kill, *pt* **cūlled**
kin, kyn, künne, cünne *n* kindred, kind, sort, *sg gen* **cünnes**, *pl gen* **cünne**, **nā kyn thyng** in no way whatever
kind *adj* pleasant
kīnde, kȳnde, kǖnde, cǖnde *n* kind, nature, *pl* **kȳndis**
kinedom(e) *n* kingdom
king, kyng, kīng *n* king, *gen* **kinges**, **kyngis**
kisse *v* kiss
kissinge *n* kissing
kitōūn *v* kitten
kīþen, kǖþen, cǖþen *v* make known, show, announce, *pres 1 sg* **cǖþe**
knarre *n* a muscular thick-set fellow
knāve *n* boy
knicht, knict *n* knight
knyght *n* knight, **knyght of the shire**=a member of Parliament
knitten *v* knit, fasten attach
knowen *v* recognize
knowth(e) *pp adj* renowned, famous
kōld *n* cold
kōūden, kunne→**can**
kōw̄þe *pp adj* known, renowned
kǖþen→**kīþen**

L

laas *n* cord used to suspend a hanging object, lace
labōūre *n* labor
lacche *v* laugh, *pt* **lauȝte**
lafte→**lēven**
laike *v* play, sport
lakken *impers* be lacking
lānd(e)→**lōnd(e)**
langage *n* language
langar→**lōng**
lanhūre *adv* at least
lap→**lēpe(n)**
large *adj* broad, *adv* broadly
lasēr *n* leisure, opportunity
lāste *v* last, continue
lāt(e)→**lēte**
late *adv* recently, newly, lately
latoun *n* latten, a mixed metal like brass
lāverd→**lōrd**

lazar *n* leper
leafden→lēve(n)
leasse→lesse
lecherīe, lecherȳe *n* lechery, debauchery
lēde(n) *v* lead
leed *n* cauldron, leaden vessel
lēf, leef *n* leaf, *pl* lēāf, lēves
lēf, lēōf *adj* dear
lefdi, leafdi *n* lady
leid(e), leyde→leye(n)
leye(n) *v* lay, put, *pt* leyde, *pp* leyd, leid(e)
leysche *n* leash
leit→lēte
lēne(n) *v* lend, grant, *pp* lēnedd
lenger *adv comp* longer
lēōfmon, lēōvemon *n* lover, mistress, lady
lēōve→lēf
lēpe(*n*) *v* leap, *pt* lēp, lap
lēre→lōre
lērnen(n) *v* learn
lēse *v* lose, *pt* lēste, *pp* lost
less *n* lie, **vithōūten less** without lie, truly
lesse, lasse, leasse *comp adv* less
lest, leste→list, listen
lēte, lāte *v* let, permit, leave, *pr sg* let, *pt* lēt(e), leit
lēte *n* appearance
lette, leten *v* stop, impede, *pt* lette, *pp* ilet
leten→lette
leðer *n* leather
Lettow *prop n* Lithuania
letuarie(s) n an electuary, remedy
lēve→lēf
lēve(n), leyve *v* grant, permit, leave cease, remain *sbj pr sg* leve, *pl* leften, leafden, *pt* leften, leafden, *pp* laft, yleft, left

lever(e) *adj* lēf(=dear, pleasant)의 비교급. rather, **him were levere**=rather, he preferred to
lewdnesse *n* stupidity
lewed *adj* lay, non-clerical, ignorant
libbe→live(n)
līcam, līcome *n* fleshly body, corpse
licenciat *adj* allowed to preach or hear confession, holder of licence
līcome→līcam
licōūr *n* moisture, liquid, sap, liquor
Lyeys *prop n* Layas, now Ayas, in Armenia
līen, lȳ *v* lie
līf, lȳf *n* life, līves (adverbial gen) alive, **on līve** alive
lyfande→live(n)
lyghtly, lyȝtlich *adv* lightly, easily
lyke *adj* like
līken *v* compare, *pp* līkned
līke(n), lȳke(n) *v impers* please, **if you līketh**=if you wish
lime *n* limb
lymitour *n* a mendicant friar who was appointed to beg, to hear confessions, preach within certain limits.
Lincol *prop n* Lincoln
lipsen *v* lisp
list, lest n pleasure, joy, lust
liste(n), lüste(n) *v impers* please, **him list(e)**=he wishes, chooses
lystes usually *pl*, lists, an enclosed area for jousting, **in lystes**=in combat
lytarge *n* white lead
lite *adj* little, unimportant, **muche and lite**=great and lowly, everyone
līt(t)el, lyttil, little *adj* little
litunge *n* color, tint
live(n), lyve(n), libbe *v* live, *prs p* lyfande
liveneþ *n* sustenance
lyveree *n* livery, uniform of a guild,

anything delivered or handed over
lodemenage *n* skill in navigation, pilotage; a course followed
lōdlich→**lōblich**
lof *n* some instrument of torture
lōʒen→**lacche**
lōke(n), looke, lōkien *v* look (about, after), take care of, *prs 1sg* **lōki**
loken→**lūke(n)**
lokkes *n pl* locks of hair
lōnd(e), land(e) *n* land
lōng, lang *adj* long, *comp* **langar**
lōnge *adv* long, *comp* **lēng, nō lēng** no longer
lōnge(n) *v* long, desire, yearn, belong
loore *n* a spiritual or religious teaching, **Cristes loore**=Christ's teaching
looth *adj* hateful, displeasing, **looth hym were**=it would be loathsome to him, he would hate
lōrd, lāverd *n* lord, *gen pl* **lōrdene**
lordynges usually *pl*, a term of polite address to superiors, sirs
lōre, lāre *n* lore
losse *n* loss
lost→**lēse**
lōþ *adj* hateful
lōthe *v impers* loathe
lōþlich, lōdlich *adj* disagreeable, loathly
lough *adj* low
love, luve, lufe *n* love, lover
love, lufe, luve, luvien *v* love, *prs 3sg* **luveþ**, *pl* **lufes**, *pt* **lovede, lufit**, *sbj prs* **luvie**, *pt sg* **lüuede**
lovedayes *n pl* days for settling disputes
loveyer *n* lover
lowely *adj* humble
luce *n* pike
lūd *adv* loud
luf-daungēre *n* love-bondage, power of love

lūke(n) *v* lock, fasten, *pp* **loken**
lust *n* pleasure, enjoyment
luste *n* lust
lüste→**list(e)**
lusty *adj* vigorous, energetic
luve, luvie(n)→**love**

M

mā→**mō**
mācod, māced, maad→**māke**
magyk *n* magic, **magyk natureel**=the knowledge of hidden natural forces (e.g. magnetism, stellar influence), and the art of using these in calculating future events, curing diseases, etc.
mai, may *v* be able to, may, *ind prs 2sg* **maht**, *3sg* **mot(e)**, *pl* **mōw̄e(n), muʒe**, *pt* **micte, mycht, myght, miʒt(e), myʒte, myhte, mihhte, maghte, moʒt, moucte, mougte, mühte(n)**, *sbj* **mōw̄e**
maid→**māke**
maid, maiden *n* maid, maiden
mair→**mōre**
mais→**māke**
maistres *n* masters
maistrie *n* power, force, mastery, excellence, **for the maistrie**=in the highest degree, extremely
māke(n), makien *v* make, *prs 3sg* **mākes, mais**, *pl* **maken**, *pt* **māked(e), mācod, maid**, *pp* **māced, māked**
male *n* bag, mail bag
malisūn *n* curse, malediction
man *n* man, *sg gen* **mannes, mannus**, *pl* **men(e)**, *pl gen* **mens, mennes**
mandement *n* command, order
maneir, maner *n* manner, kind
mani(e), many, monie *adj* many
manrēd *n* homage

marchal *n* an official in a royal or noble household in charge of ceremonies, protocol, seating service, etc.
marchant *n* merchant
marybones *n pl* marrow bones
marre *v* mar, *prs 2sg* **marreʒ**
martyr *n* martyr
māse *n* confusion
ma(u)nciple *n* a purchaser of provisions for inn of court or other institutions, purveyor
Maure *n* St. Maur
me *interj* why, now
mē→**ich, men**
mēde *n* mead, meadow
medlee *adj* of a mixed color
meede *n* desert, merit, meed, reward
meiht→**mai**
meistrīe *n* mastery, great deed
mekill→**mikel**
mellying *n* meeting, fight, melee
men, me *indef pron* one, people, they
men(e), mennes→**man**
mēne(n) *v* mean, *prs 3sg* **mēnebb**
menge *v* agitate, *prs 3sg* **meinb,** *pp* **meynd, imend**
menʒe *n* company of followers, army, host
mercenarie *n* hireling
mere *n* mare
mery, myrr, mürie *adj* merry, lovely, beautiful
meschief *n* misfortune
mēshe *v* crush
messe *n* mass
messebōc *n* mass-book, missal
messegēre *n* mass-gear
mēte *n* a particular meal, usually the first main meal of the day taken before or about noon; lunch, midday dinner, **at mēte**=at table.

mēte(n) *v* meet, *pt* **met**
micel→**mikel(l)**
mycht, miht(e) *n* might, power, *pl* **mihten**
micte, mycht→**mai**
mid, myd *prep* with
Middleburgh *prop n* Middelburg, in Holland
myght, myʒte, myhte, mihte→**mai**
mihti *adj* mighty
mikel(l), mykel, mekill, muchel, micel *adj, adv* big, great, much
mīlde *adj* mild, gentle
mīle *n* mile, long time
mī(n), my→**ich**
mynystralcȳe *n* merry-making, minstrelsy
mirācle *n* miracle
myry→**mery**
myrie *adj* merry
mirke *adj* dark
mȳs→**mōūs**
myscarien *v* suffer harm, go bad, go wrong
mysse *v* miss, be rid of
myster *n* occupation, profession, trade, craft
mō, mā *adv, comp* more
moche, muche *adj, adv* much
mōd *n* mood, temper
moghte, moʒt→**mai**
moyste *adj* moist
mōlde *n* earth, *gen* **mōldeʒ**
mōne *n* moon
monie, mony→**mani**
monk(e) *n* monk, *pl* **monekes**
mo(o)ten *v* be allowed (to~), can, must, in an oath
mōre, māre, mair *adj, adv comp* more
mormal *n* gangrene
morne *n* morrow, morning
morne-milk *n* morning-milk
morne-song *n* morning song
mortreux *n* a kind of stew, a dish of

mōse n titmouse
mōste *adj, adv sup* most, greatest
mōte *v* must, may, can
mottelee, motteleye *n* parti-colored fabric, motley
moucte, mouhte→mai
mōūl *n* moud, earth
mōūs, mūs *n* mouse, *pl* mys
mōūth *n* mouth
mōw̄e(n)→mai
muche and lite *adj* great and small, important and unimportant
muchel *adj* much
muʒe, mūhte(n)→mai
mülne *n* mill
müngunge *n* memory, remembrance, commemoration
mürie, murye→mery
murierly *adv comp* more merrily
mūs→mōūs
muwe *n* cage, (originally a cage where hawks were kept while moulting)

N

nā→nōn
nacioun *n* nation
nader *n* adder, viper
nǣvre→nēver(e)
nākit *pp adj* naked, unarmed
nam, nāmen→nime(n)
nāme *n* name
namō, namōre, namoore *adv* no more
nān→nōn
narette, nearette *v* do not repute, or account
narew, nareu, narwe *adj* narrow
nas < ne was

natheless *adv* nevertheless
natureel *adj* natural
nāveþ, nāveð→hāve(n)
ne *adv* not, no, *conj* nor
nearow→narew
neb *n* face
nēde *n* need nēdeʒ (*adverbial gen*) needs, necessarily
nēde(n) *impers* it is necessary
neet *collect* livestock, esp. cattle
nēh→nīʒ
nekke *n* neck
nēr, nēor, neir *adv* near *comp* nēorre
nēre→bē(n)
nes→bē(n)
nēse *n* nose
nest(e) *n* nest
nēve *n* nephew *pl* nēves
nēver(e), nēuer, nǣvre *adv* never
ny *adv* nigh, nearly, as ny as ever(e) he kan=as closely as he can
nyce *adj* fastidious, fussy
nieʒ→nīʒ
nightertale *n* nighttime
nīʒ, nieʒ, *adv* nigh, near, nearly
niʒt, niht *n* night, *adverbial gen* nightes
niʒtingāle *n* nightingale
nime(n) *v* take *pt sg* nam *pt pl* nāmen
niste→wite(n)
nō, na *adj* no *adv* not, not at all
noghte, noʒt, nouʒt(e), nout *adv* not
nolde(s)→wille
nōn, nān *indef pron* none
nones→for
nōnes-weis *adv* not at all, in no way
nonne *n* nun
noon *adj* none
noot < ne woot
norþ *n* north
norrissyng *n* nutritiousness
nōse, noyse *n* nose

nosethirles *n* nostrils
note *n* nut
not heed *n* close cropped head
nouȝt(e), nout→**noghte**
nōw̄(e), nū *adv* now
nōwiderwardes *adv* in no way
nowthe *adv* now, **as nowthe**=at this time, for now
nūþe *adv* now

O

o→**on**
ō→**ōn, of**
of, off(e) *prep* of, concerning, by, because of, with, off
offertoire *n* an antiphon sung or said in the mass during the collection of the offering
office *n* secular employment as clerk
offrynge *n* offertory
ofgōn *v* win
oft(e) *adv* oft, frequent
oftesȳthes *adv* often
oghte *indef pron* aught, anything, something
oynement *n* medical salve, ointment
oynon *n* onion
oystre *n* oyster
ōld *adj* old
on, o *adv, prep* on, in
ōn(e), ō, ān, āne *indef pron, adj* one, *fem sg dat* **ōre,** *adverbial gen* **ōnes, at ōnes** at once, **ōnne**(*adverbial acc*) only, with difficulty
ondswerien, andswarien *v* answer, *pt* **andswarede,** *pp* **iondsweret**
onōh→**inōȝ(e)**
ooth *n* oath
ōpen, upen *adj* open, uncovered, evident
or *conj* or

ōr→**ēr**
ordyre *n* order
ordres *n pl* religious orders
Orewelle *prop n* Orwell
oryent *n* orient
ōþe, āthe *n* oath
ōther, ōther, ōthir, ōthyr *adj* other, second
ōther, outhire, owthire *conj* or, **outhire (owthire)**⋯**or** either⋯or
ōtherwhīle *adv* at other times
oughte→**owen**
ounce *n* a tiny bunch
oune→**owen**
our→**ōver**
ōūr(e), ōw̄re, ūre pron our
ōūte, ōw̄te, ūt *adv* out
outhir→**ōþer**
outrely *adv* absolutely, utterly, quite
outridere *n* an office of an abbey or convent who rides out to do the external affairs
ōver, ōfer, our *prep* over
over-al *adv* everywhere, generally
overeste *adj* uppermost
ōverheghede *pp* carried too high up
ōverkumen *v* overcome
ōverlēpe *v* leap upon *pp* **ōverlēpe**
ōverlyttil *adv* too little
ōvermekill *adv* too much
ōversēon *v* look down upon, *pt* **oversēȝ**
oversithon *adv* too frequently
ōverspradde *pp* spread over, covered
ōwel *n* flesh-hook
owen *v* possess, own, *pt* **ouhte, aucht, āhte**
owen, oun(e) *adj* own
ōwer *adv* anywhere
ōw̄er→**our**
ōwher *adv* anywhere
ōw̄re→**wē**
ōw̄te→**ōūte**

owthire→ōþer
Oxen(e)fōrd *prop n* Oxford

P

pa(a)s *n* a walking pace
pade *n* toad
paye *n* liking, pleasure
painen *refl* take pains
Palatye *prop n* Palathia
palfrey *n* riding horse
palmere *n* a pilgrim, originally a pilgrim to the Holy land
paramūr *adv* as a lover
pardee *interj* by God, indeed, cf. F. par dieu
pardoner *n* seller of 'pardons'
pardoun *n* a document granting indulgence
parfit *adj* perfect
parisshen *n* parishioner
parvys *n* an enclosure, portico, or porch in front of a church, especially St. Paul's, where lawyers meet
passe(n) *v* pass, *prs pl* passes, *pp* ypassed
patente *n* patent, bi patente=by the authority of the king's letters patent
patriark *n* patriarch
pecock *n* peacock
pees *n* peace
peire *n* pair, set
penaunce *n* penance, yeven penaunce= impose penance
pērce(n) *v* pierce
pērde *interj* truly, indeed
pēre *n* peer, equal
pēre(n) *v* appear
perfay *adv* by faith
perilōūslīch *adv* perilously
perle *n* pearl
pers *adj* blue, *n* cloth of bluish color

persāve *v* perceive, *pt* persāvit
persoun *n* parson, rector
pese-hole *n* pease-hull, pea-pod
philosophie *n* knowledge
philosophre *n* philosoper, especially an alchemist or magician
piled *pp* deprived of hair, bald, plucked, scanty
pilwe-beer *n* pillow-case
pynched *pp* pleated
pynchen *v* cavil at, find fault with
pīne *n* pain, torture
pīne *v* torture, *pt* pīned
pīning *n* torture, suffering
pīpe *n* pipe, whistle
pitaunce *n* portion of food
pitous *adj* pitiful
plaiding *n* dispute
plaie, playe→pleye(n)
plait *n* argument, dispute
pleye(n), plaie, playe *v* play, jest, *pt* pleyde
pleyn *adv* fully
plesaunt(e) *adj* pleasing
poynaunt *adj* pungent
poynte *n* point, in good poynte=in good condition
pomely *adj* spotted, dappled with spots
pōpe *n* pope
poraille *n* poor people
porciōūn *n* portion
port *n* bearing, deportment, demeanor
portraien *v* draw or paint pictures
posshen *v* push, *pt* possed
post *n* pillar
poudre-marchant *n* a kind of spice or mixture of spices, flavoring powder
poure *v* pore
pouren *v* read (a book) intently
pōvre *adj* poor
praye *v* pray, *prs p* prayand

praktisour *n* practitioner
precios *adj* precious
preie, preye, prye *v* pray, supplicate, ask
press *n* condition of being hard pressed, danger
presse *n* curling iron, closet for clothes
prēst *n* priest
preven *v* prove, testify
prȳde *n* pride
prikasour *n* horseman, mounted hunter, hard rider
prike(n) *v* prick, incite, stimulate
priking *n* tracking the hare by its footmarks
prynce *n* prince
prȳs *n* renown
prīse, *v* praise, *pp* **prīsit,** *n* prize, price
prisūn n prison
pryuy *adj* familiar, secret, special
propre *adj* (one's) own, proper
proue(n) *v* prove, discover, *pt sg* **proued**
Pruce *prop n* Prussia
pulle *v* pluck
pultrye *n* poultry
purchacen *v* make gains, become rich
purchas *n* (illegal) gain, earning
purchasyng *n* acquisition of property
purchasour *n* purchaser
purtreye→**portraien**
putte(n) *v* put, *prs 3sg* **puttes,** *pp* put

Q

quarterne *n* prison-cell
quab→**quēthe(n)**
queme *adj* agreeable, pleasing
quēresoēver *conj* wheresoever
quēthe(n) *v* say, speak, *pt* **quab, quod**
quhat→**what**
quhen→**whan**

quhīll→**whīle**
quyken *v* bring to life, quicken
quiste *n* bequest, testament
quiten *v* requite
quod→**quēthe(n)**

R

rachentēges *n pl* fetters
ragen *v* romp, frolic
raiss→**rīse**
ran→**renne(n)**
ratōn, ratōūn *n* rat
rāþe *adv* quickly
raughte→**recchen**
rǣve(n)→**rēve(n)**
rēād→**rēd(e)**
rebel *adj* disobedient
recche *v* care, desire
recchelees *adj* negligent of duty, careless
reccehen *v* reach, hold out the hand, *pt* raughte
recorden *v* recall
rēd(e) *n* counsel, advice
rēde v read, *prs p* **rēdande**
rēd(e), reed, rēād *adj* red
re(e)d *n* counsellor, adviser, advice
reʒhelibōc *n* rule-book, book of canons
reherce *v* declare, pronounce
rehercen v repeat
reyn *n* rain
reysen *v* go on a military expedition
reken *adj* radiant
rekene *v* reckon
rekenynges *n* reckoning, **maken rekenynges**= pay the bill
remenaunt *n* the rest or remainder
rēnable *adj* loquacious, eloquent
rēnde *v* rend, tear
renke *n* man

renne(n), ryn(ne) *v* run, *prs 3sg* **renneth**, *pt* **ran**, *pp* **runne, yronne**
rennyng *n* running, **at a rennyng**=at one rush
renōn *n* renown
rent *n* (regular) income
reportour *n* umpire, reporter
resceyve *v* receive
rēsōn *n* reason, discourse, reasoning
reso(u)n *pl* words, remarks
rest, ryste *n* rest
reste(n), ryste *v* rest, *prs 3sg* **rest**, *pl* **rystes**
reule *n* rule
reulen *v* rule, **reuled bēn**=be directed, be controlled
reuþe *n* sorrow, misfortune
rēve *n* a reeve, officer responsible for managing the manor, steward
rēve(n) *v* rob, pillage, ravage
reverence *n* respect, honor
rewme *n* realm
riche, rice *adj* powerful, of high rank, rich
ryche3 *n* riches
richelīke *adv* richly
richt→ri3t(e)
rīde(n), rȳde(n) *v* ride, run here and there *prs 3sg* **ritt**, *pt sg* **rood**, *pl* **ryden**, *prs p* **rīdend**
right *adv* very
ryghtwȳse *adj* righteous
rigorōūsly *adv* rigorously
ri3t, richt *adv* just, rightly, properly
ri3te, richt *n* right, property
ringe(n) *v* ring, resound, *prs 3sg* **ringes**
rīs *n* twigs, small branches
rīse, ryss *v* rise, *pt* **raiss**
rīsing *n* rising, getting up
rōde, rood(e) *n* rood, cross
roialliche *adv* royally

rood(e)→rōde
rot *n* decay
rōte *n* a kind of fiddle, a small harp
rote *n* **bi rote**=by heart
rōþe *n* counsel, advice
rouncy *n* riding horse, hack, nag
rōūnde *adj* round
rōūnded *pp* in a rounded form
rōūte *n* rout, company
rōw̄te *n* heavy blow or stroke
Ruce *prop n* Russian
rudeliche *adv* rudely
ryde *v* ride
ryse *v* rise

S

sā→sō
sǣ, sē, šǣ, sēā *n* sea
say(e), said(e), sais→seye(n)
sāk *n* sake
sal→shal
samne(n) *v* gather, collect, **pp sammnedd**
sange→sōng
sangwyn *n* sanguine (of complexion), a clothe of glood-red color
sannt *n* saint
sāre→sōre
sat→sitte(n)
Satalie *prop n* Attalia
saucefleem *adj* affected with red pimples
saugh→seen
saule(s), sawle→soule
sautrie *n* psaltery, small harp
saw→sē(n)
sawcefleem *adj* pimpled
scærp(e)→sharp
scaled *pp* scabbled, scurfy
scarsly *adv* thriftily, economically
scater *v* scatter

scathe *n* pity, harm, misfortune
schal→**shal**
schăme→**shēme**
scharp→**sharp**
schawde, schawin→**schewe(n)**
scheawede, schewand→**shewe(n)**
schewen, shæwen, schawin *v* show, *pt* schawde
schīlde(n) *v* shield, protect
schȳneʒ→**shīne**
schȳr *adj* bright, shining
science *n* knowledge
sclendre *adj* slender
schō *pron 3sg fem* she
scholde(st)→**shal**
schort, scort→**short**
schōt, schūt→**shōte**
sclendre *adj* slender
scole *n* school
scoleyen *v* study, attend school
sculde→**shal**
sē→**šē(n)**
sēche(n) *v* seek, *prs pl* **sēcheþ**
sēde *n* seed
sēd(e)→**seye(n)**
seege *n* siege
se(e)ke, sike *adj* sick
seen *v* see, *pt* **saugh, seigh**
segge *n* sedge
segge *n* man
segge→**seye(n)**
seye(n), seyn, segge, say *v* say, *prs 2sg* **seist**, *3sg* **sais**, *pt* **sēd(e), seide, seyde**, said, *pt pl* **seyden**, *sbj prs 2sg segge*
seigh→**sēn**
seyl *n* sail
sēke(n) *v* seek, visit
self, sülf *pron, adj,* emphatic self
sēlde *adv* seldom
selle *v* sell
sēme *v* seem *prs pl* **sēmes**

sēm(e)ly *adj* suitable, proper, seemly, good-looking, *adv* becomingly, properly
semycope *n* short cloak
sen *conj* since
sē(n), sēon *v* see, *imper* **sē**, *prs 1sg* **sēo**, *pt* **saw, isēʒ, seigh**, *pp* **seyn, isein**
sendal *n* fine silk
sēnde(n) *v* send, *pt* **sēnde**
sengeley *adv* singly, separately apart (from others)
sentence *n* (moral) significance, meaning
sēr *adj* separate, several
Serebeŗi Salisbury
sergeant *n* a member of the superior class of barristers
servȳs *n* service
servysable *adj* willing to serve
seson *n* season
sessioun(s) n the session of the justice of the peace
sett(e) *v* set, be seated, *pt* **sette**, *pp* **set**, *prs p* **settand**
shal, schall, sall *v* shall, must, will, *prs 2sg* **shallt, shalt**, *pt 2sg* **scholdest**, *pt* **sholde, shollde, scholde, sculde, suld(e)**
shăme, schăme *n* shame *sg ge* **scheome**
shăme *v* be ashamed
shămefastnesse *n* modesty
shāpe(n) *v* shape, create, prepare, *pp* **shāped**
shaply *adj* fit, well-suited
sharp, scharp, scærp *adj* sharp
sheef *n* sheaf
sheeld *n* a french coin (escu)
sheeld *n* French coin
sheene *adj* bright, shining, beautiful
shēren *v* cut, *pp* **yshorn**
shewe(n), schewen, scheawe(n) *v* show, *prs 3sg* **sheweth**, *pt* **schawde**, *prs p* **schewand**
shīne, schȳne *v* shine, *prs pl* **schȳneʒ**,

pt **shoon**
shīre *n* shire
shirreve *n* a sheriff, chief executive officer of the Crown in each shire
shiten *pp* befouled
shō *n* shoe
shonye *v* shun
shoon→**shīne**
short, schort, scort *adj* short
shorte *v* shorten
shortly *adv* in short
shōte, schōte, schūt *v* shoot, *pt* **ishōte, schōt**
shōūr *n* shower
shrewe, schrewe *n* malignant man, villain
shrīven *v* shrive, *pp* **shriven**
sib *adj* related by blood, akin, *pl* **sybbe**
sic→**such**
sīde, sȳde *n* side, *pl* **sīden, sȳdeȝ**
syghte *n* sight
signe *n* a token, indication
significavit *n* a form of document issued by the Chancery for the arrest of an excommunicated person
sike *adj* sick
sikerly *adv* assuredly, without doubt
sikerlīke *adv* surely, certainly
sylver *n* silver
symphonīe *n* music
syn *conj* since, considering that, **syn that**= from the time that
syn(e) *n* sin
singe(n) *v* sing, *prs 3sg* **singes**, *pt* **sōng**
syngulēre *n* singleness, uniqueness
sinndenn→**bē(n)**
sīre *n* sire, father
sitte(n), sitte *v* sit, *prs 3sg* **sit**, *pt* **sat**, *pp* **sitte, set, sittyn**
siþen, syþen, sythyn *adv* then, since then, *conj* since
slē(n), slā *v* slay, *pt* **slew**, *pp* **islein**, **slayn, slāne**
sleight(e) *adj* cunning, trickery, deceit
slēpen *v* sleep, *pt* **sleep**
smal *adj* small
smālt→**smīte(n)**
smerten *impers* pain, hurt
smertly *adv* quickly, suddenly
smīte(n) *v* smite, *pp* **smǣt**, *pt* **smoot**
smōþ *adj* smooth
smoot→**smīten**
snāke *n* snake
snewen *v* snow, abound
snybben *v* reprove, chide, snub
sō, swō, swā, sā, se *adv* so, in such a way, *conj* as, **riȝt swō** just as if
soft *adj* soft, mild
soyn→**sōne**
solaas *n* solace
solempne *adj* of great dignity, important, stately
solempnely *adv* gravely
some(e), sum, somme, summe *pron, adj* some (one), a certain
som-del *adv* somewhat
somer *n* summer
somet *adv* together
somonour *n* summoner of offenders to the church courts
somtyme *adv* once on a time
sondry *adj* sundry, various
sōn(e), soyn *adv* soon, right away, immediately, **sōn so**=as soon as, *comp* **sōnner**
sone, sonn, sune *n* son
sōnd *n* envoy, messenger, *pl* **sōnden**
sōng→**singe(n)**
sōng(e), sange *n* song
sonne *n* sun
soore *adv* sorely
soote→**swēte**
so(o)th(e) n truth, **for soothe**=truly, **soothe**

to seyn=to tell the truth
soothly *adv* truly
sop *n* bread dipped in wine
soper *n* supper
sōre, sāre *adv* sorely, bitterly, a lot, much
sort *n* fate, lot
sorwe, soreȝe *n* sorrow
sotlīce *adv* foolishly
sōþ *n* truth, **to sōþe**=for a certainty
soule, saule, sawle *n* soul, *sg gen* **sawle**
souple *adj* supple
sovereygne *adj* sovereign, supreme
sownen *v* sound (an instrument), *prs p* **sownyng(e)**
space *n* space of time, spare time, opportunity
sparwe *n* sparrow
spec→**spēken**
spēche *n* speech, law-suit, plea
specially *adv* in particular
spēde *n* success
spēde *v* *reflex* hasten, *pt* **sped**
spēdely *adv* speedily
spēke(n) *v* speak, *pt sg* **spec**, *pt pl* **spōken**
spēkyng *n* speaking, discourse
spellen *v* tell, proclaim, preach
spēre *n* spear
spēre(n) *v* fasten, lock in, imprison *pp* **sperd**
spēten *v* spit
spȳce *n* spice, *pl* **spyceȝ, spȳseȝ**
spiced *adj* seasoned with the natural flavor obscured
spinne(n) *v* shoot or spring up, *sbj pt* **sponne**
spīre *n* reeds
spore *n* spur
spot *n* spot, blemish
sprēde(n) *v* spread, *pp* **ispread**
sprynge(n) *v* spring, grow up, *pt* **sprange**, *prs p* **spryngande**
squier *n* squire

staat→**(e)sta(a)t**
stābylness *n* stableness
stad *pp adj* placed (in peril)
stān *n* stone
stāne-dēd *adj* stone-dead
stannt→**stonde(n)**
stāre *v* stare, *prs 2sg* **stārest**
stark, starc *adj* stark, strong
stēde *n* steed
stēde, stide, stüde *n* place
stēle *v* steal
stēmen *v* glow
stēpe *adj* brilliant, glaring, bright
sterre *n* star
sterte, stirte *v* start, jump, *pt* **sterte, stirt**
stif *adj* stiff, fierce
styll *adj* still, quiet
stirt→**sterte**
styward *n* steward
stoc *n* stock, tree-stump
stonde(n) *v* stand, *prs 3sg* **stannt**, *pt* **stōd(e)**
stoon *n* stone
stoor *n* livestock
storke *n* stork
stot *n* horse, cob
stōünde moment, hour
straung(e) *adj* strange, foreign
streit *adj* rigorous, strict, narrow
strem *n* stream
strēng *n* cord
strīke *v* strike, move forward *pt* **strōke, strāk**
strōnd *n* shore, country, region, strand
strong *adj* strong
strūcyō *n* ostrich
stüde→**stēde**
studien *v* deliberate
stūnde *adv* at once, for the time
stuw *n* fishpond, stew
substaunce *n* means, wealth

subtilly *adv* cunningly, craftily
succōūr, sukurs *n* succor, help, supplies
such, sic, swylk *pron, adj* such
suencten→**swenche(n)**
suffisaunce *n* sufficiency
suffre *v* suffer, allow
suīke→**swīke**
surcoat *n* overcoat
suȳðe→**swīþe**
sülf, sülve→**self**
sumere *n* summer, **sumere dāle**=summer valley
sum(me)→**som(e)**
sum-wīle *adv* sometimes
sunne *n* sun
suōren→**swēre(n)**
superfluitee *n* excess, superfluity
surcōte *n* outer coat
sūþ *n* south
swā→**sō**
swā-sum *conj* as
swelle(n) *v* swell *pt* **swal**
sweyn *n* swain, servant
swenche(*n***)** *v* oppress, *pt* **suencten**
swēore *n* neck
swērd *n* sword, *pl* **swērdis**
swēre(n) *v* swear, *pt pl* **suōren, swōr**, *sbj prs* **swēre**
swēte, soote *adj* sweet
swētelīche *adv* sweetly, agreeably
swettnes *n* sweetness
swich, swych, suich *adj/pron* such
swīke, suike *n* traitor
swylk→**such**
swyn *n* swine
swynk *n* labor, toil
swynken *v* labor, toil
swynkere *n* a loose upper garment, laborer
swūþe, swȳþe, swȳðe, swū̃þe *adj* great, strong, *adv* very, greatly

T

tā→**tāke(n)**
tabard *n* a sleeveless coat for a laborer
tǣr→**bēr**
tǣronne *adv* thereon
taffata *n* taffeta, fine silk
taill *n* tail
taille *n* tally, credit, account scored on wood, **by taille**=on credit
takel *n* archery-gear, arrows, tackle
tāke(n), taken, tāk, tā *v* take, *pt* **tōk, tūk**, *pp* **tākenn**
tāle *n* talk, conversation
tālen *v* tell tales
tapycer *n* carpet or tapestry maker
tappestere *n* tapster, barmaid
targe *n* light shield
tart *adj* biting, pungent
tartre *n* tartar
tatt→**bat**
te, tē→**þe, þū**
tēche *v* teach
tēken(n) *adv* besides, in addition
telle(n) *v* tell, *pt* **talde**
temptatiūn *n* temptation
temple *n* inn of court, college of lawyers
terme *n* term, **in terme**=in terms, precisely
tendre *adj* tender
tēne, tēone *n* reproach, grief, hardship
tēre *n* tear
than(ne) *adv* then
tharray *n* array
thencrees *n* increase
thēr *adv* there, **thēr as**=(to/at/in the place) where
thērto *adv* in addition, thereto
thērwithal *adv* with it
thylke→**ilke**
thyng *n* a legal document
thō *pron* those

thombe *n* thumb
thries *adv* thrice
thriftily *adv* appropriately
tīde *n* (canonical) hour
til, till *prep* to, **til þat**=until, *conj* till
tile(n) *v* till, cultivate
tīme, tȳme *n* time
typet *n* tippet, hood
tō, te *prep* to, in order to, **tō ðæt** until
tō *adv* too, very much
tōdēle(n) *v* divide, distribute, *pt* **tōdēld**
toft *n* tuft, bunch
tōgadere, tōgedere *adv* together
tōlde→telle(n)
tollen *v* take toll
tonge, tunge *n* tongue
top *n* head, **top our taill**=head over heels, upside down
tōtōse *v* tear in pieces
toþer *pron* (the) other
tōward, tōwart *prep* toward
travayle *n* labor, travail, *v* labor, work
treo, trē *n* tree
treothe→trewbe
trēsōr *n* treasure
tretys *adj* well-proportioned, shapely
trēwe *adj* true, *sup* **trewest**
trewnesse *n* loyalty, trueness
trewþe, trowwþe, trēothe *n* truth, faith
trompe *n* trumpet
trow(w)en(n) *v* believe, *pt* **trowede**
trussed *pp* packed
tū→þū
tūkien *v* ill-treat, *pp* **itūked**
tukked *pp* tucked up
tukken *v* tuck up
tūne *n* town
tunge→tonge
tūre *n* tower
turneiment *n* tournament
turne(n), turnnenn *v* turn, translate

tweie *num adj* two, twain
tweinen, twynne *v* depart, go
twō, twā *num* two

þ, Th

þā→þe, þō
þǣrinne→þērinne
thai *dem pron pl* those
þay, thai, thay, þaym, thaim, thaym, þair(e), þām(e) thāme→þei
thāme→þei
þamselfe *intens pron* themselves
þan, þan(n)e, than, þen, þenne, þeonne *adv* then, *conj* when, than
þanken *v* thank
þar, ðat, that, tatt, þet *dem pron* that, *rel pron* that, which, who, what, *conj* the fact that, in order that, so that
thār, þār(e)→þe, þei, þēr
þār-after *adv* thereafter, after that
þārmid *rel adv* with which
thārof→þērof
þauh→þouȝ
þe, the, te *def article* the, *fem dat gen* **þāre**, *pl* **þā, þō**
þe *rel particle* that, who, **þe þe**=he who
þē, thē→þōū
þēd *n* people, nation
þeȝ→þouȝ
þei, thei, þay, thay *pron 3pl* they, *poss* **þeȝȝre, þeire, theyre, þair(e), thair(e), thār**, *dat/acc* **þaym, thaym, thaim, þām(e), thām(e)**
þen, þenne→þan
þenke(n), thenke(n), þenche(n) *v* think *pt* **þoȝte, thoucht**, *pt 2sg* **þohhtesst**, *pp* **thoughte**
þeonne→þan
þēos→þes
þēr(e), thēr, þār, thār(e), tǣr *adv* there,

278 · Middle English

rel *adv* where, *conj* where
þērin *adv* therein
þērinne, þǣrinne *adv* therein
þērof, þēroff, thārof *adv* thereof
þēran, þron *adv* on, from this, thereon
þērtil *adv* thereto
þēr-whīle *conj* while
þes, þis(s) *dem pron, adj* this, *fem sg* **þēos**, *pl* **þēse**
þicke *adj* thick
þilke *dem adj* this
þīn(e), þī→**þōū**
thying, þīng *n* thing, affair, business *pl* **þīng**
thynke(n) *v impers* seem, appear, *prs 3sg* **thynketh, þinc þē**=how does it seem to you, *pt* **þoȝt, þuȝte, thouȝte**, *prs p* **thynkande**
thir *dem adj* these
thyrde→**þridde**
þis(s)→**þes**
þō, þā *adv* then, *conj* when, **þā···þā**= when···then
þoȝt(e), thoucht, thouȝte, thoughte→**þenke(n), thynke(n)**
þōle(n), þōlien *v* suffer
þonk *n* thought, mind, **hire þonkes** willingly
þoru→**þurȝ**
þōū, þū, tū *pron* thou, *poss* **þī, þīn(e)**, *dat/acc* **þē, thē, tē**
thoughte, thought, þohht *n* thought
þouȝ, thouȝ, þeȝ, þa(u)h *adv* yet, however, *conj* though, however
þōūsande, þūsen(d) *n* thousand
þrange *adv* narrowly, grievously
þrē, thrē *num* three
þrengen *v* press, *pt* **þrengde**
þrēte *n* threat
þrēte(n) *v* threaten, *prs 2sg* **þrētest**
þrych *v* crush, oppress
þridde, thrid, thyrde *num* third

þron→**þēron**
þrōte, thrōte *n* throat
þū→**þōū**
þuften *n* handmaid
þuȝte, þuhte→**þenke(n), thynke(n)**
þurȝ, þur(u)h, þurrh, þoru *prep* through
þurlin, þürlin *v* pierce, *pp* **iþürlet**
þus, thus *adv* thus
þūsen(d)→**þōūsande**

U

ūche→**ēch**
ūle *n* owl
umwhīle, umwīle *adv* awhile, momently
unblēndid *pp* unblended, unmixed
unclēnē *adj* unclean
uncōūpled *pp adj* uncoupled, free
undēp *adj* not deep, shallow
underfangen→**underfō(n)**
underfōn, undervōngen *v* accept, receive, *pt* **underfēng**, *pp* **underfāngen**
undergēte(n) *v* perceive, understand, *pt pl* **undergǣton**
undergrowe *pp* underdeveloped
undertāk(en), undirtāk *v* undertake, run a risk, assert, wager, **I undertāke**=I assure you, *sbj pt sg* **undertōke**
undirstandynge *n* understanding
unhardy *adj* not bold, not daring
unimēte *adv* immesurably
unmīlde *adj* cruel
unnc→**wit(t)**
unrecheless *adj* heedless, indifferent
unryghtwȳsely *adv* unrighteously
untellendlic *adj* inexpressible
untrewe *adj* untrue
unwiȝt *n* monster
uōte→**fōt(e)**
up, vp *adv, prep* up, upon

ūs→wē
usāge *n* craft, skill
ūt→ōūte
ūtrely *adv* utterly
ūvel→ēvel

V

vachit→wache
vay→wey(e)
vayne *adj* vain
vaire→fair
vān→fō
vanitē *n* vanity
vār→bē(n)
vavasour *n* a sub-vassal ranking immediately below baron, landholder
vch, ūch(e)→ēch
veyne *n* vein
veirest→fair
veyne *v* vein
venerie *n* hunting
venesōūn *n* venison
vengeans *n* vengeance
vent→wēnde(n)
veole→fēle
verdit *n* verdict
vernicle *n* the picture or representation of the face of Christ said to be impressed upon the handkerchief or sudarium of St. Veronica, any similar picture of Christ's face
verray *adj* true, very
vertu *n* virtue, power
ves→bē(n)
viage *n* journey, voyage
vicht→wicht
vigilie(s) *n* wake, devotional watching
vīle *adj* vile
vileynye *n* rude words, ill-breeding, baseness, rudeness, anything unbecoming a gentleman
vīss→wīs, wīse
vitaille *n* food, provisions
vith→with
vithōūten→withōūten
vode→wode
voirdict *n* verdict, decision
vōlde *n* way
vōn→fō
vor→for
vorþī→forþī
vouch sauf *v* agree, vouchsafe
vp→up
vūl→fūl

W

wacche *v* watch, *pp* vachit
wǣren, wǣron→bē(n)
waye→wey(e)
wayte, waiten *v* wait, waiten after=expect, look forward to
wāke(n) *v* wake, watch
wan→winne
wantown *adj* jovial, sportive
wantownesse *n* affectation, caprice
war *adj* wary, prudent
wār, wāren→bē(n)
wareine *n* warren, game preserve
waren *refl impers sg* beware
warie(n) *v* condemn, curse, *sbj sg* warie, *pp* waried
warne(n) *v* warn
wārsǣ→whērsō
wārtō→whērtō
was, watȝ→bē(n)
wāste *n* waste, uncultivated open place
wastel-breed *n* finest white bread
waterlees *adj* out of water

wē *pron* we, *dat/acc* **ūs**, *poss* **ōwre**
wēane *n* misery, woe
webbe *n* weaver
wey(e), way, vay *n* way, taken (one's) way=take one"s way, set out on a journey, by the way=on the way
wē *pron* we, det/acc **ūs**, poss **ōwre**
wēanne *n* misery, *adv* well, very
weyeden→**weien**
weien *v* weigh, *pt pl* **weyeden**
wēl, well, weil *adv* well, very
wēle *n* happiness, precious thing
wēl-nēʒ *adv* wellnigh
wende(n) *v* turn, go, *pt* went, vent, translate, *pp* **wennd**
wēne, wēn *n* hope, expectation
wēne *v* think, expect, hope *prs 2sg* **wēnst**, *pt* **wēnde**, *pt pl* **wēnden**
wenge→**winge**
wēpen *v* weep, *pt pl* **wēpen**
wēre(n)→**bē(n)**
werk, werre *n* work
werken *v* work, fashion, pt wro(u)ghte
werpen *v* cast, throw, *pt sg* **warp**
werrien *v* wage war, attack, *pp* **iweorret**
werse, wrs *comp adj* worse
werte *n* wart
wes→**bē(n)**
wex *n* wax
whan, hwan, hwon, when, quhen, wonne *conj* when, **quhen at** when
whār(e)→**whēre**
whārfōre *adv* wherefore
what, hwat, quhat *inter, rel pron* what
whelkes *pl* pimples, swellings
whelp *n* puppy
whēre *conj* whether
whēre, whār(e) *inter, rel adv, conj* where
whērsō, wārsǣ, hwerseeaver *adv/conj* everywhere, wheresoever
whērtō, wārtō, hwērtō *interr adv* for what? why?
whērwith *adv* wherewith
whēte *n* wheat
whī *inter ad* why
which *rel pron* which, of what kind
whīle, quhill *n* while, time, þe **whīle**=during
whȳle, hwīl(e), wīle *conj* while, *adv* formerly
whīlom *adv* once (upon a time), formerly
white *adj* white
whō, hwō, hō *inter pron* who, *indef pron* whoever
whōsō *indef pron* whosoever, no matter who
wicht, vicht *adj* brave, valiant
wydwe *m* widow
wīf *n* wife, woman, **good wīf**=the mistress of a household
wiʒt(e) *n* creature, man, person cf. ModE wight
wike *adj* wicked
wylke *rel adj* which
wille, wilen *v* desire, want to, will, *prs* **will(e), wile, wülle** *1sg* **chülle**, *2sg* **wilt, wült**, *pt* **wolde, wollde, wilde, nolde**(=ne wolde), *2sg* **woldest, naldest** (=ne woldest)
wimmen→**womman**
wympul *n* wimple, a covering for the neck
wȳn, wīn *n* wine
wȳnde *n* wind
winge, wenge *n* wing
wynne, wyn, vyn *v* win, gain, *pt* **wan**, *pp* **wonne**
wynning *n* gain, profit
winter *n* winter, year
wirken, wyrke *v* work, compose, *pt* **wrahte**
wīs, vīss *adj* wise
wīse, wīss, vīss *n* tune, melody, key, manner, wise

wisse *v* guide
wyste *v pt* knew, reckoned
wysshe *v* wish, *prs p* **wyschande**
wit→wiþ
wite *v* guard
wite(n) *v* know, *prs sg* wōt, wāt, *pt* wiste, wüste, niste(=ne wiste)
withholden *v* support
witnesse *v* witness, *prs 3sg* **witnisseth**
wit(t) *pron dual* two of us, *dat/acc* **unnc**
witnien *v* witness, bear witness
witt(e) *n* wit, intelligence
wiþ, wiþþ, wit, vith *prep* with, against
wiþinnen *prep* within
wythōuten, wiþūte(n), withūten, vithōūten *prep* without
withseyen *v* oppose
withstonde *v* withstand
withtāke *v* reproach, *prs p* **withtākand**
wō *n* woe, sorrow
wode, vode *n* wood
wōhlech *n* courtship
wol *v* will, *pt sg* wolde, *pl* **wolden**
wolde(n) *v pt* would
wom(m)an *n* woman, *pl* **wimmen, womene**
wonderly *adv* wonderfully
wone *v* dwell
wone *n* custom, habit, habitual action, wont
wone *n* dwelling, *pl* **woneʒ**
wonen *v* live, dwell
wōng *n* plain, field
wōnyng *n* dwelling
wōnynge *pres p* living
wont *pp adj* wont, accustomed
wood *adj* mad, crazy
woot→witen
wōrd *n* word
wōre→bē(n)
worth *adj* worth, worth while
worþe *v* become, be

worthy *adj* brave, respectable
wōt(e)→wite(n)
wrahte→wirken
wrange *n* woe
wrātte *v impers* get angry
wreah→wrīen
wrecce *adj* wretched, poor
wrecched *n* misery
wrīen *v* cover, hide, *pt* **wreah**
wrighte *n* craftsman, workman
writelinge *n* trilling, warbling
wrȳthen *v* writhe, twist, *pp* **wrythen**
wrooth *adj* wroth, indignant
wrōþ *adj* wroth, angry
wrouhte→wirken
wrs→werse
wūnde *n* wound
wunder *n* wonder, atrocities, **tō wundre**= cruelly, *adj* astonishing
wunderlich *adj* wonderful
wurþa *adj* worth

Y

yaf→ʒive(n)
ybouʒt→bȳe
ybōunden→bīnde
ycleped *pp* called
ȳdil *adj* idle
ȳdilness *n* idleness
ye→eye
yeddyng(es) *n* ballad
yeldehalle *n* guildhall
yelding *n* yielding, produce, crop
yeman *n* yeoman
yemanly *adv* yeomanly
yēme *v* govern, take care of
yerde *n* rod, stick
yette(n) *v* pour, *pt sg* **yot**
yeven *v* give

yfalle *pp* fallen
ygo *pp* gone
yif(e)→**ȝif**
ylad *pp* led, carted
ylike *adv* alike
ymage *n* astrological figure, talismatic image
ynesche *adj* tender, soft
ynogh *adv* enough
yonge *adj* young
yot→**yette(n)**
yow *pron* you
ypreved *pp* proved
ypurfiled *pp* trimmed
yronne→**renne(n)**
ys *v* is
yshadwed *pp* shaded
yshryve *pp* shriven
yteyd *pp* tied
yung, yong(e) *adj* young
ȳvel→**ēvel**
ywār *adj* aware, on guard
ywimpled *adj* covered as to the neck, wearing a wimple